UNVEILING

The

BRIDE

THE NEW COVENANT CHURCH

"And I saw the holy city, the new Jerusalem,
coming down out of heaven from God,
prepared as a bride beautifully adorned
for her husband." Revelation 21:2

PETER NEWMAN

For God's Elect
The Bride of Christ

"To Him who loves us and has freed us
from our sins by His blood, and has
made us to be a kingdom of priests
to serve His God and Father –
to Him be the glory and the power
forever and ever!   Amen."
Revelation 1:5-6

Contents

INTRODUCTION

The Bible uses several terms to describe the church; for example, the city of God, the temple of the Spirit, and the body of Christ. However, the "bride of Christ" may best describe the divine relationship God desires the church to have with His Son. For it was always in God's heart from before time to obtain a holy bride and eternal companion for His Son. The Bible says that, as a husband loves his wife, Christ loved the church and gave His life for her, so that He might "present to Himself a glorious church, having no spot or wrinkle or any such thing; but that she would be holy and blameless (Ephesians 5:27)." However, our present day church has fallen far short of fulfilling God's desire to obtain a holy and blameless bride for His Son. Instead of overcoming this ungodly world, the church has been overcome by the sin of the world. Although God does not expect us to be sinless, He does expect us and commands us to stop practicing chronic sin. Yet most Christians attending church are hopelessly entangled in habitual sins (some evident and others secret), which means they either do not know Christ or they are not abiding in Christ.

As a result, the only difference between today's church and the world is that those in church believe they are forgiven. Since even the world recognizes this is religious hypocrisy, the church has lost its spiritual salt and light to influence secular society. If we are honest before God, we must admit that the modern church is not acting like the holy bride of Christ; it is behaving more like a spiritual harlot who loves the world and the things of the world. This certainly is not the church that God envisioned and His Son gave His life for. Two thousand years after Jesus Christ died and rose from the dead, how did the church end up in this fallen spiritual state, and is it too late to resuscitate the church from this spiritual death?

This book attempts to answer this critical question by surveying the development of the church beginning with its birth on the Day of Pentecost and its early church life; through the Middle Ages; to the Reformation period; and up to our present time. This overview of church history reveals the purity and power of the church is directly connected to the purity and power of the gospel that is preached and practiced. A prime example of this connection is the thousand year downward spiral of the church through the Middle Ages when the gospel of Christ had become distorted and corrupted. Another example of the connection between the gospel that is preached and the life of the church can be seen in the Protestant Reformation. The spiritual breakthrough of the Reformation only restored half of the gospel. In practice, the Reformation restored the gospel of how "the righteous are saved by faith," but never restored the whole gospel of how "the righteous will live by faith." There is a vast difference. As a result of the work of the Reformation, the church knows Christ's Atonement has provided believers with forgiveness from the penalty of their sins. Yet because of the Reformation's critical shortfall, the church does not know that Christ's death on the cross has also provided believers with freedom from the power of sin by removing their sinful nature. The result is most Christians do not know how to overcome sin and live by faith in Jesus Christ who indwells them by His Spirit. Yet this is the central purpose of Christ's death on the cross and the cornerstone of the New Covenant church.

What is urgently needed is a complete restoration of the whole gospel. This is not an academic book written for seminary professors and students. This book is written for all Christians who know something is tragically wrong with today's church and desperately long for something much better – the glorious church that God has promised us in His Word. In addition to diagnosing the crux of the problem facing today's church, this book presents the remedy - a model of how the New Covenant church would work based on the complete gospel of Christ and Scriptural principles concerning church life. Five hundred years have passed since the Holy Spirit began to restore the power of the cross of Christ and the keys of the kingdom to Christ's church. Our hope and prayer is that this book will help the church recover the whole gospel of Christ, which will ignite a fire of the Holy Spirit in the hearts of all believers – a fire that will spread all over the world to restore the purity and power of the New Covenant church – a fire that will not be quenched and cannot be stopped until the bride of Christ has made herself ready for her Bridegroom, the Lamb of God, our Lord Jesus.

At the end of this overview of church history, we have included notes for those Christians who are eager to embrace the cross of Christ and desire to restore the New Covenant church to all its glory. These endnotes address many matters of practical concern, such as how to walk by faith and overcome sin; how to carry your own cross and lose your soul-life for Christ and His church; how to hear and obey the voice of the Lord; how to function as a member of Christ's holy priesthood; how to exercise the gifts of the Holy Spirit in the church; and how the New Covenant church works under the headship of Jesus Christ. These endnotes can serve as practical instruction for those Christians who desire to fellowship and function together as God intended - as Christ's New Covenant church and holy bride. If you are interested in learning more about the cross of Christ and the New Covenant church, we invite you to visit our website at www.ChristCrucified.info.

Peter Newman
October 31, 2017

THE BIRTH OF THE BRIDE

In God's divine order, everything reproduces after its own kind. Plants reproduce plants, animals reproduce animals and humans reproduce humans. In the same way, just as earthly seed reproduces the image of the earthly, only heavenly seed can reproduce the image of the heavenly. According to God's plan of redemption, Jesus Christ is the heavenly seed that reproduces His church. Jesus said, "Unless a grain of wheat falls into the earth and dies, it remains only a single seed; but if it dies, it produces much fruit (John 12:24)." Jesus spoke here of His death on the cross by which He would birth His church and bring many sons and daughters into His glory (Hebrews 2:10). The Bible says, "Christ loved the church and gave Himself up for her to make her holy... and present to Himself a glorious church (Ephesians 5:25-27)." This divine union between Christ and the church is the eternal purpose of God the Father (Ephesians 3:10-11). For it was always in God's heart from before time to obtain a holy bride and companion for His Son and heavenly family for Himself. In the Book of Genesis, we see that God created Adam, the first man, in His image to have fellowship with him and to have Adam rule over the earth (Genesis 1:26-28).

But instead of preserving his friendship with God and his dominion over the earth, Adam disobeyed God and fell under Satan's domain. Adam's rebellion against God affected all mankind and, as a consequence, the entire human race inherited his sinful nature (Romans 5:19). Yet despite Adam's fall, God did not change His divine plan. At the right time, God sent His Son, born as a man, to destroy Satan's power and restore mankind to Himself and to His eternal purpose. Thus Jesus Christ came to earth with one over-riding mission - to die on the cross in order to rescue us from Satan's rule and reconcile us to God (Colossians 1:13, 19-20). What Adam had lost through his disobedience, Christ then regained for us by His obedience, even to the point of death on the cross. The crucifixion of Jesus Christ is, therefore, the most momentous event in human history and the triumph of the ages.

THE DIVINE ROMANCE

Thus God's plan of redemption is the unfolding love story of the divine romance between Christ and the church. The Bible uses several terms to describe the church; for example, the city of God, the temple of the Spirit, and the body of Christ. However, the "bride of Christ" may best describe the divine relationship God desires the church to have with His Son. For just as a husband loves his wife, Christ loved the church and gave His life for her. Just as Eve was created from Adam's body to be his bride and glory, God created the church from Christ's body to be His bride and glory. And as Eve was created as Adam's companion and helpmate to reign over the earth, God created the church to be Christ's companion and co-regent to reign with Him in the age to come (Genesis 2:18-24; Revelation 19:6-7; 20:6). As Paul revealed to the first century church, "I betrothed you to one husband, so that to Christ I might present you as a pure virgin… and the two will become one flesh. This mystery is great; but I am speaking about Christ and the church (2 Corinthians 11:2; Ephesians 5:31-32).

Just as there was a betrothal period in Biblical times between the bride and the bridegroom until their wedding ceremony, so the church is now betrothed to Jesus Christ. Through water baptism, new believers declare their betrothal to their bridegroom, Jesus Christ, and their union with His death, burial and resurrection. According to Biblical custom, this betrothal is a binding commitment or covenant that can only be broken by infidelity. And by Biblical tradition, the bride remains veiled until her marriage. At the right time, after the second coming of Christ, the bride will be revealed, the wedding feast will take place and the eternal union of the Lamb of God and His bride will be consummated (Revelation 21:1-2, 9-10).

Two Kinds Of Life
Two Kinds Of Church

However, we see two kinds of church today – the false church, which bears the image of the earthly (man) and the true church, which bears the image of the heavenly (Christ). The Bible says, "You have come to... the city of the living God, the heavenly Jerusalem... the church of the firstborn who are enrolled in heaven (Hebrews 12:22-23)." We see from the Scriptures that the true church is the city of the living God, the new Jerusalem - the bride of Christ. The Bible says, "God placed all things under Christ's feet and appointed Him to be head over everything for the church, which is His body, the fullness of Him who fills all in all... just as the husband is head of the wife, Christ is also the head of the church... you are Christ's body and individually members of it (Ephesians 1:22-23; 5:23; 1 Corinthians 12:27)."

The primary difference that separates the true church, which is the body of Christ, from the false church is the kind of life it has. In this regard, the New Testament describes two different kinds of life. First, there is *psychē* or *soul*-life, from which we get the English word psychology. This is the life Jesus described when He said, "Whoever finds his *soul*-life will lose it, but whoever loses his *soul*-life for My sake will find it (Matthew 10:39)." What is our soul-life? This is the life which springs from our natural personality (and its inherent attitudes, affections and abilities). In other words, the person who loses (gives up) fulfilling his natural soul-life in this world will find eternal life in Christ, but the person who fulfills his natural soul-life in this world will lose eternal life. As Jesus said, "What will it profit a man if he gains the whole world, and yet loses or forfeits his very life?" (Luke 9:25)

The New Testament Greek word used for eternal life is *zoē*. Of the two kinds of life, *psychē* or soul-life originates from man, but only *zoē*-life originates from God and is divine. This is the divine life Jesus described when He said, "I have come that they may have *zoē*-life, and have it more abundantly (John 10:10)." This is the life the apostle John referred to when he wrote, "He who has the Son has the *zoē*-life; he who does not have the Son of God does not have the *zoē*-life (1 John 5:12)." Before Jesus saved us, we did not have *zoē*-life. Jesus said, "I tell you the truth, unless you eat of the flesh of the Son of Man and drink His blood, you have no *zoē*-life within yourselves (John 6:53)."

Consequently, our life before Christ consisted of our soul-life, which we inherited from our natural parents; and our inward sinful nature, which we spiritually inherited from Adam, the first man. However, when we are born again of God's Spirit, we receive Christ's resurrection *zoe*-life into our spirit. As Jesus said, "That which is born of the flesh is flesh, and that which is born of the Spirit is spirit (John 3:6)." This resurrection *zoē*-life that inhabits and sets apart the true church is the free gift of the New Covenant, which was purchased for us by Jesus' sacrifice on the cross (Romans 6:23). Thus the New Covenant church is a divine organism – a spiritual body - filled with Christ's resurrection *zoē*-life.

THE TRUE CHURCH HEARS AND OBEYS
THE VOICE OF HER BRIDEGROOM

In the natural realm, when any of the body's major organic systems (such as the cardiovascular or respiratory systems) become blocked or obstructed, the body quickly loses its vitality. Its immune system becomes compromised; its members stop functioning; and the body itself can die. In the same manner, if the members of Christ's body continue to live and function by relying on their own natural soulish *(psychikos)* ability instead of staying spiritually connected to their head Jesus Christ, they block the power of Christ's *zoē*-life from vitally nourishing and strengthening them. The outcome is spiritual degeneration and death. How does the body stay connected to its head Jesus Christ? The Bible says the true church - the bride - responds to Christ's headship by hearing and obeying His voice. This is God's love language. Jesus said, "If you love Me, you will obey My commands... whoever has My commands and obeys them, he is the one who loves Me (John 14:15, 21)."

The apostle John affirmed this when he wrote, "We know that we have come to know Him if we obey His commands. The one who says, 'I know Him,' but does not obey His commands, is a liar, and the truth is not in Him. But if anyone obeys His Word, the love of God is truly complete in him (2 John 3-5)." Jesus further emphasized this vital aspect of fellowship and connection to Him when He said, "My sheep hear My voice, and they know Me, and follow Me... he who has an ear, let him hear what the Spirit says to the churches (John 10:27; Revelation 2:7)." Because the New Covenant church's source of life is the head of the body, Jesus Christ; it follows that its membership, unity, growth and direction originate and are sustained by the Spirit of God. "For all who are being led by the Spirit of God, these are sons of God (Romans 8:14)." This is the New Covenant church – a spiritual body - born, grown and governed by Jesus Christ Himself.

THE FALSE CHURCH
DOES NOT HAVE CHRIST'S LIFE

However, the false church is not submitted to Christ's headship; therefore, it does not hear and obey His voice. This is the counterfeit church – an earthly organization - born, grown and governed by men who do not know Jesus Christ. As a result, worldly-minded men plan, direct and coordinate the affairs of the false church by their natural ability and wisdom. The counterfeit church's membership, unity, growth and direction are soulish *(psychikos)* and function just like any other institution controlled by man. Without the resurrection *zoē*-life of Jesus Christ as its source and direction, the counterfeit church is only a "Christian" culture club with conforming customs and dues (a ten percent church tax on its members' gross income called tithes). Some false churches may have originally started in the heavenly power of the Spirit, but then abandoned their "first love" for their Bridegroom, Jesus Christ, and ended up religiously functioning in man's earthly soul-power (Revelation 2:1-5).

History records that when the church fails to hear and obey Christ's voice, its connection and fellowship with Him is broken and lost. Just as the body without the spirit is dead, when Jesus removes His Spirit from the carnal church, it is spiritually dead. However, since the counterfeit church can continue to run on its corporate soul-power and natural resources without relying on Christ's Spirit, it can keep functioning as a lifeless institution without missing an earthly step. There are many churches that appear to be alive to those lacking spiritual discernment. They may even be physically growing in terms of people, property and programs. They may seem to have charismatic ministers, dynamic preaching and inspiring worship. However, there is a conspicuous absence of Christ's *zoē*-life in these false churches. As Jesus said, "You have a reputation of being alive, but you are dead (Revelation 3:1)." Tragically, this has occurred countless times in church history as well as in our day.

THE KEYS TO THE KINGDOM
UNLOCK THE POWER OF THE CROSS

Before we go on, let us go back to the very beginning of the church's birth, growth and subsequent spiritual decline. One of the more dramatic moments in Jesus' ministry occurred when He asked His disciples who they thought He was. Peter boldly responded that Jesus was the Christ, the Son of the living God (Matthew 16:13-19). Jesus said Peter received this divine revelation from God, and proclaimed that His church would be built on this foundation or bedrock of God's revelation of His Son, Jesus Christ. Jesus then promised to give Peter (and the other apostles) the keys to His kingdom and declared the powers of hell would not prevail against His church. The fulfillment of Jesus' two promises – receiving the keys to the kingdom of God and overcoming Satan - are coupled together. Without Christ's keys to the kingdom, the church lacks Christ's power to overcome Satan and sin. And unless the church overcomes sin, she cannot abide in Christ and fulfill God's eternal purpose (1 John 3:6).

What are the keys to the kingdom of God? They are the keys to understanding the mystery of Christ's Atonement. The Bible says the message of the cross contains the power of God to redeem us from sin (1 Corinthians 1:18). The Bible also says that if the spiritual forces of darkness had known the mystery of the cross, they never would have crucified the Son of God (1 Corinthians 2:6-8). Therefore, spiritually understanding the purpose and power of Christ's crucifixion is the key to unlocking the power of Christ's resurrection life in His church.

GOD'S DIVINE HEART TRANSPLANT
THE PROMISE OF THE NEW COVENANT

Following His resurrection, Jesus gave the apostles more divine understanding concerning the meaning of His crucifixion and the divine provisions of His New Covenant. He showed them how His death on the cross as the Lamb of God provided them with forgiveness from the penalty of sin. He also showed them how His death on the cross provided them with freedom from the power of sin. How did God accomplish this? Since we were born into sin, we had to die to be freed from sin. God accomplished this by spiritually including us in His Son's death, so that we could be born again into His Son's resurrection life (Romans 6:3-5). When we received Jesus Christ as our Lord and Savior, God spiritually immersed us into Christ's death in order to perform what we might call a "divine heart transplant." God used His Son's sacrificial death on the cross to spiritually remove our terminally sin-sick heart and replace it with His Son's divine heart (Romans 6:6; 1 Corinthians 5:21; 2 Corinthians 13:5; Colossians 2:11-12).

This New Covenant divine heart transplant was foretold by the prophet Ezekiel six centuries before Christ's birth when Ezekiel declared that God would remove our sin-hardened heart and replace it with a new spiritual heart when He put His Spirit within us (Ezekiel 36:26-27; see also Jeremiah 31:31-34). Therefore, by the divine operation of the cross of Christ, God delivered us from indwelling sin by removing our sin nature, so that His Son would dwell in us by His Spirit (Romans 8:9; Galatians 2:20; Colossians 2:11-12). The Bible says, "God has sent the Spirit of His Son into our hearts, crying, 'Abba! Father!' (Galatians 4:6)." Thus God included us in His Son's death so that His resurrected Son might live in us (Colossians 1:27).

This divine heart transplant is the miracle of our new birth, the promise of the New Covenant, the purpose of Christ's Atonement and the power of Christ's gospel. We see that God's way to permanently deal with our chronic sinning was to remove the sinner (the sin factory) from within us and substitute Christ in his place.[1] Whereas we were once sinners by nature, God now calls us His saints or "holy ones," who are partakers of His divine nature, and members of His Son's holy bride. This is the spiritual lesson that God wants every new believer to learn when they are baptized (buried) into a watery "grave" and emerge as a new person in Christ (Romans 6:4; 2 Corinthians 5:17). Water baptism outwardly expresses the divine transformation that occurred in a believer when they were born again of the Spirit. Through baptism, new believers declare their union with Jesus Christ and His death and resurrection. Thus water baptism is the betrothal or commitment ceremony of new members of the bride of Christ to Jesus, their Bridegroom. And so from His Son's death and resurrection, God has created a people for His own possession - the body of Christ, His church – who are destined to be conformed to His Son's glorious image and be eternally united with Him as His holy bride (Romans 8:29; Revelation 19:6-7).

SALVATION IS ONLY THE BEGINNING NOT THE END OF GOD'S PURPOSE

Salvation is only the beginning and not the end of God's divine purpose for His elect. Remember that God has chosen us to be a pure and holy bride for His Son. The Bible says, "God has saved us and called us to be a holy people... it is God's will that you should be holy... for God did not call us to be impure but to live a holy life... like the Holy One who called you, be holy yourselves in all your behavior; because it is written, 'You shall be holy for I am holy' (2 Timothy 1:9; 1 Thessalonians 4:3, 7; 1 Peter 1:15-16)." If you are a Christian, there are no exceptions to God's call to live a pure and holy life. But how can we keep ourselves pure and undefiled from sin while living in this sin-sick world, so that we can fulfill God's eternal purpose to be a holy bride for His Son? Although God does not expect us to be sinless, He does expect us to stop practicing chronic sin. Otherwise, we cannot know Him or abide in Him (1 John 3:6).

This is the great dilemma that has challenged all Christians through the centuries to this day. After Christ saves us, how can we be His witnesses in the world without being overcome by the sin of the world? Although we now have God's Spirit indwelling us, our soul-life (our natural personality with its inherent attitudes, affections and abilities) was not instantly transformed into Christ's image when we were saved (Ephesians 4:22-24). Although we do not have to repeatedly crucify our old *Adam sinful nature* (since God has already put it to death and removed it), we still have to contend with our old *Adam way of thinking* (the sinful thoughts of our natural and *unconverted* soul-life). Most Christians mistake their unrenewed carnal mind for their old sinful nature. This lack of Scriptural discernment has had detrimental consequences to many Christians' sanctification and relationship with the Lord. There is a great difference between our old sinful nature (now dead and gone) and our *unconverted* natural soul-life *(our unrenewed mind)*. Our *unconverted* soul-life does not have the power of the old sinful nature, which was like a sin factory within us, continually producing sinful attitudes and actions and enslaving us to its power (Ephesians 2:1-3).

Since God has freed us from captivity to sin by destroying and removing our sin nature/the sin factory, we are now capable of living a sanctified or holy life. Our co-crucifixion with Christ when we were saved is not merely positional, conceptual or symbolic. When we were born again, God actually removed our sin nature, which was at the very core of our inner being and the root of our self-identity and rebellion toward God. Since sin is no longer our master, we are able by faith to bring our thought-life into submission to Christ. In this way, our minds can be renewed and transformed daily as we believe and act on the grace and truth of God's Word (Romans 12:2; 2 Corinthians 10:5).[2] Now that Satan no longer has a foothold within us through our old sin nature, and our new nature has the power of the Holy Spirit indwelling us, we are able by faith (in Christ's triumph on the cross) to put off our old soulish way of thinking and acting, and put on Christ's way of thinking and acting (1 Corinthians 2:16; Ephesians 4:22-24; Colossians 3:9-10). Thus the power of Christ's gospel is able to not only save sinners, it is able to sanctify them as saints of God - His New Covenant church, the bride of Christ.[3]

THE CRUCIFIXION OF JESUS CHRIST IS THE FOUNDATION OF THE CHURCH

Once Jesus had given the apostles this divine understanding on how His death on the cross had freed them from slavery to sin, the gospel of "Christ crucified" became the apostles' triumphant proclamation and foundational teaching for the New Testament church (1 Corinthians 1:23; 2:2). The message of the cross of Christ speaks of the totality of Christ's triumph over sin and death through His crucifixion and resurrection. It also speaks of our victory over sin and death through our union with Christ's death and resurrection when we were born again. Paul summed up this gospel with his personal testimony: "I have been crucified with Christ and I no longer live, but Christ lives in me; and the life that I now live in the body, I live by faith in the Son of God who loved me and gave Himself up for me (Galatians 2:20)." After the birth of the church on the Day of Pentecost, it was this divine revelation of the cross of Christ that empowered the New Covenant church in the first century. Therefore, it is by believing and acting daily on this truth of the gospel *(our old self no longer lives, but Christ now lives in us)* that we are able to lose our old soulish identity (that originated in Adam) and find our new spiritual identity in Christ. This should be our normal Christian life.

It is our divine union with Jesus Christ that gives us a deep inward security and eternal sense of belonging to His body, which neither heaven nor earth can shake and neither Satan nor sin can steal and destroy (Romans 8:31-39; Hebrews 12:26-29). Jesus said, "The glory that You have given to Me I have given to them, that they may be one just as We are one; I in them and You in Me, that they may be in perfect union, so that the world may know that You sent Me, and loved them even as You have loved Me (John 17:22-23)." However, the apostles had to constantly be on guard and contend for the gospel to ensure this glorious truth of Christ's completed work on the cross was not subverted and compromised (Galatians 1:6-9; Jude 3-4). For if Satan could not extinguish Christianity, He would certainly try to distort and corrupt it.

THE MEANING OF THE CROSS WAS LOST THROUGH THE CENTURIES

Consequently, at the end of the first century with the death of the last of the original twelve apostles, the truth of the gospel came under relentless attack from Satan to nullify the power of the cross. Tragically, as a result of this devilish onslaught, the spiritual meaning of Christ's crucifixion (the keys to the kingdom of God) began to be obscured within just a few generations.[4] The key that was lost first was the divine truth that God freed us from the power of sin by replacing our sinful nature with Christ's divine nature when we were saved. Once the church no longer believed and acted on this Biblical truth that it had died in Christ, its spiritual life and identity were no longer rooted in Christ. Instead of submitting to God's righteousness that comes solely through faith in Christ and His completed work on the cross, the church sought to establish its own righteousness and religious identity by relying on its own corporate soul strength. The church then began to depend on its organizational power and natural resources to do Christ's work.

When Christians began to trust in their soulish *(psychikos)* ability instead of Christ's completed work on the cross to be holy and serve God, it produced a counterfeit version of Christianity (that we might call Churchianity), which appeared outwardly righteous but was inwardly lawless, hypocritical and deceived (Matthew 23:28).[5] Church leaders then increasingly relied on their own earthly religious authority to ensure there was obedience, unity and doctrinal purity in the ranks of their church members. These carnal-minded religious leaders suppressed the spontaneity, freedom and sovereign direction of the Holy Spirit in the church; therefore it should be no surprise that the supernatural gifts of the Holy Spirit soon faded away from common use.[6]

As this downward spiral continued for the next few centuries, the church became even more preoccupied with its clerical hierarchy, temple-like building programs, and growing wealth and political influence rather than the indwelling Lordship and Life of Jesus Christ. The church lowered God's standard of holiness in order to increase church attendance and membership rolls, and church leaders became carnally focused on their clergy status to protect, promote and profit from their religious positions. These misguided clergy nullified the Scriptures and wrongly interpreted and divided the Biblical role of elders into three separate, tiered offices – bishops, pastors and elders.[7] The Catholic church later added two more layers – cardinals and the pope – to this pyramidal hierarchy. By the fifth century, this religious monarchy had completely destroyed the New Covenant's priesthood of all believers and replaced it with a special caste of paid professional priests (now called "pastors" in the Protestant church). This self-serving false priesthood then reinstated the obsolete Old Covenant practice of tithing to support themselves and their cathedral "temples."[8]

THE CHURCH'S LONG SPIRITUAL DECLINE

This protracted decline into unbelief and spiritual darkness continued until the sixth century when the now State-sanctioned, institutional church (also known as the Catholic church by this time) eventually lost even the first key to enter the kingdom of heaven - the basic truth of saving faith in Christ's Atonement. The spiritually worthless ritual of the Catholic Mass had replaced the saving power of the cross of Christ. The monarchal and monolithic Catholic church had become a spiritually empty cathedral of pomp and ceremony guarded by unsaved, self-ambitious, self-profiting, corrupt clergy who gave lip service to God but whose deeds denied the reality and power of Christ's crucifixion and resurrection (2 Timothy 3:5).[9] In the case of these false shepherds, Jesus' rebuke is fitting: "Woe to you... for you have taken away the key to knowledge; you yourselves did not enter, and you have hindered those who were entering (Luke 11:52)."

However, throughout these long centuries of church apostasy, God continued to faithfully reveal His Son and the fullness of His completed work on the cross to any believer who earnestly sought to know Him and obey Him. While the false church was steeped in darkness, this faithful remnant of Christ's bride served as God's lamplight in the world and "suffered reproach with Christ outside the camp," and often endured severe persecution since the false church born of the flesh always persecutes the true church born of the Spirit (Hebrews 13:12; Galatians 4:29). It is no wonder that historians have called much of this era "the Dark Ages."

The Protestant Reformation
A Spiritual Breakthrough

Then, in the early 1500s, after a thousand years of spiritual decline in the institutional church, a momentous event occurred. God's divine sunrise dawned once again as the Holy Spirit began to restore the liberating truth of Christ's gospel and the keys of the kingdom to the church at large. A major breakthrough came when God mercifully gave a Catholic monk named Martin Luther divine revelation on Romans 1:17: "The righteous will live by faith." The movement that arose from this divinely restored truth of the gospel of Christ became historically known as the Protestant Reformation. The

Reformation restored the authority of the Scriptures and illuminated man's need to be saved by faith in Jesus Christ alone. This brought into focus once again Christ's Atonement for the forgiveness of sins and the need to be born again of the Spirit. Thus, by God's grace, this key to the kingdom, which had been largely lost for nearly a millennium, was miraculously recovered. This restored key to entering the kingdom of heaven – salvation by faith in Christ alone - became the torch that spread the fires of evangelism to the whole world.

Yet the Protestant Reformation only partially restored the mystery of the cross to the church. For the past five hundred years, the church has only acted on half of the gospel. In practice, the Protestant Reformation restored the gospel of how "the righteous are *saved by faith*," but never restored the whole gospel of how "the righteous will *live by faith*."[10] There is a vast difference. As a result of the work of the Reformation, the church knows Christ's Atonement has provided believers with forgiveness from the penalty of their sins. Yet because of the Reformation's critical short-fall, most Christians do not know that Christ's death on the cross has also provided believers with freedom from the power of sin by removing their sinful nature. God's people can be ignorant about many things, but when they are ignorant about the full purpose and power of the cross, they are in real trouble. Note that, in Biblical terms, "knowing" God's truth does not mean merely mentally assenting to it.[11] It means believing and acting on it and wholeheartedly obeying it (Romans 6:17).

THE REFORMATION RECOVERED ONLY HALF THE GOSPEL

The result is most Christians believe their sins are forgiven, but they do not know how to stop practicing sin and live by faith in Jesus Christ who indwells them by His Spirit. Yet this is the central purpose of Christ's

Atonement and the cornerstone of the New Covenant church. Without possessing this crucial key to God's kingdom, many Christians are compromised by sin and are spiritually weak and sick to the point of perishing. Because of their spiritual ignorance, most Christians mistakenly believe they still have a debilitating sinful nature even after they have been born again of the Holy Spirit. Consequently, they trust Jesus as their Savior and hope one day to go to heaven; but, in their daily lives, they inwardly struggle in frustration and resigned discouragement beset with entangling sins. Of course, there are many Christians in our day who experience no such struggle and discouragement, because the Holy Spirit is unable to convict them of their sins. Their conscience has become hardened so that they now accept their sinful attitudes and behavior as a normal way of life. This easy acceptance of sin in their lives by the present generation of Christians is one of the greatest problems confronting the church today. The root of this problem can be summarized in one word - unbelief, which manifests itself in a lack of the fear of God, and is the essence of disobedience. This is tragic because the Son of God sacrificed His life on the cross so that we would not be defeated by sin.

What sort of salvation would we have if God only saved us from the penalty of our sins, and then left us on our own to deal with the demonic power and deception of sin? How could God have destroyed Satan's foothold in us if we still had a hostile and evil sinful nature living within us? How could we spiritually overcome our enemy, the devil, if we still had an enemy allied to him waging guerilla warfare within us? This would be a pitiful and incomplete redemption that would not fulfill God's eternal purpose to have a pure and uncompromised bride who is wholeheartedly devoted to His Son. Yet most Christians are defeated by sin and the devil because they think this is as far as God went when, in actuality, this is as far as their faith and knowledge of the truth of the gospel has gone.

THE PROTESTANT CHURCH FOLLOWS THE CUSTOMS OF THE CATHOLIC CHURCH

Since the Protestant Reformation did not recover the whole gospel of Christ, the "reformers" did not know (and believe and act on) the truth that they (that is, their inward sinful nature) had died in Christ to the world, including religious worldliness (Galatians 6:14). Therefore, they did not know how to lose (or lay down) their *psychē* soul-life daily by faith in order to find their spiritual identity and resurrection *zoē*-life in Christ. As a result, the Protestant church carried forward many of the carnal and obsolete religious traditions and practices identified with the Catholic church. Much of the Protestant church today practices a separate and distinct paid priesthood (or professional clergy). And many Protestant churches practice the old Judaic system of tithing (the ten percent income tax for membership) to support their paid priesthood and physical buildings. Surveys reveal that the typical Protestant church spends over eighty percent of its incoming revenue in order to maintain its paid staff, physical buildings and internal programs. Less than twenty percent of their income goes to evangelical outreach. Thus many Protestant churches today practice a form of cathedral or temple worship, where the physical building is their center of worship, and the heart of their religious service to God. When most Christians say they are going to church, they mean they are going to a special building (or temple) to worship. However, under the New Covenant, God's people do not go to church; they *are* the church – they *are* God's building and God's temple (1 Corinthians 3:4: Ephesians 2:19-22). This is not just semantics; it reveals a certain mindset and the way people think and act about church.

What does the word "church" actually mean? The modern English word "church" is phonetically derived from the Middle English word *chirche,* which was derived over time from the Greek word *kuriakos,* which means "to belong to the Lord." However, in the New Testament, the word "church" is directly translated from the Greek word *ekklesia,* which means an assembly or congregation (Matthew 16:18), and whose root meaning is "called out from." In the New Testament, the word "church," or *ekklesia,* is always used in reference to a gathering together of Christ's disciples, and is never used in reference to a physical building (Matthew 18:17-20; Romans 16:5; 1 Corinthians 16:19; Colossians 4:15; Philemon 1:2). Therefore, the church consists of all people who have been called out from the world to gather together in service and worship to the Lord. And the Bible says that the spiritual service of worship which God accepts is when we present ourselves as a living and holy sacrifice to Him (Romans 12:1). As Paul taught, "We are the temple of the living God; just as God has said, 'I will dwell in them and walk among them; and I will be their God, and they will be My people. Therefore, come out from them and be separate,' says the Lord. 'And do not touch what is unclean, and I will welcome you, and I will be a Father to you, and you will be My sons and daughters,' says the Lord Almighty (see 2 Corinthians 6:16-18)."

All of the Protestant religious practices mentioned above are throwbacks to the Old Covenant and the Mosaic Law. Even the single pastor system is a continuation of the Catholic tradition of having a parish priest who administers the sacraments and interprets the Bible to the laity. And the senior pastor system is also a reversion to the Old Covenant high priest system when a single "anointed" man was needed to intervene and interpret God for the rest of the congregation. But under the New Covenant, the church has only one High Priest, Jesus Christ, who intercedes for us and teaches us all things by His Spirit who lives in us (Romans 8:26-27; Hebrews 3:1; 4:14-15; 7:23-28; 10:21; 1 John 2:27). In effect, many churches today say they preach a New Covenant salvation but, in actuality, they practice a form of Old Covenant religion. Whenever a church practices a form of temple worship; supports a salaried professional clergy separate and distinct from the laity; practices the law of tithing; and suppresses the miraculous gifts of the Holy Spirit from being freely expressed in their meetings by the priesthood of believers, it is a sure sign that church does not love God and is not submitted to Christ's headship. Remember that to love God is to obey His Son and His commands. How can we be true servants of Christ's New Covenant if we observe a form of Old Covenant religion? Practicing Old Covenant religious customs and suppressing the Holy Spirit is also a sure sign that church is not walking by faith in Christ's completed work on the cross and that its spiritual life and identity are not found in Christ. In other words, based on the clear instructions of Scripture, that church is not a legitimate New Covenant church. Why would God ever pour the precious new wine of His Spirit into that old, brittle, unyielding and corrupted wineskin?

PRACTICING OLD COVENANT RELIGIOUS CUSTOMS NULLIFIES GOD'S NEW COVENANT GRACE

The Old Covenant religious practices of the false church may seem harmless to the undiscerning because they have now become "institutionalized," "traditional" and "normative." However, being immersed week after week in religious practices that are rooted in Old Covenant Mosaic Law is spiritually harmful, and can even be spiritually deadly to those who continually participate in them because they can be lulled into falsely thinking that their righteousness is based on practicing these Old Covenant religious traditions and practices. This is why the Bible calls practicing the Old Covenant Law and customs the "ministry of death and condemnation (2 Corinthians 3:6-9)." This is why Peter called practicing the Mosaic Law "a yoke which neither our fathers nor we have been able to bear (Acts 15:10)." This is why Paul wrote concerning the Mosaic Law: "It was for freedom that Christ has set us free. Stand firm, then, and do not be burdened again by a yoke of bondage (Galatians 5:1)." This is also why Paul warned others that they must never allow themselves to come under the yoke of the Law, not even a part of the Law: "You have been severed from Christ, you who are seeking to be justified by the Law; you have fallen from grace (Galatians 5:4)." The Bible goes as far as to say that anyone who practices even a part of the Old Covenant Mosaic Law and its religious customs in order to be righteous is under a curse and subject to God's wrath (James 2:10; Romans 4:15; Galatians 3:10).

The Bible states, "'The righteous will live by faith,' however, the Law is not based on faith; on the contrary, 'He who practices these things will live by them' (Galatians 3:11-12)." In other words, those who practice even parts of the Old Covenant Law will be judged by the Law and not by grace. For a professing Christian to religiously practice even parts of the Old Covenant Law (whether it is the false church's version of the Levitical priesthood; or the Mosaic Law of tithing; or a form of temple worship that takes the place of the true New Covenant church) in order to be righteous is to "nullify the grace of God, for if righteousness comes through the Law, then Christ died for nothing (Galatians 2:21)."[12]

Many of the Old Covenant-based religious traditions and practices that have developed over the centuries in the false church are the result of men not knowing (and believing and acting on) the grace and truth of the gospel of Jesus Christ and the freedom and power of His New Covenant. Jesus said, "You nullify the Word of God by your tradition that you have handed down (Mark 7:13)." When you do not believe and act on the gospel that you were crucified with Christ and have died to the world (since you no longer have a sinful nature), your "Christian" identity and "church" identity will, by the natural course of events, be based on worldly religious principles, including Old Covenant religious practices, that are contrary to the resurrection *zoē*-life of Christ. In the beginning, this may only seem like a little of the religious world's way of doing things; however, if not spiritually dealt with, it eventually compromises the whole church. As Paul said, "Do you not know that a little leaven leavens the whole lump of dough? (1 Corinthians 5:6)." Thus the counterfeit church's clerical aristocracy; its programmed and tightly controlled order-of-service; its ever-expanding building programs; and its constant appetite for more and more money are soulishly inspired and driven. The "fully-matured" false church is like a diseased and cancerous body, and many of its religious traditions and practices are actually the malignant symptoms of a much deeper soul-sickness caused by not having its identity rooted in Christ, which is a direct consequence of not being submitted to Christ's sovereignty. In the first century, the foundation or ABCs of the church was simply, but powerfully, the gospel of "Christ crucified." There was no other foundation. However, as someone has aptly said, the ABCs of the false church are Attendance, Buildings and Cash.

THE CHURCH MUST STAY CONNECTED TO CHRIST TO LIVE

To sum up, if the church is to have Christ's resurrection life, it must "stay connected to the head *(Christ)*, from whom the whole body, being supported and held together by its joints and ligaments, grows with a growth which is from God (Colossians 2:19)." From this Scripture, we can conclude that when a church truly loves God and is properly submitted to Christ's sovereignty, it will have Christ's resurrection life that enables it to be spiritually held together by its joints and ligaments, and God will cause the whole body to grow and produce spiritual fruit. What are these spiritual joints and ligaments that hold the true church together? The New Testament Greek word for joints in this verse is *haphē*, which are the points at which parts of the body are connected together. As members of the body of Christ, we are joined and connected together by our Christian fellowship (the New Testament Greek word for fellowship is *koinonia*, which also means to be joined in communion to one another). The New Testament Greek word for ligaments in this verse is *syndesmos*, which are the connecting bands that hold our joints together. Without these strong bonding ligaments, our joints would separate under stress. These ligaments are a picture of the spiritual bonds of love and peace which hold our Christian fellowship *(koinonia)* together. The Bible says, "Make every effort to keep the unity of the Spirit through the bond *(syndesmos)* of peace… beyond all things, put on love, which is the perfect bond *(syndesmos)* of unity (Ephesians 4:3; Colossians 3:14)."

When the New Covenant church stays connected to its head, Jesus Christ, the members of His body will have the spiritual bonds of love and peace needed to hold their Christian fellowship together in unity even during difficult and stressful times, and God will cause the church to spiritually grow and multiply. If, however, a church does not love God and does not stay connected to Christ, it will not have the spiritual bonds of love and peace needed to keep its fellowship spiritually together and alive. Does this sound unworkable and impractical? Based on the world's way of doing business, it is impossible. However, in God's kingdom, this spiritual dynamic is profoundly wise. Jesus said, "What is highly esteemed by men is detestable in the sight of God (Luke 16:16)." In the eyes of men, relying on the bonds of love and peace to hold the church together is weak and fragile; however, in the eyes of God, this guarantees His New Covenant church – the bride of Christ - will always be dependent on the headship of Jesus Christ to be nourished by His *zoē*-life, in order to produce the spiritual fruit of love and peace. These are the ties that bind the church together in true *koinonia* fellowship. As Paul taught, "If you have any encouragement from being united with Christ, if any comfort from His love, if any fellowship of the Spirit, if any affection and compassion, then make my joy complete by being of the same mind, maintaining the same love, united in spirit, intent on one purpose. Do nothing out of selfish ambition or vain conceit, but with humility of mind regard one another as more important than your-selves. Do not merely look out for your own personal interests, but also for the interests of others. Have this attitude in yourselves which was also in Christ Jesus (Philippians 2:1-5)."

Once again, this does not necessarily mean that a spiritually dead church that is not submitted to Christ will cease to function, since the nature of the false church is such that it can operate without Christ's *zoē*-life and without the spiritual bonds of love and peace. As long as the false church maintains a physical building, a paid pastor and is financed by weekly tithes (religious taxes), it will continue to appeal to less than sincere, so-called "Christians" that are attracted to an outward form of Christianity and the false security of a "religion" and "community" that does not demand them to surrender their lives daily to Christ's sovereignty. The spiritual bankruptcy of these false churches would become very apparent if they ceased collecting the tithe taxes. As soon as this unBiblical cash flow stopped, almost all of these churches would cease doing business and close their doors.

FIVE FEATURES OF THE NEW COVENANT CHURCH

Now let us take a closer look at the true church. According to the Scriptures, the New Covenant church has the following features:

- The New Covenant church normally meets in believers' homes and whenever the church grows too large to meet in one member's home, it simply multiplies from house to house throughout its geographic locality (Acts 2:46; 5:42; 20:20; Romans 16:5; 1 Corinthians 16:19; Colossians 4:15; Philemon 1:2). This eliminates the need to raise large amounts of money to buy, build and maintain church facili-ties. This helps ensure that God (not men and their money) will cause the growth of the church (1 Corinthians 3:6-7). This informal, home setting also encourages open participatory meetings; helps the church function in a more personal and loving way as God's family; and enables the saints to practice hospitality toward other believers and visitors (Romans 12:13; Hebrews 13:2; 1 Peter 4:9). Thus the New Covenant church in each city or community is essentially an informal network of home-based meetings. An exception to these weekly home meetings might be to occasionally rent a building, auditorium or conference room for a city-wide meeting of house churches and/or to facilitate the outreach ministry of a visiting apostle, prophet, evangelist or teacher (Acts 19:9).

- The New Covenant church experiences intimate spiritual fellowship with the Father and His Son and experiences close-knit community life among the believers who are committed to laying down their self-will and giving up their natural *unconverted* soul-lives in *agapē* love for one another (Acts 2:42-47; 4:32-33; 1 Corinthians 12:12-27; Ephesians 4:15-16; Philippians 2:1-5; 1 John 1:3; 3:16). As members of God's household, the saints' lives are closely intertwined with one another as brothers and sisters and mothers and fathers in Christ (1 Corinthians 4:15; 1 Thessalonians 2:11; 1 Timothy 5:1-2; Titus 2:3-4; 1 John 2:12-14). This encourages mentoring and discipleship relationships to naturally develop. On the Lord's Day (Sunday), the local believers often meet together in their homes to share "the Lord's Supper" as a full fellowship meal (Acts 20:7; 1 Corinthians 11:20). The primary purpose of eating this communal meal together is to remember (with thanksgiving and rejoicing) the New Covenant provisions of the Lord's death by sharing "the bread and the cup" together, and to reaffirm the believers' bonds of love and peace with one another as God's family (1 Corinthians 11:23-26). This is why this fellowship meal is also called an "*agapē* love feast" (Jude 1:12).

- The New Covenant church has a vibrant, functioning priesthood of all believers (both men and women) who passionately love our Lord Jesus Christ, and are gifted and equipped by the Holy Spirit to do the work of the ministry together and build up the body of Christ in love.[13] Every member of this royal priesthood personally knows and serves Jesus Christ, our High Priest, and has a vital and unique ministry role in His body (Romans 12:3-8; 1 Corinthians 12:1-12; Ephesians 4:11-13, 15-16; Colossians 2:19; 1 Peter 2:9; 4:10-11; Revelation 1:6; 5:10). Consequently, when the church meets together under Christ's headship, one member might be led by the Holy Spirit to share a prayer or a song; another member a word of knowledge or wisdom; another member an exhortation or a teaching; another member the gifts of healing or miracles; and another member might share a prophecy or a message in tongues with its interpretation - all done in an orderly, peaceful and loving manner for the benefit of the whole body (1 Corinthians 14:26-33).

  This dynamic priesthood of all the believers is one of the fundamental building stones ("living stones") of the New Covenant church (1 Peter 2:4-5).[14] This spiritual freedom and responsibility in the New Covenant church enables every member to grow into fully knowing God, and also helps each member learn how to exercise their individual gifts to effectively serve and care for God's family. It also enables Christ, as the head of the church, to lead His body (through a variety of members with a variety of gifts) as all the saints learn to fix their eyes on Jesus and hear and obey His voice.[15]

- The New Covenant church has a compassionate commission to employ a variety of means to reach others with the gospel of Christ (Mark 16:15; Acts 4:20; 11:20-21; Philippians 1:5). This reflects the heart of God's love for the lost and enables Jesus Christ to employ the multi-gifted members of His church as coworkers to advance His gospel and bring His elect into the kingdom, and this outreach of *agape* love toward others also helps keep the church from becoming insular and isolated. This divine commission goes beyond just bringing new converts into the church. Jesus specifically commanded the church to make disciples who obey His commands (Matthew 28:19-20). This is why it is essential to feed newborn lambs the milk of God's Word followed by more solid food for training in righteousness as soon as they are able to digest it, so that they can exercise faith in the truth of God's Word in order to overcome Satan and sin, and be Christ's witnesses in this world (1 Corinthians 3:2; Hebrews 5:12-14; 1 Peter 2:2-3; 1 John 2:12-14).

- The New Covenant church is normally shepherded in each locality by a number of spiritually mature and humble brothers called elders.[16][17] As servant-leaders, the elders are unpaid and accountable to the church and to Jesus Christ, the head of the church, to be godly examples of faithfulness; provide wise oversight (not micromanagement) to the church; help train and equip the priesthood of believers to do their God-given ministries; and provide loving pastoral care to members of God's local flock (Acts 20:17, 28; Ephesians 4:11-13; 2 Timothy 3:1-7; James 5:14; 1 Peter 5:1-4). Since Jesus is the Chief Shepherd, He personally calls, trains and, at the right time, appoints these mature brothers as His undershepherds in the local church. When a church reaches a certain size and spiritual maturity, these elder brothers will naturally emerge and be recognized by the saints, and may also be confirmed by the "laying on of hands" of visiting apostles and prophets (Acts 14:23; Titus 1:5-9).

This plurality of shared leadership helps prevent carnal authoritarian rule; stifles a "personality cult" from developing around a sole or senior pastor; and helps keep the church singularly focused on Jesus Christ as the Chief Shepherd who personally leads His body by His Spirit. This New Covenant form of local church leadership only works if the elders are truly submitted to Christ their head and to one another in the humility of the Holy Spirit (Philippians 2:1-5). This law of the Spirit ensures these elders (shepherds) in the New Covenant church must stay vitally connected to Christ to have His resurrection life, so they can stay united in Spirit to properly care for God's flock with His wisdom, power and love; and be spiritually sensitive to discern and follow (not interfere with) the Holy Spirit's prompting and leading of the saints.

- The New Covenant church does not practice Old Covenant tithing to subsidize a special, paid priesthood or clergy (Hebrews 7:5, 12); instead its members practice voluntary giving (according to their financial means as God has blessed them) to further the outreach of the gospel and help those members of the body who are financially suffering and in need (Acts 4:34-35; 11:29; Romans 12:13; 1 Corinthians 16:1-2; 2 Corinthians 9:6-7; 1 John 3:17). This eliminates the mandatory Mosaic religious tax placed upon God's people to finance a professional clergy who are separate from the laity.[18] It also helps ensure the basic needs of members of God's family are not lacking while other members are experiencing abundance (2 Corinthians 8:1-15; 9:6-7). This fulfills the divine command: "Bear one another's burdens, and thereby fulfill the law of Christ... when one member suffers, all members suffer together (Galatians 6:2; 1 Corinthians 12:26; see also 1 John 3:17)."

PRACTICING NEW COVENANT CHURCH PRINCIPLES IS NOT ENOUGH

These are the basic features that form the New Covenant church. We believe the Holy Spirit led the first century apostles to establish the New Covenant church on these basic principles to protect the simplicity and purity of the gospel of Christ, and safeguard the church from worldliness as much as possible (2 Corinthians 11:3). However, just following the New Covenant church pattern and principles is not enough. A church that looks like it has the form and features of the New Covenant church may still not have Christ's *zoē*-life. No, there is far more required than just New Covenant form: as we have said earlier, the church – the bride - must steadfastly abide in union with Christ, her Bridegroom. In the Scriptures, Jesus Christ inseparably links abiding (staying rooted) in Him with carrying our own cross for His sake. Jesus said, "Whoever does not carry his own cross and follow Me, cannot be My disciple (Luke 14:27)." The cross of Christ, which was the implement of His death, must now become the implement of our *own* death (the death of our self-willed, self-governed soul-life).

Therefore, the cross is not just His; it must by faith become ours as we turn away from fulfilling our *psychē* soul-life daily. Jesus said, "The man who loves his soul-life in this world will lose it, while the man who hates *(turns away from)* his soul-life in this world will find eternal *zoē*-life (John 12:25)." Let us be clear: God does not want to destroy our soul; He wants to restore our soul to His original divine purpose. God wants our soul to be governed by His Spirit and transformed by His Word as each day we put off sinful thoughts that originate from our unrenewed mind, and put on the mind of Jesus Christ who lives in us (1 Corinthians 2:16). This is God's divine expectation for His people after they are saved. As Paul wrote, "Work out your salvation with fear and trembling, for God is at work in you to both will and to act according to His good purpose (Philippians 2:12-13)."

THE ISSUE IS ONE OF SOVEREIGNTY
WILL WE GIVE UP OUR SOUL-LIFE FOR CHRIST?

The issue is simply one of ownership: will we continue to be enslaved to our unconverted soul's natural desires, or will we be enslaved to God in sanctification? This means that when we are faced with a choice of doing God's will or our will, we will obey (if we have the heart of the bride) the Holy Spirit within us instead of following our natural soulish *(psychikos)* temperament, preferences and inclinations (Romans 6:13-19). Allowing God's Word (His Sword of the Spirit) to have this decisive authority and transforming power in our life has a far-reaching, penetrating and pruning impact over all our natural affections, associations and activities. Sometimes we will turn away from worldly attitudes and activities when God's Word convicts us. Other times, God will use difficult situations to discipline and prune us. "For God disciplines us for our good, so we may share His holiness (Hebrews 12:10)." The bride of Christ simply cannot be prepared for eternal union and co-regency with Christ apart from undergoing God's training in righteousness, which involves suffering for Christ's sake.[19] The Bible says: "If we suffer, we will also reign with Him (2 Timothy 2:12)." Losing our soul-life means we give up our whole being completely to Christ's Sovereignty. Every believer who lays down their soul-life for Christ's sake overcomes the world, and everyone who overcomes the world will be dressed in readiness for the marriage supper of the Lamb, and will reign with Christ over the nations in the age to come (Revelation 2:26-27).

Tragically, many professing Christians are not wearing their wedding garments. They think they are spiritually dressed to meet Christ when they are actually stark naked. Jesus said, "You do not know that you are naked. Buy from Me white garments so that you may clothe yourself and the shame of your nakedness will not be revealed (Revelation 3:17-18)." It is important to note that Jesus was speaking to those in the church and not to unbelievers.

In Biblical times, the bridegroom traditionally paid a "bride price" to marry the bride, and also paid all expenses for the wedding, including furnishing the traditional wedding garments. In keeping with this Biblical custom of the bridegroom paying a price to marry his bride, Jesus paid the ultimate price for His bride, the church. The price that Jesus paid was His own life blood. It was because of this purchase price that Paul wrote, "Do you not know that...you are not your own? For you have been bought with a price: therefore glorify God in your body (1 Corinthians 6:19-20)." Even though He furnishes the heavenly wedding garments, Jesus said we must "buy" them. What does this mean? The Bible says the wedding garments signify the righteous acts of faith done by the saints (Revelation 19:8). Although Jesus paid the ultimate price on the cross to clothe us in His righteousness, it is our works done in faith that enable us to wear His garments of righteousness. Thus, for two thousand years, God has never changed the price that the bride of Christ must pay to obtain her divine wedding clothes. The cost is always the same – the price is our soul-life, which we must give up if we want to walk by faith in God's true righteousness and do His good works.

Jesus said, "If anyone wishes to come after Me, he must deny himself and take up his cross and follow Me. For whoever wishes to save his soul-life will lose it, but whoever loses his soul-life for My sake and the gospel's will find it (Mark 8:34-35)." In other words, we must put to death (by faith in the cross of Christ) our natural, unconverted soul's love of the world in order to receive God's righteous wedding garments that distinguish and identify us as Christ's eternal bride. As Jesus told one church, "You have a few people... who have not soiled their clothes. They will walk with Me, dressed in white, for they are worthy. He who overcomes will, like them, be dressed in white. I will never blot out his name from the Book of Life, but will acknowledge his name before My Father (Revelation 3:4-5)." Many professing Christians, however, are not ready for the wedding supper of the Lamb. If they do not obtain their wedding garments soon by believing and acting on the truth of the cross and giving up their soul-life for Christ's sake, they will be speechless when God throws them out of His Son's wedding, for they will have proven themselves unworthy and shamefully unclothed (Matthew 22:11-14).

WHEN THE CHURCH ABIDES IN CHRIST THE CHURCH BEARS HIS FRUIT

Jesus said, "Every good tree bears good fruit, but the bad tree bears bad fruit. A good tree cannot produce bad fruit, nor can a bad tree produce good fruit (Matthew 7:17-18)." God has grafted us into His Son; this is our glorious salvation, but this is just the beginning of God's pruning and sanctifying work in our lives. If we abide in Christ and He abides in us, we will bear fruit that has His fragrance. If we still think we can bear fruit by our own doing, then we do not need the power of the cross working in our life. When a church is planted and stays rooted in the whole truth of the gospel, it is like a healthy branch growing from the tree of life (Jesus Christ), and that branch will produce good fruit (John 15:1-8). As the Bible says, "If the root (*Christ*) be holy, so also are the branches (Romans 11:16)." The New Covenant church will then experience community (*koinonia*) resurrection life together as the living body of Christ instead of organizational or institutional life, which is really no life at all.

If, however, a church has not been planted in the true gospel of Christ, it cannot produce good fruit. For if the members of a church do not know (and believe and act on) the divine fact that they died in Christ, they cannot expect to live in Christ, nor can Christ be expected to sovereignly live in them. They then have no alternative than to try to live and function together as a church by the best of their soulish (*psychikos*) ability and understanding. They will tragically mistake their soulish enthusiasm for faith and their soulish energy for Christ's *zoē*-life. The Bible says, "Only the Spirit gives *zoē*-life;

our soulish energy has no spiritual value (John 6:63)." Until we know that we have died in Christ and have found our life in Christ (Colossians 3:3), our soul's irresistible need is for self-identity and self-fulfillment instead of walking in obedience to God and His Word by faith. Much of what the false church has done in Jesus' name has been to satisfy this driving soulish need for identity since its spiritual life and identity are not in Jesus Christ.

THE TRUE CHURCH IS THE BRIDE OF CHRIST
THE FALSE CHURCH IS THE HARLOT OF SATAN

Consequently, the false church has failed to fulfill God's divine purpose because it has tried to do in the power of its soul what could only be done in the power of Christ's death and resurrection. Once again, this is not harmless; the Bible says that whatever is not done from faith is sin, and whoever practices sin is under control of the devil (Romans 14:23; John 8:34 & 44; 1 John 3:8). The natural soulish *(psychikos)* life that is not submitted to the Holy Spirit is a *psychic* gateway leading to demonic deception and control (James 3:5). If we do not live daily by faith in the grace and truth of the cross (by putting off our unconverted soul-life and putting on the Lord Jesus Christ who lives in us), we will not have God's discernment to recognize the difference between what is soulish and what is spiritual (Romans 13:12-14; Hebrews 4:12; 5:14).

In the beginning, this demonic deception may seem relatively harmless because the deception is subtle. But over time, this deception leads to greater darkness and even greater deception and eventual enslavement to Satan. This is the way deception works: well-meaning new Christians who zealously want to serve God do not envision they will end up serving the false church of Satan. For the true church is the bride of Christ and belongs to the kingdom of God; whereas the false church is, by its very nature and functioning, the harlot of Satan and belongs to the kingdom of Babylon.[20]

Some Christians might ask: how can an errant and unbelieving church be the church of Satan when it seems to be filled with so many "good" people trying to do "good" deeds? However, remember "the road to hell is paved with good intentions;" and the Bible says that an unbelieving heart is an evil heart, and those who practice sin are of the devil (Hebrews 3:12; 1 John 3:8). The Bible also says that the face of evil is often masked with false "goodness," since Satan himself masquerades as an angel of light and his agents masquerade as ministers of morality (2 Corinthians 11:14-15). True goodness is demonstrated by faithfully obeying the whole truth of Christ's gospel and walking in the freedom and power of the New Covenant.

If you are in a false church that is practicing an Old Covenant religion (even remnants of it), get out now! We pray that every true child of God would wake up and heed the Holy Spirit's warning and come out of the false church and its curse before they are overcome by its deception and perish with it (Revelation 18:4). Of course, the false brethren do not want anyone to leave that false church and, like the devil, they will twist God's Word, citing Hebrews 10:25, which exhorts us to not stop meeting together for spiritual fellowship and encouragement. However, now is the time for God's elect to obey God, and not follow false pastors and try to fellowship with false brethren. The Bible clearly states that we can only spiritually fellowship with other Christians who walk in the light and live by the truth (1 John 1:6-7). The Bible is not talking about the difference between those who are mature or immature; the Bible is talking about the difference between those who are obedient or disobedient; between those who walk in sanctification and light or in sin and darkness. God expressly commands us to not fellowship with anyone who is habitually practicing sin and unbelief (1 Corinthians 5:11). The false church is a house of cards built on religious traditions and unbelief rather than on faith in the truth of the cross of Christ. How can there possibly be any genuine spiritual fellowship and true spiritual encouragement in the false church?

We fully recognize that finding a true New Covenant church these days is as difficult as finding a treasure hidden in a field. However, it would be far better to meet together for fellowship with just two or three other Christians who sincerely want to obey the whole gospel of Christ and live in the spiritual blessings of the New Covenant than to be part of the false church and its practices. Jesus said, "Wherever two or three gather together in My name, I am there with them (Matthew 18:20)." And if you cannot find another Christian of true faith, it would even be better to suffer hardship and be alone with the Lord than to participate in the sins and deception of the false church and eventually experience God's wrath against it. The Bible says that in the last days perilous times will come: men will be lovers of self, lovers of money and lovers of pleasure rather than lovers of God: "having a form of godliness, but denying its power. Have nothing to do with these men (2 Timothy 3:1-5)."

BUILDING THE CHURCH
IS LIKE BUILDING A FAMILY

In closing, building the church is just like building a marriage and a family. It might sound daunting, but God has invited and enabled every saint to join in building His family, so that together we can "be fruitful and multiply" (Genesis 1:28). Just as the marriage covenant can only survive and thrive when both husband and wife are properly submitted to their spiritual head, Jesus Christ; in the same way, the New Covenant church can only survive and thrive when she is properly submitted to her Bridegroom and Husband, Jesus Christ (Ephesians 5:23). Thank God that we are able, by the Spirit of Christ who lives in us, to lay down our unconverted natural soul-life (with its self-will and selfish desires) for the sake of building the New Covenant church, which is God's family and Christ's bride, so that the Father and His Son can make their home with us.[21] Jesus said, "If anyone loves Me, He will obey My Word, and My Father will love him, and We will come to him, and make our home with him (John 14:23)."

As someone has insightfully remarked, "In God's service, what matters most is the man; not the methods. Unless the man is right, right methods will be of no use to him or his work; for carnal men to use spiritual methods will only result in failure... the real danger to the work of God is our soul-life and natural energy, untamed and uncontrolled by the Holy Spirit." For, ultimately, it is not New Covenant principles and methods that matter; it is whether the work of the cross has accomplished its divine purpose within us. Therefore, everyone who aspires to build the Lord's house, His church, should ask themselves: "By faith in the power of cross (knowing that I am a new creation in Christ and no longer enslaved to sin), am I putting to death daily the sinful attitudes and actions of my unsubmitted natural soul-life, so that I might love Christ Jesus and serve His church by the Spirit and not by the flesh?" Otherwise, we will only produce soulish converts and soulish churches and, in doing so, render the cross of Christ void of its power. As the Bible says, "Unless the Lord builds the house, its builders labor in vain (Psalm 127:1)."

THE TRUE CHURCH HAS THE HEART OF THE BRIDE

What then is a New Covenant church? Is it a church that applies New Covenant principles to how it meets together? Yes, but much more. Above all, a New Covenant church exalts the Lord Jesus Christ by believing and acting on the divine provisions of the New Covenant that Christ purchased for us by His death, so that the saints can fellowship and function in the freedom and power of Christ's resurrection life. For Christ not only died to set us free from the penalty of sin, He also died to set us free from the power of our sin nature (by removing it), so that He might sovereignly live in us - His church, His bride. This is the gospel of Christ that empowered the New Covenant church in the first century, and this should be the normal Christian church life in our day. Although

God does not expect His people to be sinless, He does expect His people and even commands His people to stop practicing chronic sin. My brothers and sisters, let me be very direct and clear: it is not enough to just change our church system from an Old Covenant style of meeting to a New Covenant style of meeting. No, much more than just changing the way we do church and meet together is needed.

If you have the heart of the bride, you will not be satisfied with just joining a church that has a New Covenant style of meeting.[22] Your heart's desire will only be fulfilled when you are joined together with other passionate, like-minded saints who have been entrusted with the true gospel of Christ and are committed to carrying their own cross and laying down their soul-lives daily for Jesus Christ, our Bridegroom, and for one another, His precious bride. For it does not matter whether a church tries to meet together according to a New Covenant pattern: if that church is not planted and rooted in the true gospel of Christ and has Christ's resurrection life, it will not bear good fruit, even if New Covenant principles seem to be present.

Jesus warned, "Every plant that My heavenly Father did not plant will be uprooted... if anyone does not abide *(stay rooted)* in Me, he is thrown away like a branch that dries up; such branches are gathered up, thrown into the fire and burned (Matthew 15:13; John 15:6)." However, to those saints who stay rooted in union with Him and stay submitted to His training in righteousness, Jesus said, "My Father is glorified by this, that you bear much fruit, and so prove yourselves to be My disciples... I chose you and appointed you to go and bear fruit - fruit that will last (John 15:8 & 16)."

THE RESTORATION OF CHRIST'S CHURCH REQUIRES THE RECOVERY OF CHRIST'S COMPLETE GOSPEL

The Protestant church was originally founded from an attempt to re-form the Catholic church. However, what is required is far more than just the Protestant attempt at reformation, which did not go nearly far enough. An incomplete gospel can be just as bad as no gospel at all. It was an incomplete Protestant gospel that opened the door to deception and distortion of the true gospel of Christ by those whose hearts are not right with God. Therefore, what is urgently needed is a complete restoration of the whole gospel of Jesus Christ. For as long as the gospel that is preached is distorted, anemic and corrupted, it has no power to transform the church into Christ's glorious image. How can we possibly hope to restore the church to its God-ordained place of purity and power if we do not believe that God removed our sinful nature through Christ's death on the cross? This divine truth is the crux of what is missing from today's church theology. Even if we attempt to restore the church to its New Covenant pattern and principles, how can we possibly restore the church to its right place with God if we still think we have a sinful nature and are chronically practicing sin, so that our own souls are not right with God? How can we spiritually fight our enemy, the devil, if we mistakenly believe we still have an enemy allied to him waging guerrilla warfare within us? How can we claim to be the virgin bride of Jesus Christ when our own spiritual garments are stained by the sin of the world? How can we be wholeheartedly devoted in love to our "magnificent obsession," our Bridegroom, Jesus Christ, if we are double-minded in the affections of our heart? How can Christ sovereignly live in us if we do not believe and act on the truth of the gospel that, through Christ, we no longer have a sinful nature and have died to sin?

Five hundred years have now passed since the Holy Spirit began to restore the power of the cross of Christ and the keys of the kingdom to Christ's church. The first key – the righteous are *saved by faith* in Christ's completed work on the cross – has been restored. We believe God, in His great mercy and eternal wisdom, will soon restore the final key – enabling the righteous to *live by faith* in Christ's completed work on the cross - so that His church might walk in the power of His Son's resurrection life during the dark and turbulent days of tribulation that lie ahead (Revelation 7:9-14).[23] The recovery of Christ's gospel and the restoration of Christ's church go hand in hand. To this end we pray that God would open the eyes of everyone who fears Him, so they might find the divine key to understanding the truth of the cross that opens the door to the fullness of their glorious inheritance in the New Covenant as the bride of Christ. This God has promised: "The secret of the Lord is for those who fear Him, and He will reveal His Covenant to them (Psalm 25:14)." Until that time, let those who are forerunners in Christ's New Covenant church continue to be faithful and devoted to their Bridegroom, their true Love and Lord, the Lamb of God, Jesus Christ.

Once the gospel of Christ and the keys to God's kingdom are fully recovered, the New Covenant church will be wholly restored in all her power and glory, and the gates of hell will not be able to stop the church from fulfilling God's divine purpose (Revelation 11:15; 12:10-11). The Holy Spirit will then write the final triumphant chapter of church history. For all history is heading toward one single event – the wedding of the Lamb to His bride. In that day, heaven and earth will see the new Jerusalem – the consummation of God's eternal purpose through the ages – the full expression of Jesus Christ revealed in His church, His bride (Revelation 19:7-8; 21:2-3).

"Hallelujah! For the Lord our God, the Almighty, reigns.
Let us rejoice and be glad and give the glory to Him!
For wedding of the Lamb has come and
His bride has made herself ready."
Revelation 19:6-7

Practical Instruction On The Gospel Of Christ And The New Covenant Church

The New Covenant Church
The Bride Of Christ
Does Not Have A Sinful Nature

1 Many born again Christians mistakenly believe they have two natures within them, a new Christ-like nature and an old sinful nature, which war against each other. They believe that their new nature loves God and wants to practice righteousness, but that their old nature loves sin and wants to practice lawlessness. They think that their Christian life reflects whichever of these two conflicting natures they yield themselves to the most. However, this "tale of two natures" is not Biblically true. Romans 6:6 plainly states that our old sinful nature was crucified and *done away with* through Christ's death on the cross. Those who mistakenly think that a born again Christian still has a sinful nature sometimes justify their opinion by focusing on the interpretation of a single Greek word, *katargeo,* as it appears in Romans 6:6: "For we know that our old self was crucified with Him, in order that our body of sin *(our sinful nature)* might be *done away with (katargeo)*, so that we would no longer be slaves to sin." In this verse, the New American Standard Bible translates the Greek word *katargeo* by the phrase, *"done away with."* This is an appropriate translation within this Scriptural context since our old sinful nature died and was buried

(done away with) by our baptism *(immersion)* into Christ's death. The King James Version translates *katargeo* in this verse as *"destroyed,"* which also fits this Scriptural context since our sinful nature (the sin factory) was destroyed by Christ's death on the cross.

However, those who mistakenly believe that the sinful nature still resides within a born again Christian think the word *katargeo* should be translated as render "inactive" or "idle." In other words, they think that a Christian's sinful nature is not irrevocably dead and extinct, but instead resides in a Christian much like an idle and dormant volcano, which can spontaneously and explosively erupt back to life and cause destruction and havoc whenever a Christian sins. However, this is neither Scriptural nor logical. A careful review of the twenty-seven times that *katargeo* is used in New Testament confirms that *"done away with"* or *"destroyed"* is the proper translation of *katargeo* in the context of Romans 6:6. In fact, *katargeo* may be accurately and more clearly translated as *"removed."* This is exactly how *katargeo* can be translated in 2 Corinthians 3:16 to describe how the Old Covenant veil that blinds Jews to seeing Jesus as their Messiah is removed *(katargeo)* whenever someone turns to Christ. This veil certainly is not rendered just inactive or idle; it is removed and taken away (see 2 Corinthians 3:14 for confirmation). As another example, Paul also uses the word *katargeo* in the following verse: "Food is for the stomach and the stomach is for food, but God will destroy *(katargeo)* them both (1 Corinthians 6:13)." Once again, the best translation of *katargeo* in this verse is to *"destroy"* or *"do away with;"* it clearly does not mean to render *"inactive or idle."* This is not just semantics; when the word *katargeo* is not translated correctly in Romans 6:6, it completely changes the meaning of the Scripture.

Many Christians also mistakenly think that Romans Chapter Seven describes the conflict between the two opposing natures that exist in every born again believer. However, this is not Biblically correct. In

Romans 7:14:24, Paul uses the "first person" to emphasize the anguish and futility of trying to keep God's Law *before you were born again* when you still had a sinful nature that was hostile toward God. It is important to remember that Paul wrote his letter to the Romans in the Greek language, a precise and expressive language which often strategically uses the present tense to dramatically describe a past action and experience. In Chapter Seven, Paul made effective use of this *historical present tense*, as it is called in the Greek language, to vividly describe the misery and hopelessness of a person who wants to serve God but finds himself continually frustrated and sabotaged by his rebellious sinful nature because he is not born again. In writing this chapter, Paul drew from his own past personal experience as a devout Pharisee before He became a born again Christian. Thus, in Romans 7:5 and 7:6, Paul contrasts the spiritual condition of a Jewish unbeliever (whose righteousness depends on keeping God's Law, but is subverted by his sinful nature because he is not born again), with the spiritual condition of a born again believer (who no longer has a sinful nature and whose righteousness now depends on faith in Christ instead of keeping the Law). Therefore, Romans 7:5 sums up the unbeliever's life, which Paul then describes in Romans 7:14-24; whereas Romans 7:6 sums up the believer's life, which Paul then describes in Romans 8:9-17. Remember there were no chapter breaks in Paul's original letter to the Romans.

God knew that man's sinful nature was his Achilles heel, which Satan could use to continually snare him in sin. This is why the Old Covenant could not accomplish God's eternal purpose since man's sinful nature prevented him from truly obeying the spirit and intent of God's commandments. Therefore, what the Mosaic Law was powerless to do because of man's sinful nature, God did in the New Covenant by sending His Son who perfectly fulfilled the Law and became sin on our behalf when He was crucified, so that we might become the righteous-ness of God in Christ (Romans 8:3; 2 Corinthians 5:21). Our sinful Adam nature, which was at the very core of our inner being and the root of our self-identity and rebellion toward God, actually died and was removed from us when we received Christ into our heart; it was not merely rendered idle or inactive. Jesus said, "No one pours new wine into old wineskins... No, new wine must be poured into a new wine-skins (Luke 5:37-38)." God could not pour His Holy Spirit into people who still had old sinful natures; no, He could only pour His new wine of the Spirit into people who had new spiritual natures.

It is a divine axiom that God's Spirit of holiness could not inhabit our old sinful nature. That is why God had to remove our sinful nature before His Spirit could indwell us. Just before Jesus was crucified, He promised His disciples: "I will ask the Father and He will give you another friend to be with you forever – the Spirit of truth. The world cannot receive Him because it does not see Him or know Him, but you know Him because He is with you, *and He will live in you* (John 14:16-17)." Even people of faith during the Old Covenant still had a sinful nature and the Holy Spirit did not indwell them. This is one of the fundamental differences between the Old Covenant and the New Covenant, and why the New Covenant is called a much better covenant (Hebrews 8:6). For under the New Covenant, after having removed our sinful nature by His Son's death on the cross, the Bible says, "God sent the Spirit of His Son into our hearts (Galatians 4:6)." Paul confirms this divine fact that God removed our sinful nature as a prerequi-site to our being raised in Christ's resurrection life: "In Him you were also circumcised with a circumcision made without hands, *by the removal of your sinful nature,* by the circumcision of Christ; having been buried with Him in baptism and raised with Him through your faith in the power of God (Colossians 2:11-12)." By linking Old Covenant circumcision with New Covenant baptism, Paul leaves no doubt that the death and removal of our sinful nature, as symbolized by circumcision, is also portrayed by the burial stage of baptism. Consequently, we can count on the divine fact that we no longer have a sinful nature and are dead to sin with the same absolute certainty that we can count on the mathematical fact that one plus one equals two (Romans 6:11).

This is basic Christianity. However, if we do not believe this Biblical truth to the point that we act on it, we will not experience the divine provision that Christ died to give us. For example, if we do not believe and act on the Biblical truth that Christ's death has completely freed us from the penalty of our sins, we will not experience freedom from condemnation of sin. In the same way, if we do not believe and act on the Biblical truth that Christ's death has completely freed us from our sinful nature (by removing it), we will not experience freedom from the power of sin. The Bible says, "For we also have had the gospel preached to us, just as they did; but the Word they heard did not profit them, because it was not united by faith in those who heard (Hebrews 4:2)." Just using Romans 6:11 as some kind of "magic mantra," and repeating, "I am dead to sin, I am dead to sin, I am dead to sin," will not work. You must be convinced that you really have died to sin (Romans 6:6). That is why the truth of Romans 6:6 comes before the truth of Romans 6:11 in spiritual progression. You simply cannot "reckon" or "count" yourself dead to sin and act on this Biblical truth, unless you first "know" that your sinful nature has been destroyed and removed when you were born again.

Some people think that when we say a born again Christian does not have a sinful nature, we are saying a Christian does not sin. This most definitely is not what we mean. We do not believe in achieving "sinless perfection." However, we do believe and teach that when you are born again, God removes your sinful nature; thereby delivering you not only from the penalty of sin, but from the power of sin. From that point on, you have the spiritual freedom and ability in Christ to overcome sin, because you are no longer enslaved to sin. If you believe and act on this Biblical truth that you have been freed from sin when you were born again, you will be able to overcome sin rather than be defeated by it. This does not mean you will be "perfect" in the sense of being faultless or sinless. However, it does means you will develop a daily habit of overcoming sin, which should be the normal Christian life. The Bible says, "If we claim to be without sin *(sinless)*, we are deceiving ourselves and the truth is not in us (1 John 1:8)." This Scripture makes it clear that God does not expect us to live a perfectly sinless Christian life; and when we do sin, we are to repent from our sins in accordance with 1 John 1:9: "If we confess our sins, He is faithful and just to forgive us our sins and purify us from all unrighteousness." However, the verses which follow also make it clear that, although God does not expect us to live a sinless life, He does expect us and commands us to live a Christian life that is free from practicing chronic sin. There is a great difference between occasionally sinning out of ignorance or immaturity, and habitually being caught in willful sin. If we chronically practice sin after we are saved, the Bible says this is convincing evidence that we do know God or abide in God (1 John 3:4-10). There is also a great difference between trying to stop practicing sin and live a righteous life by our natural self-discipline, and living a righteous life that is the spiritual outgrowth of our steadfast faith in Christ's completed work on the cross. The Bible says the latter is the only kind of Christian life that pleases God and is approved by God (Romans 9:30-10:6; Hebrews 11:1-6).

Most Christians mistake their unrenewed carnal mind for their old sinful nature. This lack of Scriptural discernment has extremely detrimental consequences to their sanctification and relationship with the Lord. There is a great difference between our old sinful nature (now dead and gone) and our *unconverted* natural soul-life *(our unrenewed mind)*. Our *unconverted* soul-life does not have the power of the old sinful nature, which was like a sin factory within us, continually producing sinful attitudes and actions and enslaving us to its power. Some Christians might ask, "Why is it not enough to just believe that I am a new creation in Christ? Why must I also believe that I no longer have a sin nature?" There is an unbreakable bond between faith and truth. The Bible says that our relationship with God must be based on faith (Hebrews 11:6), and our faith must be based on a knowledge of Biblical truth to be real and effective (2 Timothy 2:25; Titus 1:1). For without true faith, we cannot see God or know God. Therefore, the more accurately we know and act on the Biblical truth, the more we can know God and the more effective we can be as His workers (2 Timothy 2:15). Conversely, without an accurate knowledge and obedience to the truth, the more the enemy can try to deceive and destroy us. As God said, "My people are destroyed for lack of knowledge (Hosea 4:6)."

The more central the truth, the more essential that truth is to our Christian faith. And there is no truth more central to our Christian faith than knowing Jesus Christ (who He is and what He accomplished for us on the cross). For example, the Deity of Jesus Christ is central to Christianity and absolutely essential to our Christian faith. If you do not believe that Jesus Christ is God, then you are not walking in the truth and your faith is not real Biblical faith. In other words, you cannot know God if you do not believe and submit to the essential truth of Jesus Christ's Deity. Another central truth is the fact that Jesus Christ died on the cross to deliver us from the penalty of sin and reconcile us to God (2 Corinthians 5:19). Knowing (and believing and acting on) this Biblical truth is essential to your Christian faith; otherwise your sins would separate you from God (Ephesians 2:1-9). However, there are many Biblical truths that are not as central to our Christian faith. In other words, they are spiritually and practically important to believe and act on, but they are not essential to your salvation and entrance into the kingdom of God. For example, whether you believe in pre-tribulation, mid-tribulation, or post-tribulation end-time theology is not essential to your salvation and sanctification.

God's new creation is the body of Christ, His church. Therefore, the fact that we are a new creation in Christ (2 Corinthians 5:17) is a very important truth, but it hinges on another more foundational truth: before God could make us a new spiritual creation (born into Christ); He had to first deal with our old spiritual creation (that we inherited from Adam). He had to not only deal with its fruit (our sinful actions); He also had to destroy and remove its very root (our Adam sinful nature). Otherwise, that bad root would always produce bad fruit. Christ's complete triumph over sin through the cross is clearly portrayed in the God-ordained ceremony of water baptism. As we said earlier, the death and burial (removal) of our old man (our sin nature) is demonstrated by the first stage of water baptism (when we are immersed or "buried" under the water). The second stage of water baptism (when we are raised up out of the water) demonstrates that we are now a new creation in Christ. Without the first stage of baptism, there would be no second stage. In other words, if God did not first remove our Adam sin nature, we could not have become a new creation in Christ.

Therefore, the miracle of our salvation fundamentally depended upon the death and removal of our sin nature. Since the destruction of our sin nature was essential to our new birth in Christ, why is this cardinal truth also critical to our Christian faith after we are saved? This is the reason: the only way you can practice true sanctification (or holiness) is if you know that God destroyed and removed your sinful nature and that, by this decisive action, God has freed you from slavery to sin. For how could you possibly be freed from the power of sin if Satan still retained an evil, sinister foothold in you through your indwelling sin nature? Therefore, the fact that God destroyed your sinful nature when you were saved is the strategic truth of the cross that enables you to daily overcome sin and live holy in the Lord. And this truth is absolutely essential to your eternal destiny, for without walking in holiness you will never know God nor inherit eternal life (Hebrews 12:14; 1 John 3:6).

There are a number of other important Biblical truths which also hinge upon this indispensable core truth of the cross (that God destroyed and removed your sinful nature when you were saved). For example, let us examine the truth that sin is no longer our master (Romans 6:19). But why is sin no longer our master? Because we were freed from the power of sin when God removed our sinful nature (Romans 6:6-7; Colossians 2:11). Another important truth is the fact that we died with Christ when we were born again. Most Christians should be familiar with this Biblical truth since it is clearly stated in the Bible (Romans 6:8, 11; 7:6; 2 Corinthians 5:14; Galatians 2:20; Colossians 2:20; 3:3; 2 Timothy 2:11). But what part of us died with Christ when we were saved? Did our body die? Certainly not! Did our soul die? No, of course not! Then what died? The Bible says that our old sinful nature irrevocably died and was decisively removed from us (Romans 6:6; Colossians 2:11). For how could we truly be dead to sin if we still had an evil sin nature living in us? Another vital truth of our Christian faith is the fact that Christ lives in us (Colossians 1:27). And how is Christ able to dwell in us? Because God had destroyed and removed our indwelling, resident sin nature.

The Bible also says that we are a temple of the Holy Spirit, but how could we possibly be a holy temple of God if we still had an evil sin nature inhabiting us? (1 Corinthians 2:16-17). The central purpose of Christ's Atonement and the New Covenant was to reconcile us to God so that we could be united with Him in one spirit (1 Corinthians 6:17; 2 Corinthians 5:17-21). But how could we truly be one spirit with Holy God if we still had an old man of sin living within us that was hostile to God? Finally, another key Biblical truth is the fact that the church is Christ's body on earth (Ephesians 1:22-23). But, once again, how could the church be the living body of Christ if it still had the cancerous presence of sin infecting it? It was imperative for God to get rid of the malignant cancer of our indwelling sin nature, so that we could be Christ's healthy and holy body. If we still had an evil old man of sin indwelling our body, it would be as though we had a killer zombie inhabiting and haunting our body. It should be clear that the erroneous belief that we still have a sinful nature inhabiting us after we are born again is neither Biblical nor logical. To sum up, the truth of the cross of Christ is the taproot of many other Biblical truths, such as "sin is no longer our master," and "we have been freed from sin," and "we have died with Christ," and "we are new creations in Christ," and "Christ lives in us," and "we are Christ's body, His church." Therefore, if you do not know that God destroyed and removed your sinful nature when you were born again, then you do not know a crucial Biblical truth, which is indispensable and pivotal to other important Biblical truths. You are then left with a partial or incomplete picture of Christ's victory on the cross. Your faith is only secure and unshakeable to the degree that you know (and believe and act on) Christ's complete triumph on the cross over all the power of the enemy.

If you do not know how to exercise faith in this strategic victory of the cross (God removed your sinful nature in order to destroy the devil's ability to keep you captive to sin), then your ignorance of this powerful Biblical truth will be your "Achilles' heel." For example, when you are tempted to sin, you may say, "I can resist sin because I am a new creation in Christ." But the devil can then say, "Yes, but you still have a sinful nature that wants to sin, don't you?" If you believe this lie (that you are still captive to sin because you have the indwelling presence of sin in your body), it will undermine your faith in Christ's victory on the cross and leave you vulnerable to the enemy's temptations to induce you to sin. The same is true for any of the other truths that also vitally depend upon this invaluable Biblical truth that you no longer have a sinful nature. If you add the lie that you still have a sinful nature to any of these other truths, then you nullify the whole truth. As Paul warned, "Do you not know that a little leaven leavens the whole lump of dough?" In other words, do you not know that one lie can undermine the whole truth? Here is another example of how this lie (that you still have a sinful nature) works to undermine the whole truth: you may say, "I can resist sin because sin is no longer master over me." But the devil can then say, "Yes, but since you still have a sinful nature, you cannot really expect to stop practicing sin, can you?" How can you possibly say "no to sin and yes to God" if you entertain this kind of deceptive, unbelieving and double-minded thinking?

Jesus said, "If you abide in My Word, then you are truly My disciples; and you will know the truth and the truth will set you free (John 8:31-32)." And what is the truth that sets you free from practicing sin? It is the simple yet powerful truth that you no longer have a sinful nature because God removed it from you through the cross of Christ. This God-given truth is our "Declaration of Independence" from the tyranny of sin. Since Christ's triumph on the cross is essential to not only our salvation, but also to our sanctification, we must believe and act on the truth of the whole gospel of Christ in order to know God; be His faithful overcomers; and inherit His eternal life. And this is the truth of the whole gospel: Christ died for us and included us in His death (in order to remove our sinful nature) so that He could sovereignly live in us (Galatians 2:20). Therefore, knowing who Jesus is and what He accomplished through His atoning, substitutionary sacrifice on the cross (both the forgiveness of our sins and the removal of our sin nature) is not only foundational but essential to our Christian faith and is the cornerstone of basic Christianity.

Unfortunately, many sincere Christians who are convicted by the Holy Spirit because of their habitual sinning, live with secret dread that their sinful nature is not irrevocably dead and removed. They mistakenly believe they have two spiritual natures within them, a new Christ-like nature and an old sinful nature, which continually wage war against each other. They believe their new nature loves God and wants to practice righteousness, but their old nature loves sin and wants to practice lawlessness. They are wrongly taught that this continual conflict of two opposing inner natures is the normal Christian life. This conflicted inner self-identity places the burden to overcome the old sinful nature and stop sinning on your shoulders and on your own ability, self-effort and work, instead of where it belongs: on Christ's shoulders and His completed work on the cross. As a result, many Christians live under an oppressive yoke of ignorance and unbelief – worried and fearful that their victory over sin hinges on whichever of these two warring inner natures they yield to the most. Tragically, for many Christians, the only way out of this constant inner turmoil and sense of frustration, failure and guilt is to harden their conscience against the Holy Spirit's conviction of sin, since they are continually defeated by what they believe is the satanic power of an indwelling sinful nature. Consequently, a countless number of Christians have become hopelessly discouraged and resigned to sin because they have swallowed this lie that they have an evil nature, while many others are deceived by self-righteousness and secret pride into thinking they can overcome the old sinful nature through willpower, self-discipline and religious methods.

At the present time, this truth of the complete gospel (that God removed our sinful nature when we were born again) is either rejected outright or simply ignored by the false church. However, there will come a time when God will enlighten the eyes of His elect to believe and act on this powerful Biblical truth. We believe the restoration of this truth of the gospel will coincide with a historic, worldwide move of the Holy Spirit. At that time, the false church (the harlot of Satan) will attempt to deviously absorb and subvert the divine truth of our co-crucifixion with Christ in order to carnally benefit and profit from this move of the Holy Spirit. Wolves in sheep's clothing will give "lip service" to this Biblical truth and falsely claim that they do not have a sinful nature and that Christ lives in them. However, Jesus said we would be able to discern these charlatans by their fruit (Matthew 7:20). It does not matter what someone claims to know or claims to have, what matters is whether they wholehearted obey the truth of the cross of Christ and bear His spiritual fruit (Romans 6:17). Jesus said that many people would falsely claim that He is Lord when, in actuality, they practice sin and do not obey Him (Matthew 7:21-23; Luke 6:46). Consequently, the true test of whether someone is walking in the truth is the quality of their spiritual fruit. Therefore, when we encounter any Christian who claims to walk in the truth of the cross, we need to be "fruit inspectors" and put them to the same test (1 John 3:10), which the apostle John used in his day: 1) Do they walk in true righteousness, which comes only from believing and acting on the Biblical truth of the cross?; and 2) Do they love *(agapao)* the true brethren who are walking in the Biblical truth of the cross? If they fail this test, it means they do not have true faith and they are false brethren whose hearts have not truly been circumcised by the Spirit of God (Romans 3:29; Colossians 2:11).

THE NEW COVENANT CHURCH HAS GRACE AND TRUTH IN CHRIST

2 The false church has a false mantra which its members live by: "It is all about grace." What they mean is that grace covers all their sins: past, present and future. They believe Christians are sinners who cannot stop habitually sinning (just like unbelievers). They think the only difference between a Christian and a non-Christian is that God's grace covers all of a Christian's sins so a Christian does not have to worry about God's judgment for their chronic sins. As one so-called "Christian" put it: "God grades on a bell curve and everyone gets a passing grade." In other

words, they mistakenly believe that some Christians may sin more than other Christians, but all Christians will still go to heaven, no matter how much they practice sin. Some Christians even go so far as to say they no longer need to ask forgiveness for the sins they commit because all their sins (past, present, and future) have already been covered by God's grace. Far too many Christians think the "good news" of the gospel is that they can receive forgiveness for their sins and yet continue in them. This philosophy may be soulishly comforting to those who cannot or do not want to stop practicing sin, but it is not Biblically true. When Jesus told people that their sins were forgiven, He also told them, "Go, and sin no more!" (John 5:14; 8:11)

It is said that every good lie has an element of truth in it. This is the reasoning behind this falsehood: "Since we could only be saved by grace, then grace must cover all of our sins; otherwise we could be saved by our works." The problem with this way of thinking is that it does not line up with the truth of God's Word. Because of spiritual ignorance, most Christians do not understand the relationship between faith and works. What does the Bible mean by "faith" and "works?" Faith is "what we believe" and works are "what we do," or the fruit of what we believe. The Bible says we are saved solely by faith in Jesus Christ because there are no works which could ever earn us righteousness. "For by grace you have been saved through faith... not by works, so that no one can boast (Ephesians 2:8-9)." But once we are saved, the Bible says we must then express our faith by our works; otherwise our faith is not valid. The Bible says, "Faith apart from works is inactive and ineffective and worthless (James 2:20)." Therefore, salvation is not a result of our works, but works must result from our salvation if our faith in Jesus Christ is authentic. Thus we are not saved by obeying God's commands; however, after we are saved, we will obey God's commands if our salvation is real. This obedience is what the Bible calls the "obedience of faith" and "works of faith" that every Christian should have if they are truly living by faith (Romans 1:5; 1 Thessalonians 1:3). As the Bible says, "What good is it, my brothers, if a man claims to have faith, but he has no works? Can that faith save him? (James 2:14)."

As a consequence of this misunderstanding about faith, many Christians are also spiritually ignorant of the true Biblical meaning and purpose of God's grace. In order to understand God's grace, we must look to the plumbline of truth, which is God's Word; otherwise man's natural tendency is to embrace some form of humanistic grace that, like soft clay, can be molded to the world's changing tides of culture, values, ethics and morals. This is why the Bible says both *grace and truth* came through Jesus Christ (John 1:17)." The Biblical truth is that we can only be saved by God's grace (not by our own works); but after we are saved, God's grace enables us to stop sinning. What does this mean? God's grace (made available through Christ's death on the cross) has given us a two-fold deliverance from the curse of sin. By God's grace, we have been freed from the penalty of sin; and by God's grace, we have also been freed from the power of sin (when God removed our sinful nature when we were saved).

However, since most Christians are spiritually ignorant of this second provision of the cross, they think they cannot stop practicing sin. As Paul said, "Come back to your senses as you should, and stop sinning; for there are some of you who are ignorant of God (1 Corinthians 15:34)." And Paul also said, "Should we go on sinning so that grace may increase? May it never be! (Romans 6:1)." God's grace must never be used by Christians as a license to keep practicing sin. The Bible says, "My brothers, you were called to be free, but do not use your freedom as an opportunity to indulge in sinful behavior... and do not use your freedom as a cover-up for evil (Galatians 5:13; 1 Peter 2:16)." God's grace (available through Christ's death on the cross) has been given to enable us to stop practicing sin. The Bible says, "The grace of God has appeared, bringing salvation to all men, and instructing us to deny ungodliness and worldly desires and to live self-controlled, upright, godly lives in this present age (Titus 2:11-12)." If we believe and act on this truth of the cross, then living a godly life is the proof that our faith in Christ is genuine. However, if we continue to habitually practice sin, the Bible says that we walk in darkness and cannot have fellowship with Jesus Christ here on earth or in heaven. "No one who abides in Him keeps on sinning. No one continues to sin has seen Him or knows Him... the one who practices sin is of the devil (1 John 3:6-8)."

The Bible says that any Christian who keeps practicing unrepentant, chronic sin after they are saved can no longer count on receiving the grace of God's forgiveness; instead they can expect to receive the wrath of God's judgment. "For if we go on sinning willfully after we have received the knowledge of the truth, there no longer remains a sacrifice for *(forgiveness of)* sins, but only a terrifying expectation of judgment (Hebrews 10:26-27)." If we never master the sins that habitually entangle us, then the grace of God made available through Christ's death on the cross will have been of no use to us. In the words of our brother Paul: "As God's fellow workers, we urge you not to receive the grace of God in vain (2 Corinthians 6:1)."

How To Carry Your Own Cross For Christ And His Church

3   The answer to the church's centuries old dilemma of how to overcome sin is found in the cross of Christ. The mystery of the cross is like the centerpiece of a divine jigsaw puzzle that is the key to understanding the whole gospel of Jesus Christ. The word of the kingdom and the word of the cross fit together to form one eternal gospel of Jesus Christ.

The word of the kingdom is the message that God the Father desires for Christ to reign as absolute King in our life. The word of the cross is the message that Christ died for us to make this possible. Coupled together, these two divine truths can be expressed as: Christ died for us and included us in His death (to remove our sinful nature) so He might sovereignly live in us. When we know (believe and act on) the complete gospel that we died with Christ and no longer have a sinful nature, we can then live by faith in the Son of God who lives in us.

Ultimately, our struggle against sin is a struggle of faith against unbelief because all sin springs from unbelief (Hebrews 3:12-19). Just as unbelief produces lawlessness and yields the fruit of death, our faith in Jesus Christ (who He is and what He accomplished for us on the cross) produces obedience and yields the fruit of holiness, and its reward – eternal life (Romans 6:20-22). Believing and acting on the truth of the cross (that we have died to sin) is the way (the only way) that God has provided for us to overcome sin. The Bible says, "For he who has died has been freed from sin (Romans 6:7)." This Biblical truth is our God-given "Declaration of Independence" from the tyranny of sin, which Jesus Christ died on the cross to give us. This is the liberating truth that Paul practiced and preached: "I *(my old self)* have been crucified with Christ, and I *(my sinful nature)* no longer live, but Christ lives in me; and the life that I now live in the body, I live by faith in the Son of God (Galatians 2:20)."

Once we are fully persuaded of this Biblical truth, we do not have to fight to gain victory over sin; instead, we can overcome sin from a secure position of victory because Jesus Christ who lives in us has already conquered sin for us by His triumph on the cross (1 John 4:4; 5:4). Just as Christ bore us (our old man of sin) on His cross to give us victory over sin, we can now bear our own cross by faith to manifest His victory in our lives and occupy the spiritual ground He has won for us, which is His "Promised Land," the Kingdom of

God. Jesus said, "Whoever does not carry his own cross and follow Me, cannot be My disciple (Luke 14:27)." What does it mean to carry our own cross? As we present ourselves to God daily, the Holy Spirit will reveal to us that our Lord's cross, which was the implement of His death, must now become the implement of our own death. Therefore, the cross is not just His; it must by faith become ours. But what is it that must die when we carry our own cross? Since the chief obstacle to our living by the Spirit is no longer our sinful Adam nature (since it was removed when we were born again); it is our old Adam way of thinking (our unrenewed mind) that must die. Our self-governing, soulish way of thinking must die to its own sovereignty and embrace submission at the feet of Jesus. The Bible declares, "Every knee will bow, in heaven and on earth and under the earth, and every tongue will confess that Jesus Christ is Lord (Philippians 2:10-11)."

There is a price to follow Jesus Christ and prove we are His disciples; the cost is carrying our own cross and losing our soul-life for Christ's sake. Jesus said, "If anyone wishes to come after Me, he must deny himself and take up his cross daily and follow Me. For whoever wishes to save his soul-life will lose it, but whoever loses his soul-life for My sake, he is the one who will save it (Luke 9:23-24)." When we are born again and take up His cross of discipleship, this process of sanctification begins in our lives. The Bible says, "Now may the God of peace sanctify you entirely; and may your spirit, soul and body be preserved complete, without blame at the coming of our Lord Jesus Christ (1 Thessalonians 5:23)." This complete sanctification - the Kingship of Christ ruling our lives - is possible if we cooperate by faith with the Spirit's daily outworking of Christ's death in our natural soul-life. As Jesus said, "Do not be afraid, little flock, for your Father has chosen gladly to give you the kingdom (Luke 12:32)."

The Bible says, "Each one is tempted when he is carried away and enticed by his own lust. Then, when lust has conceived, it gives birth to sin; and when sin is fully matured, it produces death (James 1:14-15)." If we allow ourselves to indulge in seemingly harmless sinful thoughts with the naïve and mistaken idea that we can always control and stop them whenever we want, we will find ourselves habitually caught in sin. The Bible says, "The little foxes ruin the vineyards (Song of Solomon 2:15)." In other words, it is the little sins that can destroy your spiritual fruit if you do not catch them and stop them. Therefore, we must exercise faith in the power of the cross and forcefully resist indulging in even the "smallest" sinful imaginations, and aggressively refuse to entertain even the "tiny" carnal thoughts that can infiltrate our mind (1 Corinthians 6:18; 10:14; 1 Timothy 6:11). For example, you may have a momentary thought of resentment toward someone who has wronged you in the past. However, if you hold onto that seed of resentment and nourish it, that seemingly harmless seed of resentment can take root and eventually bear the fruit of bitterness in your soul. Or, if you are a Christian brother, you may fleetingly look at women with sexual desire. However, if you continue to nourish that seed of lust, it can take root and lead you into pornography and other sexual immorality. This is why we must put to death even tiny seeds of sin as soon as we become aware of them if we want to walk in the Lord's holiness and be able to experience close intimacy with Him.

True Christianity is not natural; it is spiritual. Jesus did not die on the cross so that Christians would remain governed by their natural instincts and carnal desires and just do whatever comes naturally to them. Just as we were born of the Spirit, we must now live by the Spirit, and not according to our natural temperament. Paul taught, "So I say, live by the Spirit and you will not carry out the desire of the flesh *(the unconverted natural soul-life)*. For the flesh *(the unsubmitted natural soul-life)* sets its desire against the Spirit, and the Spirit against the flesh *(the unsubmitted natural soul-life); for* these are in conflict with one another (Galatians 5:16-17; see also 6:7-8)." If you remain controlled by your natural temperament and carnal desires and are not governed by the Holy Spirit, you will be of no use to God and

His kingdom. However, if you are submitted to Christ's sovereignty, then God can transform your soul-life (your natural attitudes and affections) by the power of His Word so that you become His sanctified vessel (Romans 12:1-2). As the indwelling Holy Spirit progressively governs your soul-life, carnal character traits such as arrogance, anger, lust, laziness, lying, gossiping and fearfulness will increasingly disappear and be replaced with Christ's attitudes and thoughts. This is how you "work out your salvation with fear and trembling; for it is God who works in you, both to will and to act according to His good purpose (Philippians 2:12-13)."

This on-going process of sanctification in our lives does not mean that we will never sin. John wrote: "If we claim to be without sin *(sinless)*, we are deceiving ourselves and the truth is not in us (1 John 1:8)." Therefore, when we do sin, we practice 1 John 1:9: we confess our sins and ask God's forgiveness for our sins. Although God does not expect us to live a fault-less or perfectly sinless life, He does expect us and commands us to not practice chronic sin. There is a great difference between occasionally sin-ning out of ignorance or immaturity, and habitually being caught in willful and unrepentant sin. The Biblical difference between God's judgement if we willfully and unrepentantly practice sin, and God's grace when we occasionally and unwittingly sin is expressed by John: "My dear children, I write this letter to you *so that you will not sin.* But *if anyone does sin*, we have an Advocate with the Father, Jesus Christ, the Righteous One. He is the atoning sacrifice for our sins, and not only for ours but for the sins of the whole world. We know that we have come to know Him if we obey His commands. The man who says, 'I know Him,' but does not do what He commands is a liar, and the truth is not in him (1 John 2:1-4)." Jesus died on the cross to free us from the seduction and snare of sin. If we inten-tionally and chronically practice sin, we disobey God's commands, and the Bible says that we cannot know God or abide in God (1 John 3:4-10).

In Christ, we do not practice self-crucifixion; instead we identify with the work of His cross by faith and make it our own. Now that we no longer have a sinful nature, our unrenewed mind can be transformed and submitted to Christ's sovereignty by believing the truth of God's Word. As Paul said, "Do not be conformed to this world, but be transformed by the renewing of your mind, so that you may prove what the will of God is, that which is good, and acceptable and perfect (Romans 12:2)." Thus by faith in Christ's completed work on the cross, we are able to replace our carnal attitudes and affections with Christ's attitudes and affections. We are now able by faith to put to death (and rid ourselves of) the carnal mind-set of our unconverted soul and put on the mind of Christ (1 Corinthians 2:26). Paul taught, "If you are living according to the flesh *(your unconverted natural soul-life)*, you will die; but if by the Spirit, you are putting to death the misdeeds of the body, you will live... do not be conformed to this world, but be transformed by the renewing of your mind, so that you may prove what is the will of God... put to death, therefore, whatever belongs to your soulish nature: sexual immorality, impurity, lust, evil desires and greed... now all those who belong to Christ Jesus have put to death on the cross the flesh *(their unconverted natural soul-life)* with its passions and desires (Romans 8:13; 12:2; Colossians 3:5; Galatians 5:24)."

This daily process of carrying your own cross and putting to death your unconverted, natural soul-life is what the Bible calls "being conformed to His death (Philippians 3:10)." If we love Christ Jesus, we will carry our cross and lay down our soul-life daily for the sake of His church, His body (1 John 3:16). It is our obligation and privilege as Christ's bride to triumphantly take up our own cross and "put to death" the attitudes and actions of our unconverted natural soul-life, so that by the sanctifying work of the Spirit within us, we might be transformed into Christ's holy bride (2 Corinthians 3:18). Every disciple who identifies with Christ's death by faith in this way will have the mark of the cross on their soul. This ongoing work of the cross in our lives and participation in His sufferings is essential if we desire to know Christ and live in the power of His resurrection life (Philippians 3:10).

For if we want to follow Jesus Christ in discipleship and carry our own cross, we must be prepared to suffer in our soul-life. Our flesh (the Greek word is *sarx*, which in this Scriptural context means both body and soul) will suffer the temporal grief and pain that accompanies the denial and loss of our self-sovereignty and carnal self-identity as we yield our soul-life to Christ in sanctification. The Bible says, "Since Christ has suffered in the flesh *(body and soul)*, arm yourselves also with the same purpose, because he who has suffered in the flesh *(our body and soul)* has ceased from sin so as to live no longer for the lusts of men but for the will of God (1 Peter 4:1-2)." Remember that God created our human soul; therefore, He does not want to destroy our soul, nor does He want us to vainly try to suppress our soul, which is man's carnal method of self-crucifixion. Instead, God wants to restore our soul to His original, eternal purpose. It is God's perfect design that each of us would have a vibrant, Holy Spirit-governed soul. The Bible says Jesus Christ is the shepherd and guardian of our soul (1 Peter 2:25). Jesus wants to save our soul (James 1:21); heal our soul (Psalm 41:4); purify our soul (1 Peter 1:21); convert our soul (Psalm 19:7); transform our soul (Romans 12:2); and restore our soul (Psalm 23:3).

The work of the cross will not annihilate our soul; we will still possess our soul and its faculties, just as we still possess our physical body with its faculties. But when the mark of the cross is imprinted on our soul, we will no longer independently assert ourselves apart from Christ's will. Instead, we will be transformed as yielded, obedient and useful vessels for God's use (2 Timothy 2:21). And like Jesus Himself was submitted to the Father, we will be able to say, "I can do nothing on my own initiative (John 5:19 &

30)." As we learn to carry our cross daily, we will increasingly experience and express the power of Jesus Christ's resurrection *zoē*-life. Paul testified, "We always carry about in our body the death of Jesus, so that the life of Jesus may also be revealed in our body (2 Corinthians 4:10)." The way of the cross is the only way of fruitfulness in Christ. Jesus said, "Truly, truly, I say to you, unless a grain of wheat falls into the earth and dies, it remains only a single seed; but if it dies, it produces much fruit. He who loves his soul-life loses it, and he who hates his soul-life in this world will keep it to life eternal (John 12:24-25)." To the carnal-minded, losing your soul-life for the sake of Christ and His gospel is a terrible waste. However, you only entertain the idea of waste when you underestimate the Lord's worth. When we see the priceless glory of Jesus Christ through the eyes of faith, we will want to sell all we have in order to know Him – the Pearl of Great Price (Matthew 13:45-46). Gaining Jesus Christ is worth far more than everything we have to sell. Knowing Jesus is worth far beyond anything we have to lose. To those who know it, the way of the cross is a precious path that leads us into a more and more intimate relationship with Jesus Christ.

It is absolutely essential that you know your sinful nature has died with Christ and been removed in Christ (Romans 6:6; Colossians 2:11) before you try to lay down your soul-life. Why? Because it is impossible to carry your own cross and lay down your soul-life without faith, and your faith must be based on Biblical truth to be real and effective. When you know (believe and act on) the divine truth that your sinful nature has been crucified with Christ and is dead and gone, you will be freed from the awful burden of protecting and promoting your natural (soulish) self-identity, and relentlessly pursuing the natural desire for soulish self-fulfillment and self-ambition (Galatians 6:14). One of the main reasons why many Christians do not allow the Holy Spirit to really convict them of their sins is because they would have to stop practicing those sins. Although they cloak themselves with false humility by saying they will always just be "sinners" saved by grace; in reality, they are using this as an excuse to keep practicing sin. When you allow the Holy Spirit to truly convict you of your sins, there is only one righteous response: you must stop practicing those sins by believing and acting on the truth of Christ's completed work on the cross. If we know that we have died to our former self (and our sinful nature), we are then spiritually secure and free to allow the power of the Holy Spirit and the truth of God's Word to convict us of our sins. We are then able by faith to purify our soul-life by putting to death all sinful attitudes and actions, so that the power of Christ's resurrection life might be revealed through us (Romans 8:13; 2 Corinthians 4:12). This is true humility in Gods eyes.

A picture of this spiritual principle may be found in the parable of the light and the lampstand (Luke 11:33-36). Jesus Christ is the light that illumines the lamp – our spirit (John 1:9; 8:12: Proverbs 20:27). Our soul (our natural personality) is like the lampshade. If we do not allow the Holy Spirit to govern our soul-life, our unsubmitted and unbroken natural personality will obscure the light of Christ from clearly shining through us. Jesus said a light hidden under a basket cannot be seen. This is similar to a smoke-blackened lampshade and illustrates what happens when a born again Christian still has an unconverted, untransformed and lawless soul-life. However, a light with a clear lampshade (a Christian who has their soul governed and transformed by God) shines brightly and Christ can be clearly seen in them. Once we know (and believe and act on) the divine truth that we have already died with Christ and no longer have a sinful nature, we are able by exercising faith in this truth of the cross to cleanse and purify our soul of all carnal attitudes and affections. The Bible says, "Therefore, having these promises, beloved, let us purify ourselves from everything that contaminates body and spirit, perfecting holiness in the fear of God (2 Corinthians 7:1)."

The more we believe and act on the power of the cross to purify and cleanse our soul (our lampshade) of all carnal spots and blemishes (Ephesians 5:27), the more the light of Christ within our spirit can be transparently seen through our individual personality. Jesus said, "If therefore your whole body is full of light, with no dark part in it, it will be wholly illumined, as when the lamp illumines you with its rays... let your light shine before men in such a way that they may see your good works, and glorify your Father who is in heaven (Luke 11:36; Matthew 5:16)." With this in mind, John wrote, "Beloved now we are children of God, and it is not yet revealed what we will be. We know that when He appears, we will be like Him, because we will see Him just as He is. And everyone who has this hope fixed on Him purifies himself, just as He is pure (1 John 3:2-3)." The consummation of this sanctifying process in the body of Christ – His bride - can be seen in the Book of Revelation: "And I saw the holy city, new Jerusalem, coming down out of heaven from God, made ready as a bride for her husband... And the city has no need of the sun or of the moon to shine on it, for the glory of God has illumined it, and the Lamb is its lamp (Revelation 21:2 & 23)."

THE BEGINNING OF THE CHURCH'S DECLINE

4 There is both Biblical and historical evidence to indicate the church began a spiritual decline within just a few generations after Jesus ascended to heaven. For example, in the middle of the first century (A.D. 50 to A.D. 60), the apostle Paul addressed letters to seven different churches. This was the "first generation" of churches following Christ's death and resurrection. Based on the historical record of Paul's letters, only two of the seven churches (Galatia and

Corinth) had serious spiritual problems; the large majority (although not perfect) appear to be faithfully fulfilling Christ's divine purpose for His church. However, within forty years, this situation had dramatically changed. In the Book of Revelation (written around A.D. 95), the apostle John has a vision in which Jesus also addressed seven churches. This was the "second generation" of churches after Christ's ascension to heaven. This time, only two of the seven churches (Smyrna and Philadelphia) received high marks. In contrast, five of the seven churches had very serious spiritual problems. This represented a significant decline in the spiritual state of the church in just one generation. However, those churches that were in serious spiritual trouble did not necessarily close their doors and "go out of business." Instead, they were in grave danger of opening their doors to people who professed to be Christians, but who did not walk in the truth of Christ.

Consequently, John wrote a letter to warn the churches of this danger. In his letter, John specifically describes the evidence or spiritual fruit that can help the church assess whether someone is a true or false Christian. John wrote, "By this the children of God and the children of the devil are obvious: anyone who does not practice righteousness is not of God, nor is the one who does not love his brother (1 John 3:10)." From this, we can conclude that if someone practices righteousness (that comes by faith) and loves their brothers and sisters in Christ, they are a true Christian. But, conversely, if they do not practice righteousness that comes by faith and do not love the body of Christ, they are a false Christian. John's letter to the churches, written at the end of the first century, marks the emergence of the false church. This satanic threat to Christianity came not in the form of persecution; instead, it came through the infiltration of many false Christians into the church, who brought with them a counterfeit Christianity (also known as Churchianity), which leavened the church.

John warned the churches that many "antichrists" were now trying to deceive Christians (1 John 2:18; 2 John 7). John wrote, "Anyone who goes too far and does not abide in the teaching of Christ, does not have God; the one who abides in the teaching, he has both the Father and the Son… these things I have written to you concerning those who are trying to deceive you (2 John 9, 26)." Note that the New Testament Greek word that John used for "antichrist" does not just mean "against" Christ; it also means "in place of" Christ; in other words, it can also mean a counterfeit Christ, or a counterfeit Christian. Jude also warned of this threat to the church: "Certain men have secretly slipped in among you… these are the men who are hidden reefs in your love feasts when they eat with you without fear, caring only for themselves. They are clouds without rain, blown along by the wind, autumn trees without fruit, uprooted – doubly dead… these are the ones who cause divisions, worldly-minded, devoid of the Spirit (Jude 4, 12, 19)." If, at the end of the first century, there were many false Christians trying to infiltrate the church and establish a counterfeit version of Christianity, how many more false Christians are sneaking into the church two thousand years later? In our present time of spiritual darkness and deception, there is a satanic army of imposters who masquerade as Christians; but who are devoid of the Holy Spirit and have the spirit of antichrist. Because these so-called Christians have a different spirit; they have a different faith, a different gospel and a different Jesus.

A review of the Scriptures and church history reveals that whether an individual Christian, or a group of Christians in a local church, or a generation of Christians will produce good fruit or bad fruit directly depends on the root of their faith. If they are abiding in the holy root, which is the truth of Jesus Christ and His finished work on the cross, they will have Christ's life and they will produce good fruit. However, if they are not abiding in the truth of Christ and His finished work on the cross, they will not have Christ's life and they will produce bad fruit.

THE PRACTICE OF METHODISM

5 Most Christians try to pursue holiness by practicing a form of "methodism." What is the practice of methodism? The practice of methodism involves the use of certain methods in order to try to live a sanctified or holy Christian life after you are saved. The practice of "methodism" became popularized in England in the early 1730s by the evangelist John Wesley and his brother Charles, when they led a group of Oxford students in a Bible study that some called the "Holy Club." The Wesley brothers and other Holy Club members came to be known as "methodists" because they practiced certain religious methods to try to be holy. The methods they used were reading the Bible, praying, fasting, witnessing, going to church, and serving others. This practice of "methodism" was not really new to the traditions of both the Catholic and Protestant church. For centuries before the Wesleys' methodical attempt to live holy, this approach was used by priests and monks who called it the practice of spiritual "exercises" or "disciplines."

The practice of "disciplines" employed the same basic methods used by the Wesley brothers. It was thought that the practice of these disciplines or methods might exercise and strengthen a person's willpower and ability to resist sin. It was also thought that these methods might serve as "means of grace," by which a person could appropriate God's grace to help them live a holy life. However, if we want to go on with God and know God, we must honestly acknowledge that the practice of methodism cannot stop us from practicing sin. Just as we could not be saved by practicing methodism, neither can we be sanctified (or made holy) by practicing methodism. In fact, many people who read the Bible regularly, pray regularly and go to church regularly are not even saved. As a case in point, John and Charles Wesley were not even born again when they practiced methodism in the early 1730s. They were not saved until 1738. How did they get saved? By faith in Christ alone, and not by practicing any religious method. John Wesley's own words explain how he was saved on May 24, 1738: "I did trust in Christ, Christ alone for salvation."

Practicing methodism can never produce a saving or sanctifying faith in you. Nor can it create in you an ability to "allow the Holy Spirit to control your daily life." Only faith in Christ alone can save you, and only faith in Christ alone can enable the power of the Holy Spirit to work within you. No method can ever set you free from practicing sin. Your willpower cannot set you free from practicing sin. Your self-discipline cannot set you free from practicing sin. Whenever we step out of faith in Christ and enter into our own effort, we take the burden for our sanctification out of God's hands and put it in our own hands. Practicing methodism places the burden to stop sinning on *your* shoulders and on *your* own ability, self-effort and work, instead of where it belongs: on Christ's shoulders and *His* completed work on the cross. In fact, practicing methodism is not much different than how a devout Pharisee during Jesus' time would have tried to be holy (Luke 18:9-12). A Pharisee who wanted to stop practicing sin would read the Scriptures more, pray more, fast more, tithe more, and go to synagogue every time it was open. However Jesus said, "Unless your righteousness surpasses that of the Pharisees and the teachers of the Law, you will not enter the kingdom of heaven (Matthew 5:20)."

If the practice of methodism were enough to be holy (in God's eyes) during the time of the Old Covenant, then Jesus Christ did not need to die on the cross in order to rescue us from the power of sin and reconcile us to God. But the Old Covenant was not enough to bring about true holiness in God's people. What then was needed? A New Covenant which enables every believer to overcome sin, the world and the devil. Practicing methodism (apart from faith in the truth of the cross) can only lead you into either self-righteousness or self-despair, depending on the measure of will-power and self-discipline you possess. Paul shared this Biblical truth with Christians who were still practicing sin: "Do you not know that you died to sin when you were saved by Christ? You died to sin when your sinful nature died and was removed from you when you were born again. Since you no longer have a sinful nature, you have been freed from sin, and sin no longer has any power over you. Therefore, you are now dead to sin but alive to God in Christ Jesus (see Romans 6:1-11)."

Until we see that God has dealt a deathblow to our sinful nature, we can mistakenly think we possess some inherent ability or virtue within ourselves to practice godliness. If we are trying to serve Christ through our natural ability or self-discipline, we are practicing a moral code apart from the cross, which nullifies the power of Christ from working in us. You can religiously devote yourself daily to practicing all the disciplines, but if you do not believe that Jesus Christ died on the cross to remove your sinful nature when you were born again, then your zealous pursuit of methodism has no power to stop you from practicing sin. Paul strongly warned the first century Christians that practicing religious rules, methods and principles had no power to stop them from indulging in sin (Colossians 2:20-23). The practice of methodism is the basic catechism of Churchianity (as opposed to true Christianity). Churchianity is just like any other man-made religion; it has no divine power to enable you to stop practicing sin, and it has no divine life to enable you to walk with God. Since methodism is works-based or performance-based, it is only natural that when you perform well (according to your standard of methodism) you would feel good or righteous, but when you perform badly, you would feel bad or unrighteous. It is also natural that you would feel impatient, resentful or even disdainful towards other Christians who are not trying as hard as you to perform according to your standard of methodism. Jesus condemned this kind of religiosity and said that people who practiced it were hypocrites who trusted in their own righteousness and regarded others with contempt (Luke 13:5; 18:9).

It may surprise many Christians that "carnal" Christian behavior (what the Bible calls "deeds of the flesh") can be expressed in two very different ways. The first way is obvious. "Now the deeds of the flesh are evident, which are immorality, impurity, sensuality, idolatry, sorcery, hatred, strife, jealously, outbursts of anger, selfish ambition, dissensions, factions, envying, drunkenness, orgies, and things like these (Galatians 5:19-21)." But the second way is more disguised. "No wonder, for Satan disguises himself as an angel of light. Therefore, is it not surprising if his servants also disguise themselves as servants of righteousness (1 Corinthians 12:14-15)." Consequently, the carnal lifestyle of a Christian is obvious if they are practicing immorality; however, if they are practicing outwardly moral behavior, even while they are inwardly lawless and unsubmitted to Christ, this kind of deception and hypocrisy can be more difficult to discern, except by the Holy Spirit. In the words of John Milton: "Neither man nor angel can discern hypocrisy, the only evil that walks invisible except to God alone." There is a great difference between a Christian who overcomes sin by believing and acting on what Christ has accomplished by His death on the cross and a Christian who tries to "overcome" sin by faith in his own willpower, natural ability, self-discipline and the practice of religious methods. Paul described religious people who practice this kind of outward moral behavior as "those who take pride in appearance (2 Corinthians 5:12)" and "want to make a good impression outwardly (Galatians 6:12)." Jesus called them lawless hypocrites (Matthew 23:25-28). Any religious morality that is derived apart from faith in the power of Christ's crucifixion is a bastard holiness that is the offspring of the flesh (man's strength) and not the fruit of the Spirit. If a professed Christian persists in habitually practicing this kind of false religious morality, it is not harmless. It is hypocritical and hostile to God because it is not of true faith (Romans 14:23; Galatians 5:17).

The practice of disciplines (or methodism) and the practice of faith are diametrically different. In man's eyes, practicing methodism (reading the Bible, praying, and attending church) by exercising self-discipline seems to be a reasonable and logical means to achieve an end purpose - to have a fruitful life for God. However, man's way of thinking is not God's way. The Bible says that true self-discipline or self-control is a fruit of the Holy Spirit (Galatians 5:22-23). Therefore, in God's eyes, having faith in Christ by abiding in His truth is the only means to produce the spiritual fruit of self-discipline. Practicing methodism as a means to produce spiritual fruit is not only backwards and wrong, it is insidious; the better you become at it, the more you will develop secret pride, which will blind you to God's truth and separate you from God's grace (James 4:6). Whenever you try to bear spiritual fruit by your self-effort through the practice of methodism, you cut yourself off from the life of the vine, which is Jesus Christ.

Does this mean that we should not read the Bible or pray or fellowship with other believers? Of course not! If combined with true faith in Christ and His completed work on the cross, then these activities are certainly beneficial for any true believer. What some call "methods" or "disciplines" should be a natural and integral part of every Christian's daily life if their love and faith in Jesus Christ is genuine. These activities are the "water and fertilizer" that nourish and strengthen our faith, as long as our faith is planted and rooted in the Biblical truth of the cross of Christ. However, unless these activities are combined with faith in the truth of the cross (which enables us to have a real and living relationship with Jesus Christ), they take the form of works and are worthless. As Paul admonished, "Are you so foolish? Having begun by the Spirit, are you now trying to perfect yourself by your human effort?" (Galatians 3:3).

The practice of methodism appeals to the unconverted natural mind; it is a carnal attempt to bypass the cross of Christ and the sovereignty of God by trying to be godly in your own willpower and self-discipline rather than by trusting in Christ's completed work on the cross and in the power of His resurrection life which indwells us. Believing and acting on the divine truth of the cross (that you have been freed from sin because you no longer have a sinful nature) is the only true "means of grace" that will enable you to stop practicing sin and walk in true holiness which pleases God.

How To Exercise The Gifts Of The Holy Spirit

6 The Bible describes the gifts of the Holy Spirit as the word of wisdom, the word of knowledge, special faith, healings, working of miracles, prophecy, discerning of spirits, various kinds of tongues and interpretation of tongues (1 Corinthians 12:4-11). Some additional spiritual gifts, such as the gifts of leadership, teaching, administration and service, are also addressed in Romans 12:6-8, 1 Peter 4:10-11, as well as other verses. Because of unbelief, ignorance and disobedience, the church has two common problems concerning the spiritual gifts – either a lack of use of the gifts, or a misuse of the gifts. Both these problems would be solved if Christians truly believed they had died with Christ and no longer relied on their natural abilities and church traditions to do God's work, but instead trusted solely in Christ to sovereignly and powerfully live through them.

Just as the fruit of the Spirit is not the same as naturally endowed virtues; the gifts of the Spirit are not naturally endowed abilities. All of the gifts of the Spirit are supernaturally endowed; they are not the product of our natural birth, effort or education. Whereas the fruit of the Spirit are attributes of God's divine character, the gifts of the Spirit are instruments of God's divine power. The spiritual gifts are the supernatural operation and manifestation of the Holy Spirit who distributes them to each member of the body of Christ according to His own will (1 Corinthians 12:11; Hebrews 2:4). For example, when the elders of the church laid hands on Timothy, the Holy Spirit gave him a spiritual gift, perhaps the gift of teaching or evangelism (1 Timothy 4:13; 2 Timothy 4:5), which was confirmed through a prophetic message (1 Timothy 4:14). It is important to note that all the spiritual gifts are distributed by the initiative of the Holy Spirit and not by man's will. The Bible says, "So then, does He who provides you with the Spirit and works miracles among you do it by the works of the law or by hearing with faith (Galatians 3:5)?" Therefore, in order to exercise the gifts of the Spirit properly, we must be submitted to Christ's authority and act only in obedience to the Holy Spirit's initiative (John 15:5). Jesus Himself never said or did anything on His own initiative; He only acted on His Father's initiative (John 5:19, 30; 8:28; 12:49). The fact that obeying God's initiative is required to properly exercise the spiritual gifts is also evident by Peter's instruction on prophecy: "No prophecy was ever made by an act of human will, but men *moved by the Holy Spirit* spoke from God (2 Peter 1:21)." Our continued daily obedience to Jesus Christ is critical because using the supernatural gifts will bring us into a new level of spiritual conflict and attacks by the devil to sabotage our increased usefulness to the Lord.

A major difference between the spiritual gifts and spiritual fruit is how they are imparted and manifested. Whereas the gifts of the Spirit are received and exercised spontaneously by an act of faith (Romans 12:3-6); the fruit of the Spirit are produced over time by abiding or persevering faith (Luke 8:15). One brother in Christ has compared this to the difference between a fruit tree and a Christmas tree. Fruit is formed slowly over time by being vitally connected to the life of the tree; whereas Christmas ornaments are like gifts, which are placed on the tree by a single act in a single instant of time. The Bible says "the gifts and the calling of God are irrevocable (Romans 11:29)." This means the gifts are not loaned out and then recalled. If someone falls away from the faith and becomes carnal and ungodly, their ability to use the gifts will not cease. For example, even though King Saul became rebellious, ungodly and depraved, he could still prophesy (1 Samuel 19:18-24). Consequently, the gifts do not necessarily reflect the spiritual character and sanctification of the person who exercises them; whereas spiritual fruit is an expression of that person's character and sanctification. As a result, the great danger for Christians who exercise the gifts is for them to think and feel that they are more "spiritual" than they really are. For this reason and because of the different nature and function of spiritual fruit and spiritual gifts, the gifts can often be misused by someone who is soulish and carnal. For example, the Corinthian church abounded in the spiritual gifts, but they sorely lacked in spiritual fruit since they remained very carnal-minded (1 Corinthians 1:7; 3:1-3; 11:17-32). Their failure to be convicted by the Holy Spirit that they were spiritually carnal and lawless even though they exercised the spiritual gifts should be a sobering warning to all of us.

Whenever Christians are more impressed with dramatic gifts rather than authentic fruit, there are major problems. We need to always keep in mind Jesus' warning, "You shall know them by their fruit." He did not say, "You shall know them by their gifts." Nor did He say, "You shall know them by their outward moral behavior." There is a great difference between man-made morality, which is naturally born and developed, and the fruit of the Spirit, which is only spiritually formed and grows from our abiding by faith in Jesus Christ and His Word. Morality apart from the cross of Christ is not true sanctification, it is just another version of the flesh. Exercising the spiritual gifts can be dangerous and backfire if you are not walking in true sanctification. If you are practicing sin and walking in a false, hypocritical morality, God cannot protect you from Satan's schemes to deceive and attack you when you function in the supernatural realm. The only way we can safely function in the spiritual gifts is if we are submitted to Christ's sovereignty and hear and obey His voice. And the only way we can be truly submitted to Christ's authority and walk in His sanctification is if we know (believe and act on) the truth that we have been crucified with Christ and our sinful nature has been removed from us. Then we can live by faith in the Son of God who indwells us by His Spirit (Romans 6:6; Galatians 2:20).

We can see all of the spiritual gifts displayed by the disciples in the Book of Acts. In every case, the results that the spiritual gifts produce are far superior to anything we could ever achieve with our natural ability. For example, someone may be a naturally eloquent speaker but that does not mean the Holy Spirit has bestowed on them the spiritual gift of teaching. Natural eloquence can never produce the spiritual results of conviction, repentance and faith that can only come from the Holy Spirit and the supernatural gift of preaching and teaching that God gives to His servants. Or, someone may be a natural born leader, but this does not mean the Holy Spirit has given them the gift of spiritual leadership. The Holy Spirit's gift of prophecy is definitely not the same as someone's "inspirational" sermon. And God's miracle of supernatural healing is only manifested as a gift of the Holy Spirit. Unfortunately, due to spiritual ignorance and unbelief about the gifts, many people are following ministers who are speaking from their own natural wisdom and acting from their own natural ability rather than from the revelatory and empowering gifts of the Holy Spirit.

Many Christians pursue the fruit of the Spirit, but neglect and even reject the gifts of the Spirit. However, from God's perspective it is not a matter of one or the other; He wants us to desire both the fruit of the Spirit and the gifts of the Spirit. The Bible says, "Follow the way of love and eagerly desire spiritual gifts (1 Corinthians 14:10)." The spiritual gifts are no substitute for spiritual fruit, and spiritual fruit is no substitute for the gifts. When Christians chronically lack spiritual fruit, they become sin-sick; but without the power of the spiritual gifts, Christians are spiritually impaired from delivering and healing those who are sin-sick. Since our warfare is not against mortal men but against the spiritual forces of darkness, our equipment, tools and weapons must also be spiritual; otherwise we will not prevail as Christ's soldiers in this demonic, evil and hostile world (2 Corinthians 10:3-4). Therefore Paul instructed, "Now concerning spiritual gifts, brethren, I do not want you to be ignorant (1 Corinthians 12:1)."

Although there may be various interpretations on the exact meaning of specific spiritual gifts, there is no question that the supernatural gifts of the Holy Spirit are valid today. Opinions that the spiritual gifts ceased with the death of the original twelve apostles in the first century are just that – man's opinions, which are not supported by Scripture. Anyone who says the gifts of the Holy Spirit are not for today has to nullify large portions of the New Testament. When you pick and choose which Scriptures you want to nullify to this extent, you are on very dangerous spiritual ground. What other major parts of the New Testament Canon would you choose to disregard if you personally did not like a certain truth or felt that truth was not for today? Consequently, arguments against the use of the spiritual gifts today are not normally based on Biblical grounds, but instead on spiritual ignorance and unbelief or a fear of abuse of the gifts (which Paul effectively deals with in 1 Corinthians, Chapter 14). The Holy Spirit has given the body of Christ these supernatural gifts to be a vital and integral part of the normal Christian church life. Consequently, the use of the spiritual gifts is not an option for any Christian who desires to walk in obedience to His Lord and Master, Jesus Christ.

There is also no Scriptural support to suggest that the spiritual gifts were only intended for men or leaders. Peter, citing the prophet Joel, declared, "And it shall be in the last days,' God says, 'That I will pour forth of My Spirit on all mankind; and *your sons and your daughters* shall prophesy… even on My bondslaves, *both men and women*, I will in those days pour forth of My Spirit and they shall prophesy (Acts 2:17-18)." The Bible clearly states that the Holy Spirit distributes the spiritual gifts to every believer for effective ministry to the church and effective evangelism to the world (Acts 4:29-30; 14:3; 1 Corinthians 12:7; Ephesians 4:12). "But one and the same Spirit works all these things, distributing *to each one individually* just as He wills (1 Corinthians 12:11)." The Bible says that the spiritual gifts are given to every believer to comfort, encourage and strengthen the body of Christ (1 Corinthians 14:3, 26). Paul wrote, "*To each one* is given the manifestation of the Spirit for the common good (1 Corinthians 12:7)."

After we are born again, how can we be empowered to use the spiritual gifts the Holy Spirit has given us? Jesus said we must be baptized (immersed) in the Holy Spirit to receive this spiritual empowerment. What is this baptism in the Holy Spirit that Jesus spoke of? During His ministry, Jesus commanded His disciples to be baptized in water (Matthew 28:19). Water baptism is the outward expression of the inward transformation that occurred within us when we were saved: our old man of sin died in Christ, and we are now reborn as a new man in Christ (Romans 6:3-11). However, after they had been saved and been baptized in water, Jesus then commanded His disciples to be baptized in the Holy Spirit (Luke 24:49; Acts 1:5 & 8). We see then that water baptism is associated with salvation, whereas Spirit baptism is associated with something more than salvation. This raises a very important question: if we received the Holy Spirit when we were saved, then why do we need to be baptized in the Holy Spirit after we are saved?

The answer can be found by comparing two key events in church history: Resurrection Sunday and Pentecost Sunday. On Resurrection Sunday, when Jesus appeared to His disciples when they were together as a group for the first time, the Bible says, "He breathed on them and said to them, 'Receive the Holy Spirit (John 20:22).'" This is the moment when the disciples passed from "Old Covenant salvation" to "New Covenant salvation." Believers in the Old Covenant were saved by looking forward in faith to Christ's redemptive work, which had not yet taken place; whereas believers in the New Covenant are saved by looking back in faith to the historic event of Christ's redemptive death and resurrection. In the Book of Romans, Paul gives two conditions for New Covenant salvation: "If you confess with your mouth the Lord Jesus and believe in your heart that God raised Him from the dead, you will be saved (Romans 10:9)." Before Resurrection Sunday, the disciples had already confessed Jesus as Lord. But now for the first time, they also believed God raised Him from the dead. Therefore, Resurrection Sunday is when the disciples were born again of the Spirit. This is the day when God removed their old Adam nature and replaced it with Christ's new nature.

Even though the disciples had received the Holy Spirit for salvation, Jesus also made it clear they also needed to be baptized (immersed) in the Holy Spirit for empowerment. Just before His ascension, Jesus gathered His disciples together and "commanded them not to leave Jerusalem, but to wait for the gift My Father had promised, which you have heard Me speak about. For John baptized in water, but in a few days you will be baptized in the Holy Spirit ... *you will receive power* when the Holy Spirit has come upon you and *you will be My witnesses* (Acts 1:5 & 8; see also Luke 24:49)." The Father's promise to baptize the disciples in the Holy Spirit was fulfilled on Pentecost Sunday when the disciples "were all *filled with the Holy Spirit* and began to speak in other tongues as the Spirit enabled them (Acts 2:4)." On that morning, Peter explained to all those present what had just occurred: "Therefore having been exalted to the right hand of God and having received from the Father *the promise of the Holy Spirit*, He (Jesus) has poured out what you now see and hear (Acts 2:33)." Thus the disciples were born again of the Holy Spirit on Resurrection Sunday, but they were baptized in the Holy Spirit seven weeks later on Pentecost Sunday. These two different events show our new birth in Jesus Christ is distinct and separate from Jesus baptizing us in the Holy Spirit. When we are born again, we receive Christ's life for salvation, but when we are baptized in the Holy Spirit, we receive Christ's power to be His witnesses and advance His kingdom in this fallen, sin-sick world.

The Greek word for baptism actually means immersion. When we are baptized in the Holy Spirit, we are completely immersed or enveloped in the power of the Holy Spirit. In the natural realm, there are two ways we can be immersed under water. We can go down under the surface of the water and then come up out of it. This is what happens when we are water baptized. The other way is if the water is poured over us until we are completely immersed and enveloped by it. In the natural, this experience would occur if we stood underneath a pouring waterfall. This is the type of immersion that occurs when we are baptized (immersed) in the Holy Spirit. This is why the Bible, when describing the baptism in the Holy Spirit, uses language such as "I will pour out My Spirit" and "He poured out this which you see and hear" and "the Holy Spirit fell upon all those who heard the Word" and "the gift of the Holy Spirit had been poured out on the Gentiles." We should also note the terms, "baptism of the Holy Spirit," "promise of the Holy Spirit" and "gift of the Holy Spirit" are used interchangeably to describe the same Biblical experience (see Luke 24:49; Acts 1:4-5; 2:33, 38; 10:44-45; 11:15-17).

After Pentecost, another Scriptural example of believers being baptized in the Holy Spirit occurred when Peter preached the gospel in Caesarea to the Roman centurion Cornelius and his household. In this event, Jesus Christ baptized Cornelius and his entire household in the Holy Spirit at the same time that they received Him as Lord and Savior (Acts 10:44-48; 11:15-18). Jesus sovereignly poured out His Spirit on them in this manner to supernaturally witness to Peter that God had granted salvation to the Gentiles. Peter knew Jesus had baptized these Gentiles in the Holy Spirit when he heard them speaking in tongues. The Bible records this event: *"The Holy Spirit fell upon all those* who were listening to the message. All the circumcised believers who came with Peter were amazed, because *the gift of the Holy Spirit had been poured out* on the Gentiles also. For they were hearing them speaking with tongues and exalting God (Acts 10:45-46)."* Recognizing that God had saved Cornelius and his household, Peter then instructed them to be immediately water baptized. Later on, Peter recounted what happened in Caesarea to the leaders of the church in Jerusalem. Peter said, *"The Holy Spirit fell upon them* just as He did upon us at the beginning. Then I remembered what the Lord had said, 'John baptized in water, but you will be *baptized in the Holy Spirit* (Acts 11:15-16)."* Yet another Scriptural example of new Christians being baptized in the Holy Spirit occurred when Paul laid his hands on new believers in Ephesus so they might receive the Holy Spirit. The Bible records this event: "And when Paul had laid his hands upon them, *the Holy Spirit came upon them*, and they began speaking with tongues and prophesying (Acts 19:6)."

From the Scriptural record, we see that Jesus commanded His disciples to be baptized in the Holy Spirit so that they would be empowered to be His witnesses. And what is the witness that confirms the gospel of Jesus Christ? Besides the fruit of the Spirit, especially *agapē* love (Galatians 5:22-23), the Bible says the witness that confirms the gospel are the supernatural gifts and miracles of the Holy Spirit. The author of Hebrews writes, "This salvation, which was first announced by the Lord, was confirmed to us by those who heard Him. God also testified to it by signs, wonders and various miracles, and by the gifts of the Holy Spirit (Hebrews 2:3-4; see also Acts 4:29-30; 8:5-7; 14:3)." If all we need is love to be God's witnesses, then why did Jesus exercise so many of the gifts of the Holy Spirit and perform so many miracles when He preached the kingdom of God? Why did Jesus also command His disciples to miraculously heal the sick and deliver those oppressed by the devil when they proclaimed the kingdom of God? (Matthew 10:1-5; Luke 9:1-2) Before He ascended to heaven, Jesus said the gifts and signs of the Holy Spirit would accompany those who believe in Him (Mark 16:17-18). If all we need is love, then why did the disciples employ the supernatural gifts of the Holy Spirit when they preached the gospel after Jesus had ascended to heaven? (Acts 4:29-30; 8:5-6; 14:3; 19:8-12)

The Bible itself gives us the answer: healing the sick and freeing those who are oppressed by the devil demonstrates God's compassionate love and the miraculous delivering power of His kingdom. The gifts and miracles of the Holy Spirit broadcast the gospel of the kingdom with an exclamation of power and authority (Mark 1:27). Regarding Jesus' ministry, the Bible says, "all the people were amazed and said to each other, 'What is this teaching? For with authority and power He commands the evil spirits and the come out (Luke 4:36; see also 9:1)." Paul confirms this supernatural witness of the gospel: "The kingdom of God does not consist of words, but of power... for our gospel did not come to you in words only, but also in power with the Holy Spirit… in mighty signs and wonders (see 1 Corinthians 4:20; 1 Thessalonians 1:5; Romans 15:19)." When John the Baptist's disciples asked Jesus if He was the expected Messiah, Jesus pointed them to these signs: "Go back and report to John what you hear and see: The blind receive sight, the lame walk, the lepers are healed, the deaf hear, the dead are raised up, and the poor have the gospel preached to them (Matthew 11:2-5)." If we reject the baptism in the Holy Spirit and the empowering (enabling) of the spiritual gifts that accompany it, we reject the supernatural provision that Jesus Christ has given us to be His witnesses to the world, as well as the spiritual gifts that He has given us to equip and empower His church.

If you have been baptized (immersed) and empowered by the Holy Spirit, how do you begin to exercise the spiritual gifts that God has given you? First of all, it greatly helps if you belong to a New Covenant church that approves of and encourages the use of the spiritual gifts. The level of faith in the Biblical truth of the gifts combined with the freedom of the Holy Spirit in these kinds of "charismatic" meetings facilitates the expression of the spiritual gifts. In contrast, if a church does not believe and approve of the present day manifestation of the spiritual gifts, there is no freedom in the Lord for the spiritual gifts to be expressed in their meetings. Even Jesus was restrained from exercising the gifts of healing and miracles in his hometown of Nazareth because of that community's unbelief (Matthew 13:58). Unfortunately, most churches in our present day are also communities of unbelief; therefore, the Holy Spirit is restrained from freely manifesting the spiritual gifts in their meetings. Second, you can practice being filled with the Holy Spirit each day. Remember the way that we are continuously filled with God's Spirit is by abiding (staying united by faith) in Jesus Christ and the truth of His completed work on the cross. Third, you can practice your faith by listening to the leading of the Holy Spirit. The Holy Spirit will let you know which gifts He has given you. It is very possible that the Holy Spirit has given you more than one spiritual gift since the gifts often seem to be distributed in "clusters" to each member of Christ's body. For example, a brother or sister who has the gift of prophecy may also have the gifts of tongues and interpretation of tongues, as well as the gift of discernment of spirits. And a brother who has the spiritual gift of teaching may also have the gifts of spiritual leadership and administration. And a brother or sister who has the spiritual gift of healing may also have the gifts of miracles and special faith. It is even possible for believers to function in all the spiritual gifts. Fourth, remember that all progress in our Christian life comes by exercising faith in the truth of the cross of Christ, and not by practicing religious methods (Romans 1:17). It takes absolutely no faith to never use the spiritual gifts that God has given you. God wants us to diligently pursue and practice using the spiritual gifts for the benefit of His body. Although the Holy Spirit will not compel you to use your spiritual gifts, He will gently prompt you to step out in faith to use your spiritual gifts. The Bible says, "The Lord God has spoken; who can but prophesy? (Amos 3:8)

Even brand new believers can exercise the gifts of the Holy Spirit (Acts 19:6). In the beginning, the Holy Spirit may lead you to just share a short prophecy or a brief teaching or a word of wisdom with the saints. Remember that any spoken *rhema* word that you share will always line up with the truth of the written *Logos* Word. So always use the Bible as your "plumbline" when exercising the spiritual gifts. Also remember that you are always in control of your spiritual gift; your gift does not control you (2 Corinthians 14:32-33). The brothers and sisters in your church who are more mature and experienced in the spiritual gifts can also give you feedback and encouragement in your use of the gifts. And the Holy Spirit may lead the elders of your church to lay hands on you to prophetically confirm your spiritual gifts (1 Timothy 4:13; 2 Timothy 1:6). As you continue in faith to use your spiritual gifts, you will become more practiced, and the Lord will increasingly use you to encourage, edify and exhort His church. The manifestation of the gifts is one of the important ways the Holy Spirit acts to sovereignly demonstrate God's purpose and power among His people. If we do not seek to wisely use the spiritual gifts that God has given us, our witness to the world and our ministry to the church will fall short because our testimony will lack God's divine power, and God will ultimately hold us responsible like the worthless servant was held accountable for not effectively using the talent his master had given him (Matthew 25:30).

THE ELDERS OF THE CHURCH

7 In the New Testament, the term "elder" is used interchangeably with the terms "pastor" and "overseer." All three of these words refer to the same person. The elders of the church are the overseers who shepherd the local church together. The Greek word for elder is *presbuteros,* which is found sixty-six times in the New Testament and translated as "elder" or "elders." The Greek word *poimen* is found eighteen times in the New Testament and always translated as "shepherd," except for once in Ephesians 4:11 where the King James Version translators used the word "pastor." Finally, the Greek word *episkopos* is normally translated as "overseer" in the New Testament. However, the translators of the King James Version of 1611 changed the word "overseer" to "bishop" to politically conform to the man-made, multi-tiered religious hierarchy of the Church of England in early 1600s.

[Note: King James the 1st of England had ordered the official translators to conform to (and do nothing to upset) the established church structure, hierarchy, theology, liturgy, practice and rituals of the Church of England when they translated the Bible. For example, in addition to changing the word "overseer" to "bishop," the King James translators also chose political correctness over Bible accuracy when they translated the Greek word *baptismos*. The word *baptismos* literally means *immersion* into a liquid, such as water. However, the Church of England only authorized sprinkling with water and not full immersion into water in its practice of this sacrament; therefore, the King James translators literally made up a new English word, the word "baptism," to obscure the Biblical truth that Jesus commanded His disciples to be fully immersed into water, and not just sprinkled with a little water. Thus Paul's statement: "We have been buried with Him *through baptism* into death (Romans 6:3)" lost its clarity and power in the King James Version because sprinkling a new Christian with a little water does not adequately depict the divinely powerful Biblical truth that your sinful nature died and was buried when you were saved, which is more accurately portrayed by your body's full immersion or burial under water when you are baptized].

Whenever the apostles established a new church, they normally appointed a plurality of elders *(presbuteros)* whom they left to take care of the local congregation (Acts 14:23; James 5:14). These elders *(presbuteros)* shared responsibility together as overseers *(episkopos)* to shepherd *(poimaino)* the local flock. For example, in Acts 20:17, we read that Paul "sent to Ephesus for the elders *(presbuteros)* of the church." Paul then told them, "Keep watch over yourselves and all the flock over which the Holy Spirit has made you overseers *(episkopos)* to shepherd *(poimaino)* the church of God, which He purchased with His own blood (Acts 20:28)." Thus the term "elders" refers to these brothers' spiritual maturity; the term "overseers" refers to their ministerial function; and the term "shepherds" refers to their spiritual gifting in the Lord (see Ephesians 4:11). For example, the Bible does not say that if we are sick we should ask the pastor of the church to pray for us; instead, the Bible says that we should ask "the elders of the church" to pray for us, since the elders (plural) are the pastors (shepherds) of the church (James 5:14). There simply is no church recorded in the New Testament that had our modern-day, man-made concept of a pastor, priest or bishop.

It was not until the second and third century that church leaders began to wrongly divide the elders' role of oversight and shepherding into three separate hierarchal religious offices. They justified this new man-made hierarchy and chain of authority as a means to deal with emerging heresies and divisions in the church. The newly diminished office of "elders" then became subordinated to the newly created office of the "senior pastor" in each local church, and the senior pastors in the local churches throughout a region then became subordinated to the newly created office of the regional "bishop." Eventually, the regional bishops became subordinated to the archbishops (or cardinals) who, in turn, were subordinated to the Archbishop of Rome, who by the sixth century had become the Pope of the Catholic church. With the introduction of this new top-down clerical hierarchy, church members were told that their spirituality and unity could be clearly observed and validated by their obedience and loyalty to this new religious system. And if anyone dissented and did not submit to this man-made chain of authority, they were considered a heretic and could be excommunicated, which according to the now false church, was tantamount to being con-demned to hell. When the Holy Spirit is no longer sovereignly present and directing the church, then inventing a man-made clerical structure and tightening its religious authority over the people in order to keep them under control is the natural and grievous outcome. See Endnote #16 for more on the subject of elders.

THE OLD TESTAMENT TITHE

8 The tithe ("a tenth" in Hebrew) refers to the Mosaic Law requirement to give a tenth of your profit (crops or animals) to support the Levitical priesthood. However, with advent of the New Covenant, God fundamentally changed His divine priesthood (for those who are the children of promise - the children of faith). The Old Covenant had a separate and distinct priesthood – the Levites who were in charge of the Temple worship and were supported with tithes by the rest of God's people. With the New Covenant, however, the temple worship ceased because the body of Christ, His church, is now the temple of God (Ephesians 2:19-22). The specialized, full-time priesthood that performed the temple service also ceased since all believers now constitute God's holy priesthood who have direct access to know God and serve Him (Hebrews 4:16; 8:11; 10:19; 1 Peter 2:5; Revelation 1:6). And the practice of the Old Covenant Mosaic Law of tithing ceased with the coming of the New Covenant because there was no longer a need for God's people to give ten percent of their income to support the Old Covenant Temple and its Levite priesthood (Romans 7:4; Hebrews 7:5). The Bible says, "For when the priesthood is changed, there must of necessity also be a change in the Law *(of tithing)* (Hebrews 7:12)." For these reasons, the New Covenant church never practiced tithing nor ever taught tithing.

Some Christians might ask, "But did not Jesus endorse tithing in Matthew 23:23?" In this passage, Jesus exposed the Pharisees as hypocrites because they neglected the important matters of the Law, such as justice, mercy and faith; yet they carefully tithed even a tenth of their spices. In rebuking the Pharisees, Jesus was certainly not endorsing tithing to the future New Covenant church. Since Jesus had not yet been crucified, the New Covenant had not yet begun. Since Jesus was born under the Old Covenant, He honored the Mosaic Law, including the Law of tithing during His lifetime. For example, in Matthew 8:2-4, Jesus instructed a leper whom He had healed to present the Levite priest with two pigeons as an offering according to the Mosaic Law. However, if we now applied this requirement of the Old Covenant Mosaic Law out of context to the New Covenant church, we would all be raising pigeons in our backyards to give to our elders (pastors) whenever God healed us. The truth is that the Mosaic Law of tithing ceased with the New Covenant just as both the Mosaic Law of the Sabbath and the Mosaic Law of circumcision ceased with the New Covenant. Of course, for those religious Jews in the first century who rejected Jesus as the Messiah of God, the Levite priesthood, the Temple worship, as well as the Sabbath, circumcision and tithing Mosaic Laws did not cease. However, this Old Covenant Judaic religious system never fully recovered after the Jewish Temple in Jerusalem was destroyed by the Romans in A.D. 70, and was subsequently never rebuilt.

THE CATHOLIC CHURCH

9 The term "Catholic church" is used in recognition that the so-called "universal" Catholic church divided in the "Great Schism" of A.D. 1054 into the Roman Catholic Church and the Eastern Orthodox Church.

THE UNSANCTIFIED LIFE OF MARTIN LUTHER

10 Martin Luther (1483-1546) is considered the founding father of the Protestant Reformation. We know that Luther understood that the Biblical truth that the righteous are *saved* by faith, but did Luther know how to *live* by faith, and did he lead the Reformation movement into this Biblical truth of sanctification? Jesus said we can discern a man's life and beliefs by his spiritual fruit; that is, by his spiritual character (Matthew 7:20; see also Galatians 5:19-24). Jesus did not say we can assess a man's life by his spiritual gifts and ministerial achievements. Therefore, we do not assess a man's walk with God simply by his ability to teach or even write Biblical truths, but rather by his personal life and conduct. Throughout his life, Luther was known by his family, friends and enemies to be self-willed, arrogant, combative, harsh, unmerciful, quarrelsome, vulgar, irreconcilable, short-tempered, and easily given to angry outbursts, which he aimed at friend and foe alike. Luther thought that anyone whom he considered to be religious "heretics," such as the Anabaptists, should be put to death. Luther strongly promoted and preached an unBiblical form of grace, or what we call "cheap grace." He wrote, "Be a sinner and sin boldly, but believe and rejoice in Christ even more boldly... as long as we are here [in this world] we have to sin... no sin will separate us from the Lamb, even though we commit fornication and murder a thousand times a day." Luther heartily approved of excessive drinking and boasted that he liked to get drunk whenever he felt depressed, which was often. From all historic accounts and later portraits, Luther had a chronic problem with the sin of gluttony and obesity that he never overcame. Luther condoned sexual immorality when he wrote that a wife had the right to take on a lover if her husband could not sexually satisfy her.

During the 1524-25 peasants' uprising in Germany, Luther strongly exhorted the feudal lords to slaughter the peasants and called it a righteous action endorsed by God. After upwards to 300,000 men, women and children were killed, thousands of peasants in southern Germany stayed in the Catholic church because they felt betrayed by Luther. Luther believed in polygamy and wrote, "I confess that I cannot forbid a person to marry several wives, for it does not contradict the Scripture. If a man wishes to marry more than one wife, he should be asked whether he is satisfied in his conscience that he may do so in accordance with the Word of God. In such a case the civil authority has nothing to do in the matter." In 1540, Luther secretly endorsed the bigamous marriage of his political patron, Philip of Hess, and then counseled Philip to brazenly lie about his bigamous relationship whenever anyone asked about it. Some of Luther's later writings were vehemently anti-Semitic, in which he strongly justified, encouraged and endorsed extreme physical violence against the Jews. Most historians believe Luther's books greatly contributed to the rise of Germany's national anti-Semitism, which endured for centuries, and his anti-Semitic writings continue to influence men of depraved minds to this day. During World War II, the Nazi regime republished and even enshrined Luther's anti-Semitic pamphlets to justify their Holocaust extermination campaign against the Jews throughout Europe.

While we owe a great debt to Luther's courage in standing up for the gospel that salvation is by faith in Christ alone (even when the Catholic church threatened to excommunicate him and burn him at the stake), we must speak the truth in love concerning Luther's obvious lack of personal sanctification. It is evident that after he was saved, Luther's attitudes and actions were not radically transformed by the truth of the Word of God, and that he continued to be governed and enslaved by his unconverted soul's sinful passions and prejudices, rather than being governed by the Spirit of God. Luther's ungodly personal beliefs and unrepentant sinful behavior were (and still are) an offensive stumbling block that has discredited the gospel in the eyes of hundreds of thousands, perhaps even millions of people; a fact which should be evident to all and strongly condemned by all. Since Luther could not master sin in his own personal life, he was not capable of leading the reformation movement into living a sanctified life by faith in Christ's completed work on the cross. At the end of his life, Luther himself candidly admitted his abject failure to accomplish this goal. Luther lamented that all his preaching for decades had produced no change in the sinful behavior of his followers.

Although he spearheaded a break away from Catholic Churchianity, it could be argued that Luther was the founding father of just another form of Churchianity, called Protestantism, which is not true Christianity, since it practices "methodism" and not the Scriptural sanctification that comes from faith alone. Luther's errant theology and poor example of unrepentant sinful behavior also laid the foundation for the heretical "cheap grace" and "once saved always saved" doctrines, which are satanic lies that have deceived and led millions of professing Christians astray from true faith in Christ. Some Christians say that Luther was simply a "man of his times," and that he should not be judged according to today's church standards of morality. It is true that Luther should not be judged by our present standards; however, he must be held accountable to the uncompromising truth of God's Word, by which all of us will also be judged by Christ. The sad truth is that Luther's lifelong practice of errant doctrine and ungodly behavior after he was saved would have disqualified him from any leadership role in God's true New Covenant church while he was alive, and may even disqualify him from future entrance into the kingdom of heaven. Luther's serious and chronic personal sins along with his ungodly beliefs and shameful writings should be a solemn warning for all of us to diligently pursue and practice the holiness that comes solely by faith *after* we are saved. As Paul said, "I discipline my body and make it my slave so that, after I have preached to others, I myself will not be disqualified (1 Corinthians 9:27)." This is why Paul exhorted Timothy to "pay close attention to your life and your teaching so that everyone may see your progress. Persevere in these things, because if you do, you will save both yourself and your hearers (1 Timothy 4:16)."

THE CURSE OF MENTAL ASSENT

11 For every person in America who is hostile to the gospel of Christ, there may be ten more who say they believe in the gospel and profess to be Christians. Of course, this is not true. Most of these people are not true followers of Christ and do not even know (let alone believe and act on) the real gospel of Christ. Why is there this shocking discrepancy? One of the reasons for this great disconnect is what we might call the "curse of mental assent." Many people think that as long as they think they know a basic Christian doctrine and mentally agree with it, it must mean they are a Christian. However, to "know" the truth in Biblical terms means you believe it enough to have personally acted on it and experienced it. The Bible says that unless you act on the truth of God's Word, your faith is worthless. Jesus said, "Why do you call Me 'Lord, Lord," and do not do what I say? Everyone who comes to Me and hears My words *and acts on them*, I will show you whom he is like: he is like man building a house who dug deep and laid a foundation on the rock; and when a flood came, the torrent struck the house but could not shake it, because it was well built (Luke 6:46-49; see also Matthew 7:24-27)."

Since Christianity is still a part of the American cultural fabric (although its influence is rapidly fading), many people mistakenly think they are Christians because they go to church and try live a moral life. If you ask the average American Christian when they became a Christian, they will usually tell you they have always been a Christian. When pressed, they will tell you that their parents were Christians and they were raised in the church. But as someone has rightly said, "God has no grandchildren." Every individual must make their own personal, conscious, free will decision to repent from their sins and receive Jesus Christ as their Lord in order to be born again by the Spirit and become a child of God (John 1:12; 3:3-7).

Faith is not mere intellectual and emotional agreement with Christian doctrine. Saving faith must involve a conscious act of your will, by which you make a total commitment for Jesus Christ to be the absolute Lord of your life. If you do not believe a Biblical truth enough to act on it and be transformed by it, it reveals that you do not really know the truth and do not have real faith. This is the spiritual difference between mentally agreeing that Jesus is the Christ and acting on this divine truth to the point that Jesus revolutionizes your entire life. For example, John Wesley, the famous British evangelist, was a missionary to the American colony of Georgia in the 1730s. While attempting to "evangelize" the Native Americans, another missionary pointedly asked John Wesley whether he was saved, and John Wesley replied that he knew Jesus was the Savior of the whole world. The other missionary then said, "Yes, it is true that Jesus is the Savior of the whole world, but has Jesus saved *you*?" This piercing question convicted Wesley and bothered his conscience for many months until, upon his return home to England; he came into a true saving faith in Jesus Christ. Ironically, John Wesley had a religious zeal for saving souls, but he did not have a personal saving knowledge of Jesus Christ (Romans 10:2-3). How many millions of professing "Christians" today have a zeal for doing Christian works of service, but they do not have a saving and sanctifying knowledge of Jesus Christ?

The Bible says that, after we are saved, our faith must produce works of obedience, which proves our true conversion (James 2:20). "For just as the body without the spirit is dead, so also *faith* without works is dead (James 2:26)." This is why true faith always follows repentance, which is demonstrated by its actions. For example, John the Baptist told the people they must "produce fruit in keeping with repentance (Matthew 3:8)." And Paul exhorted that men everywhere "should repent and turn to God, performing deeds appropriate to repentance (Acts 26:20)." Unfortunately, many Christians mistake remorse for repentance. The Greek word for repent is *metanoeo,* which means to change your way of thinking and reverse your past way of living, whereas remorse just means you feel sorry about your sins, but never change your sinful habits. For example, Judas "felt remorse" for betraying Jesus Christ, but he did not truly repent (change the direction of his life), so that he could receive forgiveness and be reconciled to Christ (Matthew 27:3). Many professing Christians feel they have repented from their habit of sinning, but what they really mean is they just feel sorry about their sinning and mentally assent to the fact that they have sinned, without actually changing their sinful behavior. If they had real repentance, it would be proven by their actions when they stop practicing sin and start practicing the righteousness that comes by faith in the cross of Christ. We cannot claim to repent and believe in Jesus Christ without corresponding action. Because they only mentally assent to a basic Christian doctrine of salvation, millions of unbelievers are deceived and think they are Christians and going to heaven when they are not, and millions of Christians who at one time received Christ are deceived and mistakenly think they are faithfully living a sanctified or holy life, and going to heaven when they are not. God has declared that the only wedding clothes that allow us to take part as the bride of Christ in the marriage of His Son and enter the kingdom of heaven are the garments of our righteous "actions," not merely our righteous "intentions" (Matthew 22:11-14; Revelation 19:7-8).

Only divine revelation can set a person free from the snare of mental assent. For example, it took divine revelation for Peter to believe and act on the truth that Jesus was the Christ, the Son of the living God, and it also took divine revelation for Paul to believe and act on the truth that Jesus was the Christ (Matthew 16:15-17; Acts 9:1-6). This is why Paul prayed that God would grant Christians "a spirit of wisdom and revelation in the knowledge of Him (Ephesians 1:17)." Another example of the difference between mental assent and divine revelation can be found in the doctrine of co-crucifixion. Many Christians mentally concur with the Biblical concept of our co-crucifixion with Christ (Romans 6:8; Galatians 2:20; Colossians 2:20; 3:3; 2 Timothy 2:11); but very few truly know (by means of divine revelation) that they personally died when they were born again (when their sinful nature died and was removed). Consequently, they do not have the inward spiritual conviction and faith required to act on this divine truth to the point that they can with confidence "count themselves dead to sin but alive to God in Christ Jesus (Romans 6:11)."

If God has made you aware that you are caught in the snare of mental assent, what can you do? Earnestly pray that God would give you divine revelation to convict you of your sin, and that He would grant you true repentance and faith to follow Jesus Christ with all your heart and soul and body. Then act on the certainty that He has heard and answered your prayer. As James said, "Prove yourselves doers of the Word, and not merely hearers who delude themselves. For if anyone is a hearer of the Word and not a doer, he is like a man who looks at his face in a mirror and, after looking at himself, he goes away and immediately forgets what he looks like. But the man who looks intently at the perfect law that gives freedom, and abides by it, not forgetting what he has heard, but doing it – this man will be blessed in what he does (James 1:22-25)."

MODERN DAY CHRISTIAN JUDAIZERS

12 Even if those in the false church say they consider their Old Covenant-based religious practices to be based on principle rather than law, it has the same effect as a law in their lives since their church practices are unchangeable (because of their own misguided religious conviction and stubborn determination). Many false churches obstinately hold on to their rigid and harmful religious traditions and practices as zealously as the Pharisees in Jesus' day held on to their inflexible and inhumane rules of the Sabbath. Not only are these false brethren in our day outwardly practicing a form of Judaism, they are inwardly practicing a form of Judaism by trying to be righteous and holy by the best of their natural ability, self-discipline and religious methods. As Paul admonished: "Are you so foolish? After beginning by the Spirit, are you now trying to perfect yourselves by your human effort?" (Galatians 3:3) These false brethren in our day are similar to the Judaizers in the first century who tried to lead new believers astray from Christ by telling them they must follow aspects of the Mosaic Law and practice certain Old Covenant traditions. Paul's exhortation to those naïve Christians who were being deceived by false brethren is still appropriate: "I am amazed that you are so quickly deserting Him who called you by the grace of Christ for a different gospel, which really is no gospel at all. Some people are throwing you into confusion and are trying to distort the gospel of Christ. But if even we or an angel from heaven should preach to you a

gospel contrary to what we have preached to you, he is to be eternally condemned (Galatians 1:6-8)."

The false brethren who promote and practice a different gospel in our day will be judged by God because they have hardened their heart to hearing and obeying the New Covenant truth that Jesus Christ died to set His people free from these obsolete religious practices, so that all the members of His body would be a royal priesthood who have direct access to know God and serve God (1 Peter 2:9; Revelation 6:9-10). The Bible says, under the New Covenant, everyone who is in Christ (whether Jew or Gentile) has been freed from observing the Old Covenant Law's religious practices so they can serve God by the Spirit as His holy priesthood (Romans 7:4, 6; 2 Corinthians 3:5-6; Ephesians 4:12-16; 1 Peter 2:5). What then was God's purpose in giving us the Law? The Bible says the Law was given for our good to lead us to faith in Christ. As Paul writes: "Therefore the Law has become our tutor to lead us to Christ, so that we may be justified by faith (Galatians 3:24)." The Law, which is God's holy standard or plumbline, places exacting demands on us to reveal that we are lawbreakers and show us that, in our own moral strength, we cannot overcome sin. Paul describes this tutoring "pre-Christian" experience in the first person since he himself had already gone through it before he was saved: "I would not have come to know sin except through the Law... so that through the Commandment, sin would become utterly sinful... the Law is spiritual, but I have a sinful nature, sold into bondage to sin... For I know that nothing good dwells in me; that is, in my sinful nature, for the willing is present in me, but the doing of good is not (Romans 7:7, 13-24, 18)." This is the reason why God gave us the Law: before God could prescribe His cure to us (which is Jesus Christ), He first had to diagnose our condition (which is indwelling sin), and also give us His prognosis (which is spiritual death). As God plainly spoke, "Behold, all souls belong to

Me... every soul who sins will die (Ezekiel 18:4)." The truth is that God knows who I am, but He also wants me to know who I am. God already knows I am a sinner before I am saved. Therefore, God gave the Law so I would also know I am a sinner and acknowledge my sin-sickness. The Bible says, "Through the Law we become conscious that we are sinners (Romans 3:20)." Remember that Jesus came to redeem those who know they are sinners, and not those who consider themselves righteous (Luke 5:31; 18:9-14). Therefore, the Law reveals our spiritual condition (we are sinners by nature), and our spiritual destiny as sinners (spiritual death and eternal separation from God). The Bible says, "I was once alive apart from the Law; but when the Commandment came, sin became alive and I died; and this Commandment, which was to result in life, proved to result in death for me; for sin, taking an opportunity through the Commandment, deceived me and through it killed me (Romans 7:9-10)." Consequently, the purpose of the Law is to reveal our utter sinfulness and the outcome of our sinfulness - spiritual death, so that we might cry out to God to save us from sinful nature by His Son, Jesus Christ.

It is God's intention that when the Law has accomplished its divine purpose and exposed your utter sinfulness and helplessness, you would come to the same spiritual place as Paul did in Romans 7:24. In this case, when you have come to the end of your own abilities and resources and your own righteousness, and realized your complete moral bankruptcy, you will cry out to God: "What a wretched sinful man I am! Who can deliver me from my sinful nature?" You no longer ask "what" method can deliver you, but "who" can deliver you. Having already gone through this experience, Paul's sure answer is, "Thanks be to God through Jesus Christ our Lord! (Romans 7:25)." For the truth is that Jesus Christ has already delivered you from your sinful nature and freed you from the tyranny of sin when you were born of the Spirit.

Therefore, the difference between the Old Covenant Law and New Covenant grace is not in God's righteous standard, but in His divine means to achieve this righteousness. The Law could not justify us (Galatians 2:16); could not impart divine life to us (Galatians 3:21); could not give us the Holy Spirit to permanently indwell us (Galatians 3:2); could not make us righteous or perfect (Galatians 5:5: Hebrews 7:18; 11:40); and could not permanently deal with sin (Hebrews 10:1-4). Although the Law had the power to expose and convict us of sin, it had no power in itself to enable us to overcome sin. Instead, the Law was designed to be a temporary guardian for God's people and foreshadowed Christ's sacrificial death on the cross to redeem us from both the penalty and power of sin. Thus the Law demonstrated God's provision for an atoning sacrifice for our sins (Leviticus 1-7; Hebrews 9:22), and provided many prophetic pictures of Christ's substitutionary death on our behalf as the Lamb of God (Isaiah Chapter 53; John 1:29; Hebrews 9:11-14). And, finally, the Law became our tutor to lead us to faith in Jesus Christ so that we might be freed from the curse of sin (Galatians 3:24). What the Old Covenant Law was unable to accomplish because of man's sinful nature, God accomplished in the New Covenant through His Son's crucifixion (Romans 8:3). Whereas man failed to keep the Law, Christ fulfilled the Law by His perfect, sinless life and His sacrificial, substitutionary death on the cross. The Bible says, "Christ is the end of the Law, so that there may be righteousness for everyone who believes (Romans 10:4)." Therefore, by Christ's death on the cross, we have not only been freed from the penalty of sin; we have also been freed from the power of sin, which the Law could never do. The Bible says, "And through Him everyone who believes is freed from all things, from which you could not be freed through the Law of Moses (Acts 13:39)."

For as long as we tried to be righteous in our own strength by obeying the Law, we were under slavery to sin (Romans 6:14; 7:9). How then were we freed from both the yoke of the Law and the yoke of sin? When we were saved by Christ, we not only died to sin (when our sinful nature died), we also died to the Law. And how did we die to the Law? When our "old man" of sin (our sinful nature) died through our spiritual union with Christ's death on the cross (Romans 6:6), we also died to the Law because, by God's design, our "old man" of sin had been wed to the Law, and was under the authority of the Law. The Bible says, "Do you not know brethren… that the Law only has authority over a man as long as he lives? (Romans 7:1)." Thus the Law had been given authority over us to convict us that we were sinners by nature, in order to lead us by faith to become spiritually married to Christ (when at the time of our salvation our "old man" of sin – our sinful nature - died, thereby releasing us from our spiritual marriage to the Law). The Bible says, "Therefore, my brethren, you have also died to the Law through the body of Christ, so that you might be joined to another, to Him who was raised from the dead, in order that we might bear fruit for God (Romans 7:4)."

As we said before, the Old Covenant Law did not have the power to enable God's people to stop practicing sin and did not have the power to impart God's divine life to them (Romans 8:2-3; Galatians 3:21). It is only when you are born again in Christ as a new spiritual person (and no longer have a sinful nature), that you can be led (governed) by His Spirit so that God can accomplish His eternal purpose in you (2 Corinthians 5:17; Galatians 6:15). The Bible says, "But now we have been released from the Law, having died to that by which we were bound, so that we serve in newness of the Spirit and not in oldness of the written code (Romans 7:6)." Practicing Old Covenant religion is spiritual death (if your righteousness is based on the requirements of the Law – even parts of the Law, then the law of sin and death is your master); whereas living by the Spirit in New Covenant grace is life and peace in Christ Jesus. God did not send His Son to die on the cross to just establish another sect of Judaism; nor is His New Covenant merely an offshoot of the Old Covenant and the Mosaic Law. No; God intended the New Covenant to completely replace the Old Covenant, which was then rendered obsolete (Hebrews 8:13). Consequently, it is hypocritical and deceptive for anyone to profess they believe in a New Covenant salvation, but then practice a form of Old Covenant religion that is hostile and heretical to the New Covenant, and a gross misrepresentation of the resurrection *zoē*-life that Jesus Christ died to freely give His church.

DEAD WORKS VS GOOD WORKS

13 Since every believer is a member of God's royal priesthood, the first and foremost aim of each Christian should be to glorify God and minister to Him. However, the devil does not want us to spend time in precious fellowship and communion with God. Therefore, one of the more devious devices of the devil is to occupy the believer with doing self-inspired works of religious service, rather than obeying by faith the Lord of glory. The devil knows that the natural (unconverted) soul-life of a Christian is restless with energy to fulfill its self-identity and self-ambition. If the devil can channel this unsatisfied carnal desire into "Christian ministry" and keep us busily engaged doing carnal "Christian" works as a substitute for communing with God (faithfully abiding in Him by only doing the works that He initiates), the devil will have achieved his goal to keep us carnal-minded.

This is the deception of dead works. This is one of the main temptations and pitfalls that befall many Christians who do not understand how (or stubbornly refuse) to walk with God by faith in the truth of the cross of Christ. If the devil cannot get you entangled in sins, he will have achieved the same goal if he can get you entangled in dead works. Tragically, much of what has been done by many Christians in Jesus' name has been to satisfy their own soulish drive for identity rather than finding their true identity in Christ by believing and acting on what Jesus has accomplished for them on the cross. One of the main reasons why so many Christians are caught in the deception of dead works is that very few Christians understand the relationship between faith and works, and particularly which works are acceptable to God and which are not acceptable. When it comes to our works, the Bible distinguishes between "dead works" and "good works." In the early church, new Christians received instruction on the need to turn away from dead religious works in order to serve the living God (Hebrews 6:1; 9:14). From a Biblical perspective, "dead works" include anything we do to establish a religious or moral identity outside of faithful obedience to Christ. Sadly, many works of service done by Christians today fall under this category.

Dead works have three major distinguishing features that separate them from what the Bible calls "good works." The source, the power and the outcome of dead works are different than the source, the power and the outcome of good works. Dead works are initiated by our natural mind, are empowered by our natural ability, produce what we can naturally achieve and get man's approval. Good works are initiated by the mind of God, are empowered by the Spirit of God, produce what only God can miraculously achieve and always result in God's divine approval. The Son of God is the perfect example of someone who always did good works according to the truth of God's Word. Jesus Christ never did any works independently of God's will and initiative. Jesus said, "Truly, truly, I say to you, the Son can do nothing of Himself, unless it is something He sees the Father doing... I can do nothing on My own initiative... because I do not seek My own will, but the will of Him who sent Me (John 5:19 & 30). By His good works, Jesus showed us that the work of God is God Himself at work. Jesus said, "The Father abiding in Me does His works (John 14:10)."

Even though Jesus was the Son of Man, He never did any works that originated from the strength of his human soul. Jesus showed us the only works acceptable to God are those initiated and empowered by the Spirit of God. "For all who are being led by the Spirit of God, these are the sons of God (Romans 8:14)." All good works must spring from true faith in Jesus Christ and what He has accomplished on the cross. When people asked Jesus what they must do to do the works of God, He replied, "This is the work of God, that you believe in Him whom He has sent (John 6:29)." If God Himself (through Christ) is not initiating or empowering the work, it is not the work of God. If we can do a work without relying on God's wisdom and power, then such a work is likely to be born out of our natural ability and initiative, rather than born out of our faith in the truth of the cross; and such a work is, therefore, void of the Spirit. The Bible says, "Whatever does not come from faith is sin (Romans 14:23)." However, if our faith were based on a true and complete knowledge of the cross, we would be delivered from all carnal need to do dead works.

Since dead works are not authorized by God, they are disobedient works (even though they may look like good works). For this reason, it is crucial for Christians to hear and obey the Holy Spirit in order to do good works and not dead works. We simply cannot do good works if we cannot hear God's voice. Jesus emphasized this truth when He said, "He who has an ear, let him hear what the Spirit says... My sheep hear My voice and they follow Me." If we cannot hear the Holy Spirit and discern the difference between good works that originate from faith and dead works that originate from our carnal religious mind and our desire for self-esteem and self-identity, we will naturally do dead works that spring from our soul but mistakenly think they are good works. They may even outwardly appear to be "Christian" works, but they are still dead works if the Spirit of God has not initiated them and empowered them. Many Christians are doing dead works because so few truly know God's Word, and particularly the truth of Christ's completed work on the cross, which would enable them to discern the difference between what is of the spirit and what is of the soul. The Bible says, "The Word of God is living and active and sharper than any two-edged sword. It penetrates even to dividing soul and spirit… it is able to judge the thoughts and intentions of the heart (Hebrews 4:12)." If we are living by the strength of our soul (our natural personality and ability) and not living by the Spirit through faith in God's Word, we can easily be deceived into thinking that our dead works are acceptable to God. In fact, other Christians may even encourage us to do dead works because they too lack discernment.

A Biblical example of the difference between dead works and works of faith can be found in the Old Testament story of Cain and Abel (Genesis 4:1-16; and 1 John 3:12). When the time came to sacrifice an offering to the Lord, Cain offered some of the fruits of his labors from farming to the Lord, whereas Abel sacrificed to the Lord a first born lamb from his flock. The Lord approved of Abel's offering, but the Lord did not approve of Cain's offering. Cain then became jealous and angry and killed his brother Abel, after which God cursed and banished Cain from His presence. What is the spiritual lesson here and why did God accept Abel's offering but not accept Cain's offering? Since Abel's sacrifice was a prophetic foreshadowing of the future sacrificial death of the Lamb of God, Jesus Christ, as an offering for our sin, it is reasonable to conclude that Able heard and obeyed the voice of the Lord to present a sacrificial lamb as an offering to God. This is confirmed by the Biblical fact that God approved of Abel's sacrifice. Therefore, Abel's offering was considered righteous and a good work of faith, since it looked forward to the cross of Christ, the Lamb of God. On the other hand, Cain's offering was considered evil, since it was the result of his own self-initiative and self-effort. Cain's sacrifice was a dead work, which was inspired by his own religious ideas and came from out of his own self-generated labors. Consequently, God did not approve of Cain's offering and considered it disobedient and worthless because it did not come from faith (by hearing and obeying the Lord). This Old Testament story of Cain and Abel is a perfect metaphor that illustrates the difference between the true church and the false church. Whereas the true church humbly and gladly hears and obeys the Lord's voice, the false church stubbornly and pridefully offers up religious worship and acts of service that are neither initiated nor approved by God. Because its deeds are evil, the false church always persecutes the true church, in a vain attempt to prevent its evil motives and deeds from being revealed by Christ's truth and light. Jesus said, "This is the judgment: the light has come into the world, and men loved the darkness rather than the light because their deeds were evil. For everyone who does evil hates the light, and will not come to the light for fear that his deeds will be exposed. But whoever practices the truth comes to the light, so that it can be clearly seen that what he has done has been done through God (John 3:19-21)."

The Bible says we must stop doing our own works to enter into God's rest and His work (Hebrews 4:10). The only way we can stop doing dead "Christian" works and enter into God's work is if we believe and act on the New Covenant truth of what Jesus procured for us by His death on the cross. If we believe that we have been crucified with Christ and our sinful nature is dead and gone (Romans 6:6), then we will have aligned our spirit with God's truth and we will be able to hear and obey Jesus Christ (who will initiate His good works through us). "For we are God's workmanship, created in Christ Jesus to do good works, which God prepared in advance for us to do (Ephesians 3:10)." At the end of this age, every Christian will appear before the judgment seat of Christ (2 Corinthians 5:10). On that day, Christ will assess our works and allot our rewards and responsibilities for the age to come (Matthew 25:21; Luke 19:17). The works we have done on earth will not only be judged for their quantity but also for their quality (1 Corinthians 3:10-15). Every good work we have done in obedience to the Holy Spirit will be viewed by God as gold, silver and precious stones, and God will reward us accordingly. But every dead work we have done will be treated as wood, hay and straw (stubble) and will be burned up because they are considered worthless by God. On that day, Christ will judge the hidden motives of everyone's heart (Romans 2:19). If your dead works were done out of spiritual ignorance, your works will be rejected but you will still be saved. But if your dead works were done to satisfy your own self-identity, self-ambition or personal profit, you will face God's judgment with the rest of the hypocrites and unbelievers (Matthew 7:21-23; 13:41-42; 25:26-30).

Our foremost priestly duty is not just to serve others, but to worship God by living a life wholly sanctified to Him and hearing and obeying His voice; and in doing so, bear the fruit of good works, which are initiated and empowered by the Holy Spirit. Our greatest need is to be engaged in true service for God and enjoy daily communion with Him, by living a life of real submission and devoted obedience to God. How can we share the joy of being devoted to the Lord if our own fellowship with Jesus has become joyless because we are overly distracted by the daily affairs of life, and the demands of our self-initiated and self-energized "Christian" ministry? Jesus said our righteousness must surpass the righteousness of the religious clergy of His day (Matthew 5:20). The religious leaders during Jesus' time had become completely detached from true communion with God; instead they were devoted to fulfilling their own religious self-identity and self-ambition by doing dead religious works rather than doing the will of God.

If we do not spend precious time with the Lord Jesus in private, how can we proclaim Him with power in public? If we were to spend more quality time alone with the Lord and walked in true obedience to Him, more people would take notice that we had "been with Jesus" (Acts 4:13). Knowing how to abide (stay united to) Jesus Christ and in the truth of His crucifixion and resurrection is the secret to possessing Christ's abundant life and walking in freedom from habitual sins as true sons and daughters of God (John 10:10; Romans 8:19-21). Of course, this does not mean that God is against ministry, but that all *true* ministry must originate from our personal ministry and obedience to the Lord first; otherwise our works will be dead works. Paul's testimony was that he served God as a priest *in his spirit* in the preaching of the gospel of His Son (Romans 1:9; 15:16). If we diligently endeavor to abide in Christ and hear and obey our Lord's voice, we too can have the same testimony: that we serve God *in our spirit* in whatever good work the Lord calls us to do. However, if we never learn to hear and obey the Lord's voice, the outcome of all our Christian service will be only dead works that we have done from our soulish ability, and we will not have served God or known God at all.

How The New Covenant Church Meets Together

14 **M**any contemporary churches today have two or three Sunday morning services, with each service allowed a one-hour program. Everyone who attends the service knows the program: first the band plays "worship" music; next there are church announcements; then the tithes and offerings are collected while the band plays some more; then the pastor gives his sermon (the same one to all three services); finally, a closing prayer is given, followed by the band playing once again. There is neither freedom nor time allowed in the sixty minute service for the Holy Spirit to lead the church any differently from this rigid and pre-planned program. Every week, the pastor directs and conducts this programmed meeting, which is usually a one-man show with him on center stage. The meeting is so predictable

and boring, it is no wonder that some people are napping, while others are texting or thinking about what they are going to have for lunch. If you think that church is spiritually dead, you are right. Jesus left that church a long time ago, if He ever was there. It should make any sane and Spirit-filled believer wonder, "Is this all there is? Is this all God has ordained and given us?" The emphatic answer is: "Absolutely not! God has given us far more than is being exhibited in the average church service today!"

Tragically, the typical pastor's complete dominance of the modern church service has trained the congregation to have a spectator mentality and cultivated a crippling dependence of the laity upon his ministry. This dependency model of pulpit-and-pew ministry directly contradicts the New Testament's teachings and practices and robs the church from having a true priesthood of gifted ministries. Whereas the word "pastor" is mentioned only once in the English translation of the Bible, there are dozens of Scriptures describing the mutual ministry that should occur among the priesthood of believers. The saints are to "love one another... serve one another... build up one another... be devoted to another... pray for one another... sing to one another... comfort one another... admonish one another... teach one another... forgive one another... give to one another." And this kind of mutual ministry to one another is not going to happen in the brief half-hour after the service while everyone is drinking coffee latte and eating donuts! As Paul wrote, "The body is not one member but many... if the whole body were an eye, where would the sense of hearing be? If the whole body were an ear, where would the sense of smell be?... As it is, there are many members but one body. The eye cannot say to the hand, 'I do not need you!' And the head cannot say to the feet, 'I do not need you!'" (1 Corinthians 12:14-21) Yet, under today's false religious system that separates the clergy from the laity, the pastor is often the sole member of the body to actively function throughout the church meeting, while the laity is ritually rendered to a silent and inactive status. It is as though one member of the body; such as the hand or foot, was always active and functioning, but the rest of the body were paralyzed and useless. This dependency model of one-man ministry is hostile to the intent of the New Covenant and strikes at the very heart of the priesthood of believers that Jesus purchased for us by His blood on the cross. If we examine with an open mind the life and ministry of the early church, as it is recorded in the New Testament, we see that there was the participation of every member present in the meetings and that this participation was brought about by the sovereign and supernatural presence of the Holy Spirit, working in and through each individual believer. However, the typical modern-day Protestant church has a rigid two-caste system, which consists of the career clergy-caste who are paid to minister to the laity, and the laity-caste who pay the clergy-caste to minister to them. This unScriptural clergy-laity dichotomy is a direct carryover from the Catholic church system and a throwback to the Old Testament priesthood.

Faced with overwhelming Biblical evidence that directly opposes this false paradigm, we must ask what motivates a pastor to continue practicing this dependency model of ministry, which keeps his flock permanently passive and anemic, but allows him total freedom to personally develop and use all his talents. Does his self-identity and self-esteem depend on this unBiblical model of ministry? Or does his financial livelihood require keeping the congregation wholly dependent upon him? Some pastors say they have a functioning priesthood of believers in their church because they allow sister Jane to sing a solo; or brother Tom to be an usher and collect the offerings; or sister Rhonda to give a testimony; or brother Jim to say a closing prayer. One mainline denomination even claims to have a functioning priesthood of believers because they encourage their members to "actively" listen to the pastor's sermon. And some pastors say this kind of "body life" is supposed to occur in their church's small cell groups that meet during the week. Yet this very rarely, if ever happens; these midweek meetings typically take the form of lifeless "Bible studies," which are not anointed by the Holy Spirit; therefore the spiritual gifts of teaching, word of wisdom, word of knowledge, prophecy, healings, miracles, etc. can find no expression even in those small group settings. Indeed, there are many denominations which profess to believe in the supernatural gifts of the Holy Spirit as part of their official creed, but if you attend any of their church services or small group meetings, you will never see any of their members exercise any of the miraculous gifts of the Spirit.

All of this falls woefully short of what God intended when He called His people of the New Covenant to be a royal priesthood of spiritually-gifted saints who together accomplish the work of the ministry (1 Peter 2:9; Ephesians 4:12). How can a brother, to whom the Spirit has given the spiritual gift of teaching, have the freedom to develop and use his ministry gift when the church excludes it because he has never been to seminary? Or, how can a sister, to whom the Spirit has given the spiritual gift of prophecy, have the freedom to develop and use her ministry gift when the pastor forbids it? A fully functioning priesthood of believers is only possible when there is freedom for the saints to step out in faith in the meetings and learn how to exercise the spiritual gifts that God has given them. As one brother has aptly said, "We have centered all our ministry in paid professionals and thereby sold our birthright for a padded pew." How is it possible that the abundant Spirit-filled New Covenant church life which Christ died for has been reduced to such cardboard Christianity?

It is not just the pastors who will be held responsible and accountable to God for promoting and perpetuating this dead church system; every Christian who participates in the false church and financially supports it will also be held accountable for not obeying the truth of God's Word. Many Christians choose to remain in the dead church system because they think it is safer to stay in rather than to leave the system, or they are afraid of the alienation and loneliness they will face if they leave the system. Many Christians stay in the false church system because they naïvely think that they can be "salt and light" and a reforming influence within the system. However, the false church system always wins in this situation and invariably influences those naïve Christians to lose their salt and light, in order to conform and not lose the unbelieving community's affection and approval. Likewise, many pastors choose to stay in the corrupt, dead church system because they are afraid of the disapproval and loss of financial support they will face if they ever leave the system. But it is never spiritually safe to be in the false church; in fact, it is quite dangerous and spiritually deadly. It is far better to face a lifetime of loneliness and hardship with God rather than to be seduced by the soulish and false "fellowship" of those who pretend to be Christians.

Other Christians decide to stay in the false church (even though they know there is something wrong with it) because they want their children to attend Sunday school programs to their liking. In this case, these naïve parents are being led by the whims and desires of their spiritually immature and carnal-minded children, instead of being led by the Spirit of God. It would be far better for these parents to have church at home with their children, and be an example of true Christianity to their children. By raising their children in the false church, they are putting their children's souls at great risk. Their children will either reject Christianity because all they have ever experienced was the counterfeit cardboard version (also known as Churchianity), or their children will stay engaged and seduced by the false church through their adulthood and eventually lead even their own children into it. Tragically, when all is said and done, the people get the pastors and the churches that they desire, and that they deserve.

In the New Covenant church, God has called every believer to be an active member of His holy priesthood and do the work of His ministry

(Ephesians 4:12; 1 Peter 2:5). The Bible says that Jesus Christ "has freed us from our sins by His blood, and has made us to be a kingdom of priests to serve His God and Father (Revelation 1:5-6)" Since each member of the body of Christ is a priest to God, the Bible exhorts each member to live a holy life (1 Peter 1:15); to be filled with the Holy Spirit (Ephesians 5:18); to put on the full armor of God (Ephesians 6:11); to take up the shield of faith and the sword of the Spirit (Ephesians 6:16-17); to be ready to share the gospel with others (2 Timothy 4:2); to pray continually for all the saints (Ephesians 6:18); to baptize new believers (Matthew 28:19); to encourage one another (Hebrews 10:24); to stimulate one another to love and good deeds (Hebrews 10:25); to lay hands on the sick so they might be healed (James 5:16); to teach new believers how to obey the Lord's commands (Matthew 28:19); and to use all their spiritual gifts to build up the body of Christ (1 Corinthians 14:1, 26). Therefore, it is the responsibility of every believer to walk in holiness (by faith in what Christ accomplished on the cross), which is their proper service to God, so that they may be fully used as priests of the Lord to minister to His people (Romans 12:1-2; 2 Timothy 2:21).

Let us now take a closer look at how a New Covenant church meeting functions. The meetings are not programmed and predictable. There are no clergy directing the meetings and no minister monopolizes every meeting. God's sheep are not passive spectators; instead, as members of God's holy priesthood, they actively participate in the meetings. The meetings are "charismatic" since the spiritual gifts (*charismata* in Greek) are regularly exercised by those present. The Bible says, "There are different kinds of gifts (*charismata*), but the same Spirit. There are different kinds of ministries, but the same Lord. There are different kinds of working, but the same God who works these things (*gifts*) in all men. Now to each one is given the manifestation of the Spirit for the common good. For to one is given the word of wisdom through the Spirit; to another the word of knowledge by the same Spirit; to another (*special*) faith by the same Spirit; to another gifts of healing by the one Spirit; to another miraculous powers; to another prophecy; to another the discernment of spirits; to another speaking in different kinds of tongues; and to still another the interpretation of tongues. For one and the same Spirit works all these things, and He gives them *(the gifts)* to each one just as He determines (1 Corinthians 12:4-11)." Note how the Holy Spirit distributes these supernatural gifts to "each one," and not to just some pastor who has gone to seminary. In this way, the will of God can be expressed through a prophecy given by one; by a teaching given by another; by the word of wisdom by yet another; or by tongues and interpretation of tongues given by others, as each member freely shares their spiritual gifts with the church as the Holy Spirit directs them. The Bible says, "Since we have gifts that differ according the grace given to us, *each of us* is to exercise them accordingly... according to the proportion of his faith (Romans 12:6)."

Since nearly all modern-day churches do not believe in or do not practice the gift of prophecy or the gifts of tongues with interpretation of tongues, it would be good to briefly explain the purpose and function of these specific spiritual gifts since Paul considered them the most useful gifts in building up the church (1 Corinthians 14:1-5). The Bible defines prophecy as God speaking through a Christian brother or sister to strengthen, encourage and comfort the church (1 Corinthians 14:3). The Bible also teaches and demonstrates that prophecy can entail foretelling future events and providing pertinent guidance concerning these events. In this regard, we have received a number of prophesies for the body of Christ concerning world events, and posted some of them on our website. In the New Testament record, we see a number of examples of brothers and sisters who exercised the gift of prophecy. For example, Judas and Silas gave lengthy prophetic messages to the church at Antioch, which strengthened and encouraged the saints (Acts 15:32). Agabus also prophesied to the church at Antioch and warned that a great famine would soon hit the entire Roman empire. This prophecy stirred up the church to start a famine relief fund in advance to assist their brothers and sisters in Judea who would be affected by the famine, which then occurred in A.D. 49-50 (Acts 11:28-29). Another time, when the saints were meeting together in Philip's house at Caesarea, Agabus gave a prophetic message to Paul warning him that he would be imprisoned when he traveled to Jerusalem, which occurred just as Agabus had foresaw (Acts 21:10-11). This particular passage of Scripture also records that Philip's four daughters exercised the gift of prophecy, which demonstrates that women are able to also prophesy in church (Acts 21:8-9).

Based on the teaching of the apostles and the example of the New Covenant church in the first century, how much should the saints today value the gift of prophecy and seek to prophesy in church? Paul exhorts the saints to "eagerly desire the spiritual gifts, especially that you may prophesy... one who speaks in tongues strengthens himself, but the one who prophesies strengthens the church. I wish that every one of you spoke in tongues, but even more that you would prophesy. The one who prophesies is greater than the one who speaks in tongues, unless he interprets so that the church may be strengthened (1 Corinthians 14:1-5)." Let us now briefly discuss the gift of tongues followed by an interpretation, which Paul mentions in this verse. When the gift of tongues followed by the gift of interpretation is properly used in the church, it is similar to the gift of prophecy (1 Corinthians 14:3). The only difference is that prophecy is not preceded by a message in an unknown language. How does the gift of tongues with interpretation work? Let me share a current day example: in one of our meetings, a Christian sister who did not speak any Chinese, gave an encouraging and strengthening message to us in the Chinese language, which was then followed by the English interpretation. Thus the Holy Spirit has given us both the gift of prophecy and the gift of tongues with interpretation to strengthen, encourage and comfort the church. The only thing that can stop the Holy Spirit from distributing these spiritual gifts when the saints meet today is our unbelief and disobedience.

Under the Holy Spirit's direction, each meeting of the New Covenant church is different and unique depending upon the ministry of the Holy Spirit and the needs of Christ's body. Although some reading and teaching from the Scriptures will normally take place whenever the saints meet together (1 Timothy 4:15; 2 Timothy 3:16); this does not mean there will always be a teaching every time there is a meeting; or that the teaching will always be given by the same person; or that the teaching will always take up the entire meeting. Therefore, whenever the church meets together, everyone should come ready to contribute their spiritual gifts for the good of the whole body. The Bible says, "One has a psalm, another has a teaching, another has a revelation; another has a tongue and another has an interpretation. All of these are to be done for the building up of the church (1 Corinthians 14:26)." This functioning priesthood of spiritually gifted believers is one of the fundamental building blocks of Christ's church. The Bible says, "You also, like living stones, are being built into a spiritual house as *a holy priesthood*, to offer up spiritual sacrifices acceptable to God through Jesus Christ (1 Peter 2:5)." What are these spiritual sacrifices that God accepts? The spiritual sacrifices that are pleasing to God are our very lives – our hearts and our souls and our bodies. As Paul taught, "Therefore, I urge you, brethren, in view of God's mercy, to offer your bodies as living sacrifices, holy and acceptable to God, which is your spiritual service of worship (Romans 12:1)."

This is the model of mutual ministry in the New Covenant church, which springs first and foremost from each saint's priestly service to the Lord. And it is through the saints' personal ministry to the Lord and their mutual ministry to one another that the grace of our Lord Jesus Christ, the love of God, and the fellowship and gifts of the Holy Spirit are revealed in His body as it gathers together in His Name. This does not mean there are no leaders present in the meeting; but it does mean the elders (the shepherds) are not the only ones who function in the meetings, and they do not dominate and overly control the meetings, but instead they listen to the Holy Spirit's leading to help guide the meeting. The Bible says, "God has allotted to each member a measure of faith. For just as we have many members in one body and all the members do not have the same function… since we have different gifts according to the grace given us, each of us is to exercise them accordingly. If a man's gift is prophesying, let him use it according to the proportion of his faith; if it is service, let him serve; if it is teaching, let him teach; if it is encouraging, let him encourage; if it is contributing to the needs of others, let him give generously; *if it is leadership, let him lead diligently*; if it is showing mercy, let him do it cheerfully (Romans 12:3-8)." Thus the gift of leadership is only one of the many spiritual gifts that God has given His multi-gifted body to reveal His mind to the church when the saints meet together.

To use the metaphor of a symphony conductor and his orchestra: Jesus, not the pastor, is the head conductor of the church meeting. When the saints come together in the fellowship of the Holy Spirit, everyone fixes their eyes of faith on Jesus Christ, the head of the church. The Holy Spirit then spontaneously prompts each member, as individual instruments of Christ's "orchestra," to share their spiritual gifts in proper order (1 Corinthians 14:40). When Jesus is the head conductor of the church, the meetings are creatively directed by the Holy Spirit who leads the saints (with their multiple gifts) to produce a spiritual "symphony" which nourishes the whole body. As Paul wrote, "We are to grow up in all aspects into Him who is the head, even Christ, from whom the whole body, being fitted and held together by what every joint supplies, *according to the proper working of each individual part*, causes the growth of the body for the building up of itself in love (Ephesians 4:15-16)." In this way, all the members actively participate in building up the body of Christ so that the church as a whole can fulfill God's eternal purpose — to express the fullness of Jesus Christ. It is clear from the record of the New Testament, that Spirit-led, open participatory meetings with the expression of multiple spiritual gifts were the main feature when the saints gathered together.

Although this is the normal pattern for a New Covenant church meeting, there are exceptions to this type of meeting. For example, the church may decide to have a special meeting where a visiting apostle or teacher or one of the local elders will teach Biblical doctrine. In that case, the meeting would be exclusively centered on the systematic teaching of God's Word (Acts 20:7-11). However, this kind of "teaching" meeting is the exception and not the norm; otherwise, God's sheep would become dependent upon always being fed by one or two others, instead of learning how to minister to Jesus, the Bread of Life, so they can be filled with the Holy Spirit and, in turn, feed their brothers and sisters by means of the spiritual gifts the Spirit has given each of them. The Bible says, "Each one should use whatever gift he has received to serve one another as good stewards of the manifold grace of God. Whoever speaks should do so as one speaking the very words of God; whoever serves should serve with the strength God provides, so that in all things God may be glorified through Jesus Christ, to whom belongs the glory and power forever and ever. Amen. (1 Peter 4:10-11)." Another exception to this kind of participatory, charismatic, Spirit-directed meeting would be an "evangelistic" meeting where the singular purpose is for an apostle or evangelist to proclaim the gospel of Christ to a group of unbelievers (Acts 13:44-49).

Some pastors would say this kind of freedom and spontaneity of the saints would only result in chaos, anarchy and heresy. However, we cannot look to the failed false church as our model; the Scriptures must be our only "rule of faith and practice" to instruct us how the New Covenant church should fellowship and function when the saints meet together. Under the Old Covenant, the high priest interceded with God on behalf of the people, and also interpreted the will of God to the people. Under the New Covenant, however, every brother and sister in Christ knows God, and can intercede with God and be taught by God and be led by God because the Holy Spirit lives in each one of us and teaches us all truth (John 14:17, 27; Hebrews 8:7-13; 1 John 2:27). One of the spiritual safeguards that God has established to prevent disorder and heresy from destroying His New Covenant church is the appointment of elders. The elders provide spiritual oversight to the church and protect the saints from false teachers and false doctrines. Paul warned that "fierce wolves will come in among you not sparing the flock (Acts 20:29)." The elders stand at the "gate" of the church and prevent these "wolves in sheep's clothing" from entering into the fellowship of the saints (John 10:1-2).

Besides warding off the wolves, the elders can help keep peace and order in many other ways. A church without an elder is like a family without a father. This does not mean the elders dominate and monopolize the meetings, but they can help moderate the meetings, as necessary. For example, the elders can encourage and prompt members of the fellowship by asking if anyone has a song or testimony or prophecy to share. Or, if a brother shares a word that is not Biblically sound, the elders can gently and lovingly correct him. The elders can also help evaluate any prophecies or tongues and interpretation of tongues that are spoken in the meetings. As Paul taught, "Do not quench the Spirit, and do not despise prophecies. But examine everything carefully; hold fast to that which is good (1 Thessalonians 19-21)." The elders can also prevent any disruptive visitor from hijacking the meetings, and restore peace and order with wisdom and patience. Of course, there are going to be growing pains as the saints learn how to properly function in the spiritual liberty of meetings based on the New Covenant pattern of 2 Corinthians 14:26; however, remember there is quiet and order in a cemetery, but there is no life there! As the church becomes more spiritually practiced in having responsible, open participatory, Spirit-led meetings, the role of the elders as moderators will naturally diminish. Ideally, in a more mature church, a visitor should normally not be able to tell who the elders are in the meetings. Unless there is a problem to be addressed or a Biblical doctrine to be taught, the elders will generally blend in like everyone else. See more on elders in Endnote #16.

Since Jesus Christ does not pour His new wine of the Spirit into old wineskins, but only into new wineskins (saints who are new creations in Christ and no longer have an old sinful nature), why would He pour His Spirit into churches that hold fast to the rituals of the old wineskins (archaic meetings based on Old Covenant laws and practices when even those of faith still had sinful natures before the advent of the New Covenant)? The old wineskins may have been good in their day, but now they are obsolete, inflexible, legalistic and not able to contain the new wine of the Spirit. The New Covenant church is a community of the Spirit, and when the saints gather together for fellowship, the freedom of the Spirit should be present. Paul declared, "It was for freedom that Christ set us free... and where the Spirit of the Lord is, there is freedom ... the glorious freedom of the children of God (Galatians 5:1; 2 Corinthians 3:17; Romans 8:21)." What did Paul mean by this declaration of freedom? Many Christians think this means Jesus has given us spiritual freedom to worship God and to freely use the gifts of the Spirit in our meetings. There is some truth to this since a congregation of Spirit-baptized believers who freely exercise the supernatural gifts in their meetings greatly differs from a congregation whose members have not received the baptism in the Holy Spirit, and do not know how to exercise the gifts of the Spirit. However, the manifestation of the spiritual gifts in our meetings should only be an outcome of the real spiritual freedom that Paul is talking about. What then is the true freedom that Jesus Christ died to give us? The Bible says that, by His death on the cross, Jesus purchased our freedom from sin's captivity (Romans 6:7, 18, 22). However, unless you believe and act on this glorious freedom, you may sound spiritual when you sing worship songs or look spiritual when you exercise the supernatural gifts in meetings, but you are not truly free. Jesus said that when He has freed you from slavery to sin, then you are really free (John 8:32-36).

The statement "where the Spirit of the Lord is, there is freedom" could also be said this way: "where the Spirit is Lord *(sovereign)*, there is freedom." In other words, true spiritual liberty is the outcome when we are submitted to Christ's authority and governed by His Spirit. This is why Paul could say, "He who was a slave when he was called by the Lord is the Lord's freedman (1 Corinthians 7:22)." No matter what your station or situation in life, you can experience true spiritual freedom when you are enslaved to God. With this in mind, Paul said, "Now that you have been set free from sin and have become slaves to God, you derive your benefit, which is sanctification (Romans 6:22)." This is true liberty; however, where the Spirit is not sovereign in a professing Christian's life, there is still bondage to sin. It is only when you believe and act on the Biblical truth that Christ set you free you from enslavement to sin when He removed your sin nature at the time of your new birth (Romans 6:3-6), that you will experience true spiritual liberty within your soul. As Paul taught, "He who has died *(whose sinful nature has died)* has been freed from sin (Romans 6:7)." Knowing and acting on this truth is real freedom!

This is why it is imperative that all new disciples be taught *how* to stop practicing sin so they can experience this spiritual freedom. When an apostle plants a church, he must lay the proper foundation of the gospel of Christ crucified so that the saints can learn how to overcome sin. Remember that you can only teach others *how* to stop practicing sin if you personally know *how* to do it and *are* doing it. And you can only truly stop practicing habitual sin by abiding (staying united by faith) in Jesus Christ and the truth of His completed work on the cross. And yet how many churches today instruct their new members how to stop practicing sin by exercising faith in the cross of Christ? How many churches even consider practicing sin a problem? The reality is that sin in the church has become a problem of epidemic proportions, yet the present day church is not under the conviction of the Holy Spirit for its chronic sins. This is clear evidence of the absence of the fear of God in today's church. Some habitual sins which Christians practice are evident for all to see, such as chronic gluttony or overeating (recent studies show that up to three-fourths of all professing Christians attending church are significantly overweight or obese); whereas other sins which Christians practice are hidden from others (but not from God), such as chronic use of pornography (recent studies reveal that up to three-fourths of all professing Christian men attending church are secretly addicted to pornography).

Under the Old Covenant Law, both of these sins – sexual immorality and gluttony - were punishable by death. However, many worldly-minded churches now wrongly teach that since grace "covers" all your sins, you do not have to be overly concerned about stopping your deadly, sinful habits as long as you keep coming to church and take communion for your sins. And most churches also teach and practice some form of religious "methodism" to overcome sinful habits, which is not based on faith at all, but instead is based on the inherent moral ability and natural self-discipline of each individual. Yet some of us have genuinely come to Christ because we desperately needed a Savior to save us from our destructive sinful habits, and not some "life coach" session or "self-help" book to help us perform better in our lives. Instead of desperately crying out for God to free them from their chronic sins, many so-called Christians would rather be entertained by false pastors whose sermons soulishly comfort them and build up their self-esteem, rather than spiritually convict and challenge them to repent, believe and act on the truth of the cross. How can we hope to overcome the satanic snares that would sabotage our Christian relationships with one another and our gathering together as the bride of Christ, if we cannot even master our individual sinful habits that still so easily entangle us, and from which Christ shed His precious blood to set us free? How can we faithfully cultivate a spiritually rich community life and genuine *agapē* fellowship with one another as God's family, if we are habitually sinning and our sins can always rear their ugly head and come between us? How can the Holy Spirit sovereignly lead and direct us in obedience to His voice during our weekly meetings together, if we cannot individually hear and obey the Holy Spirit every day by putting to death the sinful attitudes and actions of our unconverted natural soul-life?

The Bible says, "If you have raced with men on foot and they have worn you out, how can you compete with horses? If you stumble in a safe country, how will you manage in the thickets of the Jordan? (Jeremiah 12:5)." If we are not practicing true holiness (by believing and acting on the truth of what Christ accomplished by His death on the cross), then our spiritually gifted (charismatic) meetings can degenerate into carnality, disorder and division, just as happened to the Corinthian church during the first century. If we have not yet learned how to stop practicing sin, then freely exercising the spiritual gifts in our meetings will be of no value, and can even be spiritually deceptive and dangerous. Many Christians who exercise the miraculous gifts of the Spirit are blinded to the fact that they woefully lack the fruit of the Spirit in their lives. And if they do not recognize they have a serious sin problem, then they will not desperately seek God's solution: to believe and act on Christ's completed work on the cross, which has freed them from their entangling sins. This is why much of the charismatic movement of the 1960s and 1970s fell into carnality and failed.

There are two other common pitfalls that can occur if a church has not yet learned how to overcome sin by faith in Christ. The first pitfall is that our meetings can fall into a weekly routine (for example, three fast praise songs followed by three slow worship songs; followed by a prophecy or tongues with an interpretation; followed by a teaching; and closing with prayer for those who need it). Or, if the members thought the Lord really ministered to them when they devoted a meeting solely to listening to someone teach, they may think every meeting should be structured this same way. Or, if the members felt the presence of the Lord was with them when they clapped and danced in a meeting, they may try to clap and dance in every meeting to re-experience the Lord's presence. Or, if God blessed them once when they raised their hands and shouted praises, they may always want to raise their hands and shout in very meeting. If we are not vigilant, we can all fall into this type of religious ritual (instead of true Spirit-led *koinonia* body life) because of spiritual ignorance, laziness or unbelief in the truth of God's Word. When we surrender our meetings to a carnal and boring ritual, we have lost our spiritual liberty and limited the Holy Spirit's sovereign, supernatural and creative direction in our meetings. We will have replaced the institutional church's printed program of ritualized service for a different kind of religious bondage. The Holy Spirit is incredibly creative: just witness God's creativity in making heaven and earth and all the living things of earth, especially man and woman. Therefore, we need to stay spiritually alert in our meetings to actively listen for the spontaneous leading of the Holy Spirit. Who knows how the Holy Spirit may lead us? Perhaps the Holy Spirit will manifest His presence in our meeting in such a strong and convicting manner that the only thing we can do in response is to fall on our knees with repentance and weeping. Of course, the Holy Spirit will always lead us in a manner that is in harmony with the written Word of God. To avoid the mundane rut of ritual, the more experienced and mature elder brothers in the fellowship may need to remind the others to keep their mind on the Spirit and actively seek to use their spiritual gifts which God has given them for the common good of the whole body.

After the apostle who plants a church leaves, it is the role of elders to instruct, and guide that church in the proper use of the spiritual gifts in their meetings. The elders should encourage those weak in faith how to use their gifts and gently admonish the unruly who misuse their gifts. The elders and prophets in the church also need to have spiritual discernment to assess whether a prophecy or other gift has genuinely come from the Holy Spirit, and not from the mind of men. The second pitfall is that our meetings can slip into being a Christian social club where earthly subjects are discussed during the entire meeting, instead of our functioning together in the Spirit and truly building up one another in Christ. Once again, this can happen because of spiritual ignorance or spiritual laziness. The primary way both these pitfalls can be avoided is if most (all is even better), of the members of a church are filled with the Holy Spirit on a daily basis, and the only way to be continuously filled with the Holy Spirit is if we know how to practice living a sanctified life by faith in Christ's completed work on the cross. In closing, how will we know what to do in our meetings? The Holy Spirit will reveal and direct us what to do and when to do it. A New Covenant church that is directed by the Holy Spirit will do the right thing at the right time, and the outcome will be spiritual liberty, love, peace and unity; which are the fruit of abiding in the Spirit.

A final word: a normal New Covenant church meeting with a fully functioning priesthood of spiritually gifted believers has not been common practice since the first century. Therefore, as we begin to gather together as a New Covenant church with one united purpose to please the Lord and hear and obey the Holy Spirit in our meetings, we need to allow ourselves the grace and patience to grow into God's desire for His church, as each member learns how to function as God originally intended for His Son's bride. As each of us individually practices walking daily in the Lord's sanctification that comes from exercising faith in the truth of the cross, and we corporately practice meeting together in accordance with the Scriptural teaching and guidelines of the New Covenant church, we will inevitably stumble at times, like a child learning to walk. However, if we persevere by faith in the grace and truth of Jesus Christ, we will steadily walk and one day run.

How To Hear And Obey The Lord

15 What does it mean to hear and obey Jesus' voice? It does not mean following some mystical feeling, because feelings (even "good" religious feelings) are prone to deception. No; our hearing and obeying must be based on the Word of God. In the Greek New Testament, there are two different words used for the "Word" of God. One is *logos*; the other is *rhema*. Although they are sometimes used interchangeably, they have two distinct meanings. *Logos* means the eternal counsel or mind of God. *Logos* can also be described as the divine blueprint of God's eternal purpose. For example, John used the word *logos* in introducing his gospel of Christ: "In the beginning was the Word *(Logos)*, and the Word *(Logos)* was with God, and the Word *(Logos)* was God… and the Word *(Logos)* became flesh (John 1:1, 17)." The *Logos* or total counsel of God is made available to us through both the written Word of God – the Bible, and the living Word of God – Jesus Christ. But the whole *Logos* of God is too vast and too comprehensive for us to grasp in its entirety and fullness. Therefore, *rhema* is the way the Holy Spirit divinely reveals a portion of His heavenly, eternal, total *Logos* to us. *Rhema* specifically means a word that is spoken in time and space. For example, Jesus used the word *rhema* when He overcame Satan in the wilderness: "Man shall not live by bread alone, but on every word *(rhema)* that proceeds out of the mouth of God (Matthew 4:4)." Jesus here speaks of a specific word *(rhema)* of God that is revealed by the breath of God, which is the Holy Spirit. In other words, through the spoken word *(rhema)* of God, the *Logos* (the mind) of God becomes real and produces faith in us (if we believe it to the point of acting on it). This is what Paul meant when he said, "Faith comes by hearing, and hearing comes by the word *(rhema)* of God (Romans 10:17)." From the context of this passage

(Romans 10:8-17), we can conclude that when someone hears and acts on the *rhema* word of God that Christ died for them (Romans 5:8), they will experience deliverance from the penalty of sin. In the same way, when someone hears and acts on the *rhema* word of God that they died with Christ (Romans 6:8), they will experience deliverance from the power of sin "because he who has died has been freed from sin (Romans 6:7)."

Now what does this have to do with our New Covenant church meetings? The purpose of our meeting together is to corporately exalt God the Father and His Son, our Lord Jesus Christ, and to hear and obey the leading of the Holy Spirit in our midst. In other words, we want to hear God's *rhema* word to us, so that we can live by God's living bread, Jesus Christ. But how can the church know the mind of Christ and discern God's will if the saints cannot hear God's *rhema* word to them? How can we effectively exercise the true gift of teaching in our meetings if we cannot hear God's *rhema* word that He wants to share with the saints? Or, how can we accurately exercise the gift of prophecy or the gifts of tongues with interpretation of tongues in our meetings if we cannot hear God speaking His *rhema* word to us? Remember that God has given us a plumbline to assess the authenticity and accuracy of any *rhema* word, and that plumbline is His *Logos* Word; for every *rhema* word that is shared in church should be judged by the prophets and elders to determine: 1) Does it agree with God's written *Logos* Word – the Bible; and 2) Does it agree with God's Spirit; for a message that is given may agree with the letter of the Word, but not be given at the right time or in the right spirit. This kind of judging should normally be done in a spirit of gentleness and encouragement with the aim of not quenching the exercise of the Spirit's gifts in the meeting.

With this in mind, there are two ways (or conditions) that can help accurately us hear and share God's *rhema* word. The first condition is to immerse ourselves (by reading and meditating) daily in the written Word

(Logos) of God. If the *Logos* Word is richly dwelling in us, it becomes easier to hear God's specific *rhema* word to us. The second condition is to obey (act on) God's *rhema* word whenever we hear it. For this is the way God works with us: if we obey His voice, our spiritual hearing will get better; however, if we disobey His voice, our hearing will get worse over time until we can no longer hear nor understand what God is speaking to us. Jesus (quoting from the prophet Isaiah) said, "You will keep on hearing but not understand. You will keep on seeing, but not perceive. For the heart of this people has become dull. They hardly hear with their ears, and they have closed their eyes. Otherwise, they might see with their eyes and hear with their ears, and understand with their hearts, and I would heal them (Matthew 13:14-15; Isaiah 6:9-10)." After a person receives Jesus Christ as their Lord and Savior, one of the very first acts of obedience they will encounter is to be baptized (immersed) in water, since water baptism is the betrothal or commitment ceremony of new members of the bride of Christ to Jesus, their beloved Bridegroom (Matthew 28:19). According to Jesus' command, the next act of obedience for a Christian is to be baptized (immersed) in the Holy Spirit (Acts 1:4-8). Once again, if someone wants to obey God and continue growing in the Christian faith, they will be baptized both in water and in the Holy Spirit. However, if they resist God's voice and dismiss the Lord's baptism in the Spirit as only something that was needed to supernaturally empower the early disciples in the Book of Acts, but not required for Christians in our day, their Christian growth will be stunted and their spiritual hearing will be impaired.

Sometimes God will speak to us with a heavenly megaphone to make sure we hear Him and follow His direction, while other times He will speak to us in a still, small voice that could easily be drowned out by the many voices in the world (even "religious" voices) that clamor for our attention. Here is the key to hearing the Lord: the more we walk in sanctification by believing and acting on the Biblical truth that we are dead to sin but alive to God in Christ, the more God can speak His *rhema* word to us and we will hear Him. We simply cannot hope to hear the voice of the Lord if we continue to walk in disobedience by habitually practicing sin (whether it is carnally evident or hidden behind a mask of false morality). Paul calls this process of daily sanctification the "obedience of faith" (Romans 1:5; 16:26). For true Biblical faith is inseparably linked with our willingness to be submitted to Christ's authority. Thus true faith is both rooted in and revealed by our obedience to Jesus Christ. The more we obey the voice of the Lord, the more He can trust our faithfulness and reveal Himself and His ways to us, and employ us as His bondservants. As Paul said, "Let men regard us as servants of Christ and stewards of the mysteries of God. Now it is required of stewards that they must prove trustworthy (1 Corinthians 4:1)." On the other hand, if we persistently refuse to obey God's will and ignore His *rhema* word to us because of unbelief and disobedience, the light and understanding we may have previously received from God will diminish and eventually disappear (Matthew 13:14-15; Acts 28:20).

When God speaks to you and gives you His light of revelation, there is a window of opportunity for you to respond to Him and believe and act on His *rhema* word. This opportunity should not be taken lightly because you never know how long the window will remain open and when it will open again. The Bible says, "From everyone who has been given much, much will be required; and from the one who has been entrusted with much, much more will be required... so take care how you listen *(hear and obey)*; for whoever has, to him more shall be given; and whoever does not have, even what he thinks he has shall be taken away from him (Luke 12:48; 8:18)." This should give all of us pause and the fear of God.

There are many people in Christian ministry today who did not obey the voice of the Lord and took a wrong turn at a major crossroads in their life. Perhaps they married a nominal Christian because they were afraid of being lonely; or they married a carnal Christian for their spouse's looks, personality, finances, connections or station in life when the Lord warned them not to. Or, perhaps they got entangled in a wrong doctrine that they still follow and preach to this day because it enabled them to have a growing ministry, even though the Lord had warned them to stay away from it. Or, out of a need to fulfill their self-ambition, they went to seminary and got into professional ministry when the Lord had not called, trained or sent them. Or, they got into public ministry to rehabilitate their former self-image and bolster their sense of self-worth. Or, they sought the approval and publicity of others to promote, network and expand their ministry rather than only seeking God's initiative and approval for their ministry. Because they have never truly repented from these wrong motives, decisions and actions, they can only minister in the flesh now, instead of in the power of the Holy Spirit. But since many in the world of Churchianity will open their doors to them and reward them with favor, fame and financial support, they have brushed aside any nagging feelings that something is not right. They now mistakenly think they are serving God, when instead it may be that God is using them to accomplish His purposes, in spite of their spiritual deafness and blindness. They may preach, they may prophesy, they may heal the sick, they may convert the lost, they may feed the homeless; but if they never see the true light of the cross and have a change of heart and direction, they may never enter the kingdom of heaven (Matthew 7:21-23).

Once again, how does the "obedience of faith" relate to our New Covenant church meetings? If we are not practicing our faith daily by believing and acting on God's *rhema* word as individual members of His body, how can we corporately hear and obey Christ's *rhema* word to us when we gather together in our meetings? The basics of hearing and obeying God's voice starts with each individual believer learning to overcome sin by faith in the cross of Christ. Christ's "School of the Spirit" begins and ends each day with our learning to "put to death" by faith the sinful attitudes and actions of our unconverted, natural soul-life, so that we can live by the power Christ's Spirit that indwells us. Have we heard and, more importantly, are we obeying God's *rhema* word to us that we have been freed from the power of sin because Christ has removed our sinful nature by His death on the cross? Are we diligently applying this truth of God's Word in our lives each day, so that we are overcoming the habitual sins that use to entangle us, and abiding (staying rooted by faith) in Jesus Christ?

Until the body of Christ masters the basics of turning away from the willful inclinations of the natural soul-life, it will not fulfill its divine destiny as the devoted bride of Christ. God wants us to be a hearing and obeying people of His New Covenant who know Him, and live in His Word and walk in His ways. Our greatest aim, therefore, as Christ's bride, should be to hear and obey the voice of our Bridegroom. The more we hear and obey Christ's *rhema* word to us (both individually and corporately), the more our Lord can share His confidence and intimacy with us, and employ us as His bondservants to be His witnesses to the world and His ministers to His church. As the prophet Isaiah said, "The Lord God has opened my ear, and I was not disobedient nor did I turn back (Isaiah 50:5)." Therefore, whenever the true saints of God gather together as Christ's church, it should be the heart's desire of every member of Christ's body to practice hearing and obeying the voice of their Bridegroom, Jesus Christ.

New Covenant Church Government And Leadership

16 When it comes to church government and leadership, believers who attempt to meet together in New Covenant-styled churches may experience one of two problems. The first kind of problem is an abuse

of leadership authority, which grieves and suppresses the Holy Spirit and keeps the saints shackled in carnal subjection, passivity and fear. The second kind of problem is no leadership authority at all, which can produce lawlessness and anarchy. Both of these problems would be solved if the members of Christ's body acted daily on the Biblical truth that they had died with Christ and no longer had a sinful nature. They would then walk in sanctification and be free to fellowship and function together from a secure knowledge of their new born again identity in Jesus Christ and His sovereign grace and wisdom in each of their lives. Let us now look at each of these leadership problems more closely. In our day, many Christians have been "burned" by bad ministers and are now wary of having any kind of spiritual leaders. Because of past wrongs they have experienced and the emotional wounds they still carry, they have a natural mistrust of authority. Consequently, they would prefer to have no elders at all, or else to "emasculate" the Biblical role of elders and relegate these elder brothers to a passive and preferably invisible role.

Others maintain the only leadership oversight the local church needs can simply be met by the occasional visit of an itinerant apostle. However, this way of thinking is an emotional reaction that is not spiritually healthy and goes against the clear instruction of Scripture and God's design for the New Covenant church. According to the Bible, there is no such thing as a leaderless church, or a church in which everyone is equally a leader, that bears lasting fruit in the kingdom of God. The Holy Spirit's appointment of elders is critical to the long-term spiritual survival of any church. The Scriptures are also clear that the oversight of the local church is not the work of itinerant apostles, but the role of elders. When Christians have been hurt by others and their wounds are not healed by faith in the Lord Jesus (and what He accomplished on the cross) but instead are left to fester, it can breed a spirit of bitterness, lawlessness and rebellion that can destroy not only that person, but like a virus also infect other brothers and sisters in the church (Hebrews 12:15).

The church at Corinth in the first century is a good example of a church in which everyone was a leader. In fact, those who believe that churches do not need elders, or that elders should be hardly seen and rarely heard, usually hold up the Corinthian church as a model for this kind of leaderless style. They reason that: 1) Paul addressed both his letters to the church at Corinth *to the saints*, instead of to the saints and *the overseers (elders)*, as he did in his letter to the church at Philippi; and 2) Paul never mentioned elders in either of his two letters to the church at Corinth. With this in mind, let us take a closer look at the church at Corinth. When this church assembled, the spiritual gifts flowed with abundance, and it seemed as if almost every member exercised their spiritual gifts at the meetings (1 Corinthians 1:7; 14:23-31).

Unfortunately, the church at Corinth also had severe problems. The church had rival factions who were quarrelling and competing for power and influence (1 Corinthians 1:11-13; 11:18). The church meetings were marred by unintelligible chaos because many members spoke in tongues out loud at the same time without interruptions or interpretations (1 Corinthians 14:5-19; 27-28). The meetings also had "dueling" prophets who added to the disorder by prophesying at the same time without allowing one another to have a proper turn (1 Corinthians 14:29-33). A number of women were also out of order, and carnally dominated and interrupted the meetings (1 Corinthians 14:34-35). And each Sunday, the sacredness of the Lord's Supper was disrupted by out-of-control gluttonous and drunken members who used the fellowship meal to inebriate and gorge themselves (1 Corinthians 3:11:20-21). And finally, church members were regularly suing each other and taking each other to court (1 Corinthians 6:6-7). As a result of all these carnal problems, Paul strongly rebuked the Corinthians, "I have no praise for you, because your meetings do more harm than good (1 Corinthians 11:17)." It is evident that the church at Corinth had a major problem with practicing sin and condoning sin (see 1 Corinthians

3:3; 5:1). Consequently, Paul wrote to the church at Corinth, "I am afraid that when I come I may not find you as I want you to be... I fear there may be quarreling, jealousy, angry tempers, slander, gossip, arrogance and disorder. I am afraid that when I come to you again... I will be grieved over many who have sinned earlier and not repented of the impurity, sexual sin and debauchery which they have practiced (2 Corinthians 12:20-21)." The Corinthian Christians were obviously not living in sanctification by faith in Christ's completed work on the cross. In fact, the church at Corinth was so lawless and disobedient to God that many of its members were getting physically sick and some were even dying as a consequence of their unbelief and sinfulness (1 Corinthians 11:30).

To sum it up, the Corinthians were very spiritually immature and extremely carnal-minded, and they seemed to have no mature older brothers in the church who were able to instruct and train them. The only father in the Lord they had was the apostle Paul who would occasionally write them a letter or come visit them when he could to deal with their problems. At one point, Paul wrote them, "I say this to shame you. Is there not a wise man among you who can settle disputes between his brothers? (1 Corinthians 6:5)." Normally, the "wise men" would naturally be the more experienced elder brothers in the church who instructed the saints how to live righteously by faith and, when necessary, helped settle any issues among them. From the New Testament record, we can conclude that the church at Corinth either had no elders at all, or the elders they did have were spiritually immature and weak. For when a church is very spiritually immature, its elders will naturally also be relatively immature since the elders emerge from among the local brethren. Even though the church at Corinth outwardly seemed to have a functioning priesthood of believers, in actuality they were disturbingly dysfunctional and lawless. If the church at Corinth is a good example of a leaderless church, or a church in which everyone is equally a leader, we might then wonder what a bad example would look like!

However, the underlying root of the Corinthians' problem was much deeper than whether they had elders or did not have elders; the real crux of their problem was that the Corinthians could not (or would not) stop practicing sin long enough to abide in Christ, which would have enabled them to produce good fruit and grow in spiritual maturity, both individually and corporately. The lesson here is that if the members of a local church are still entangled in their daily habits of sin and do not know how to truly submit to Christ's headship, their so-called "priesthood" of believers will be unspiritual and dysfunctional no matter how many supernatural gifts they display in their meetings. This is why it is essential that the members of a local church learn the purpose and power of Christ's death on the cross, so they can master sin in their own soul-life and learn to walk by faith in Christ's resurrection life. Every member of God's priesthood is ordained to be a living and holy stone that builds up the church; however, the only way you can live by the Spirit and be a living and holy stone in God's house is if you know *how to* "reckon yourself *dead* to sin, but *alive* to God in Christ Jesus (Romans 6:11)." This is why training disciples to overcome sin by faith in Christ's completed work on the cross (so they can abide in Christ and bear His fruit), should be one of the foremost priorities of an apostle when he plants a church, and should also be one of the continuing priorities of the elders after they have been appointed in the local church.

And so we see that Jesus Christ, our Chief Shepherd, has given the church shepherds (elders) as His ministry "gifts" to train and equip the saints, so they can do the work of God's ministry (John 21:15-17; Acts 20:28; Ephesians 4:11-12). Note that the role of the elders is to train the saints to do the work of the ministry; not try to single-handedly perform the work of the ministry on behalf of the saints. Although women are equally vital and valuable members of God's divine priesthood, the Scriptures limit the appointment of elders to men (1 Timothy 3:2-5; Titus 1:5-6). Paul wrote that the work of an elder is a noble undertaking for brothers in Christ to aspire to (1 Timothy 3:1; see also 5:17). The brothers whom Jesus calls to be elders are trained in the school of the Holy Spirit (not in man's theological seminaries) to do the work of shepherding His flock. They learn how to shepherd God's church before they are even appointed elders by first shepherding their own families and by serving the other saints in the church (1 Timothy 3:4-5). Thus the elders are mature family men who are full of faith and the Spirit and grounded in the sound doctrine of the Word (1 Timothy 3:2; Titus 1:9). An elder's motivation to shepherd God's flock should spring from his love for Jesus Christ and Christ's love for His sheep. This is illustrated in John 21:16 by the Lord Jesus when He asked Simon Peter, "'Simon son of John, do you love Me?' And Simon answered, 'Yes Lord, you know that I love You.' Jesus then said to him, 'Shepherd My sheep.'"

A church does not have to have elders recognized and appointed to function as a church in its early developmental stage, but if a church grows both in numbers and spiritual maturity, then God will normally raise up elders to shepherd His flock. However, we should only consider appointing elders at the direction and timing of the Holy Spirit, and not just to check off a mandatory box on someone's "church growth" agenda. Thus the elders whom the Holy Spirit chooses and the body of Christ confirms and recognizes are mature brothers who naturally emerge from within their local church; they are not a seminary-trained "pastors" imported from another geographic locality or ordained and sent by their denomination, as is the modern-day custom of the false church. In this regard, each local New Covenant church is autonomous and self-governing under the headship of Christ. They may be spiritual "cousins" in *koinonia* relationship with other New Covenant churches, but they are not part of some larger, formal organization with a centralized headquarters and hierarchy. This kind of "denominationalism" is not supported by Scripture, and is a guaranteed spiritual death sentence for those churches who submit to it.

Do Christians who want to meet together as a New Covenant church need to have an apostle/church planter come to their locality in order to train them and "jump-start" their meetings, and then appoint elders for them? Although this might be helpful; it is not essential, and the risks in our day may outweigh any hoped for benefits. In our present time of great darkness and deception, it might be much safer to meet together with a few sincere Christians whom you know and trust, than to naïvely invite "wolves in sheep's clothing" into your fellowship. In our day, many of those who claim to be apostles, prophets, evangelists, pastors and teachers are actually imposters who masquerade as ministers of Christ and promote a false gospel. The primary qualification for any group of Christians who desire to meet together in their homes according to God's New Testament pattern is that they are true disciples of Christ who know the basics of how to carry their own cross daily and lay down their natural, unconverted soul-life by faith in Christ's completed work on the cross (Matthew 16:24-15). Biblical teaching on this God-given, proven process of sanctification can be found in this book, as well as on our website. If any Christians have embraced this life of the cross of Christ and desire to meet together as a New Covenant church, practical instruction can be found in this book on how a New Covenant church works under the headship of Christ. Remember that God is your Heavenly Father, Jesus Christ is your Great Shepherd, and the Holy Spirit is your Best Teacher. Our Triune God will guide you into green pastures and quiet waters, and protect you from all evil, so that you can dwell in the house of the Lord together (Psalm 23).

The elders whom the Holy Spirit will raise up and train and appoint are given to each church to guide, advise, encourage, equip, exhort, train, coach, correct, warn and protect the saints. As mature brothers, they are called by the Spirit to lead, not lord it over the flock; serve, not dominate the saints; and persuade, not coerce the saints; and the best means of persuasion is their example to others in living the Christian faith (1 Peter 5:3). It could be said that, ultimately, the goal of an elder is to work himself out of the ministry by training and equipping the saints to do the work of the ministry until the whole body matures into Christ's fullness (Ephesians 4:13). This is the same way the goal of a good parent should be to "work themselves out of a job" by raising their children into full maturity and adulthood, instead of fostering their children's continual dependency upon them. As Paul said, "My dear children, for whom I am again in labor until Christ is formed in you... we proclaim Him, admonishing and teaching everyone with all wisdom, so that we may present every man complete *(mature)* in Christ. For this purpose I labor... (Galatians 4:19; Colossians 1:28-29)."

Jesus Christ, the head of the church, hates the teachings and practices of the Nicolaitans, which in Greek means *"those who lord it over the people"* (Revelation 2:6, 15). To "lord it over" means to be domineering, demeaning, condescending and subjugating. It also means to misuse the role of authority as a way to exert control over others, rather than spiritually building them up and setting them free to spiritually grow in Christ. Jesus said, "You know that the rulers of the Gentiles *lord it over them*, and their high officials *exercise authority over them*. It is not this way among you. Instead, whoever wants to become great among you must be your servant, and whoever wants to be first among you must be your slave – just as the Son of Man did not come to be served but to serve and to give His life as a ransom for many (Matthew 20:25-28)." Our Lord is not the head of a business or government organization with a command and control hierarchy; He is the head of His body of believers and every member has a personal relationship and direct connection and communion with Him, which is based on their individual free will and faith. Therefore, the elders can advise, teach, persuade, entreat, encourage and exhort, but they cannot coerce or bully any member to obey against their will. With this in mind, Peter instructed the elders in his day: "Be shepherds of God's flock that is under your care… *not lording it over* those who are entrusted to your charge, but proving to be examples to the flock (1 Peter 5:2-3)." And Paul said, "We *do not lord it over* your faith, but we work with you for your joy, because it is by your faith that you are standing firm (2 Corinthians 1:24)."

In a formal organization like the military, members are legally obligated to obey orders, but in the body of Christ, there is no such institutional compulsion. In the New Covenant church, submission to the elders and to one another is on the basis of a believer's free will and love for Jesus Christ. As Paul said, "The love of Christ compels us (2 Corinthians 5:14)." This is why Jesus also expressly forbids those in ministry from being called by formal "honorific" religious titles (Matthew 23:6-12; see also Mark 10:42-45). And yet the false church violates Jesus' command and insists on using religious titles and calling their ministers Pastor Bill, Reverend Charles, Father Mike, Bishop Tom, Prophet Steve or Apostle Joe, which promotes and breeds a carnal elitist attitude toward those in "ministry," and sets the clergy apart as the exalted "chosen few" who are stationed above the other saints in religious rank. These self-promoting "honorific" ministers will be accountable to God and His judgment because the Bible warns those who seek and receive the honor of men cannot be servants of Christ (Galatians 1:10; see also John 5:44). In the first century New Covenant church, the believers did not use religious titles to address those in ministry; they simply called each other by their first names, such as Peter, Paul, John, Luke and Matthew. Becoming an elder in the true New Covenant church is not a way to enhance your self-esteem and gain the honor of others. Becoming an elder is a major step up in responsibility to lay down your life to serve the family of God, just as becoming a father is a major step up in responsibility to lay down your life to serve your family. Becoming an elder in Christ's true church is not a responsibility the natural man would choose; it is a work of sacrificial service to the saints, not a position of ease and prestige; and in many places in the world, the elders of the church suffer persecution, imprisonment and even death, as a result of their courageous example and witness for Christ.

Jesus is well aware that no man, even an elder, is infallible; therefore, He has instituted checks and balances in the New Covenant church to protect His body if an elder selfishly abuses his leadership role and tries to religiously lord it over others. Consequently, the Bible instructs us that no one should ever be appointed as an elder unless he is above reproach and first meets all the rigorous qualifications of an elder, and his faith and character have been tested and proven (1 Timothy 3:1-7; 4:6; 5:21; Titus 1:5-9). Paul warns that a new or spiritually immature Christian should never be appointed as an elder lest he become conceited and deceived by the devil (1 Timothy 3:6). Furthermore, if the local church at any time finds an elder guilty of abusing his leadership role or practicing other sin, our Lord Jesus has established a somber but simple way for the church to counsel the elder; and, if he is unrepentant, to "fire" him (1 Timothy 5:19-21; Matthew 18:15-17). We completely emphasize with and pray for every Christian who has been spiritually and emotionally hurt by ungodly pastors and ministers; however, at the same time, we cannot throw out "the baby with the bathwater." Jesus Christ wants His body to come into spiritual health and freedom from all past hurts and injustices, and this is one of the reasons why He gives the New Covenant church godly shepherds with a heart for God's people to protect His flock from "wolves in sheep's clothing" and lead them into "green pastures and quiet waters."

Within the New Covenant church, submission to Jesus Christ, the head of the church, and mutual submission to one another is the divine rule. All members of Christ's body are to "submit to one another in the fear of Christ (Ephesians 5:21)." Within this divine mandate of mutual submission, the younger members of Christ's body are to honor and respect those who are older, and all the saints are to submit to their spiritual leaders in the church. Paul also writes, "Now we ask you, brothers, to respect those who diligently labor among you, and have charge over you in the Lord and give you instruction, and that you hold them in high esteem because of their work (1 Thessalonians 5:12-13; see also 1 Corinthians 16:15-16)." The Bible exhorts believers to "*obey* your leaders and *submit* to their authority, for they keep watch over your souls as men who will give an account (Hebrews 13:17)." This Scripture reveals the spirit and intent of what it means to "submit and obey" within the New Covenant church. The New Testament Greek word used for "obey" in this verse is *peitho,* which in this context means to "allow yourself to be persuaded." In other words, following the elders' leadership does not mean blindly and mindlessly obeying them without reservation; instead, it means the elders have to persuade the saints to adopt their point of view, and the saints have to be willing to yield to the elders' persuasiveness. The elders' ability to persuade the saints to follow their lead is based on the elders' wisdom and example, and above all on the final plumbline test of the Scriptures. The New Testament Greek word used for "submit" in this verse is *hupeko,* which in this context means to "yield after a vigorous dialogue." Consequently, if the saints are not sufficiently persuaded to follow the elders' direction after sufficient dialogue and debate, then the elders have no one to follow their lead. In this regard, it is important to once again remember that the elders *function among the brethren* in the church, they are *not set above the brethren.* The elders' leadership gift is only one of the Spirit-endowed gifts set in the church; therefore, their leadership must always be exercised within the context of mutual submission to the rest of Christ's body, through whom the Holy Spirit can also speak. An example of this dynamic of mutual submission can be found in the Old Testament when David, whom God had appointed and spiritually gifted with leadership ability as the King of Israel, was personally confronted for his terrible sins by Nathan, whom God had appointed and spiritually gifted as a prophet to Israel. Even though Nathan respected and submitted to David's royal leadership, David humbly submitted to Nathan's prophetic authority, and then deeply repented before God for his sins (2 Samuel 12:1-15; Psalm 51).

Thus the Bible exhorts those who are spiritually mature and in leadership roles to love, honor and respect all the members of Christ's body, and not to lord it over and treat condescendingly those members who are weaker and not spiritually mature; otherwise they would sin not only against the body of Christ, they would sin against Christ Himself (1 Corinthians 8:12; 12:14-25; Galatians 6:1-3). This is the way a healthy family should function: the children honor and respect their parents, and the parents treat their children with dignity, kindness and patience, not bullying them or mistreating them in any way. This divine order set within the divine framework of mutual submission to one another is well-stated by Peter: "You younger men, in the same way, be submissive to your elders; and all of you, clothe yourselves with humility toward one another (1 Peter 5:5)." In other words, the law of Christ – the royal law of love – is to rule all our relationships in the New Covenant church. Of course, true love and humility and submission to one another is only possible if we are first truly submitted from the heart to the headship of our Lord Jesus Christ. Because every member of the body is to be equally submitted to Christ's headship and mutually submitted to one another, there is no place for either willful individualism or oppressive authoritarianism in the New Covenant church.

In Christ's church, true leadership is not based on the power of one's position nor is it based on the power of one's personality; it is based solely on the power of Christ in us. As Christ Himself said, "My power is made perfect in your weakness (2 Corinthians 12:9)." Thus the cross is the only basis for all true spiritual ministry: what Christ has already accomplished for us by His death on the cross, and what Christ now accomplishes in us, if *by the power of His Spirit* we carry our own cross daily and *put no confidence* in our natural soul-life; but instead *put to death* the sinful desires and behavior of our unconverted, natural soul-life for Christ's sake and His body's sake (Luke 9:23-24; Romans 8:13; Philippians 3:3). Although God may choose to use our natural strengths and talents, He does not want us to have any confidence in our natural strengths and talents to either produce His spiritual fruit, or to lead His flock. Exercising faith in the truth of the cross is the only way we can intimately know Jesus and walk in the power of His resurrection life (Philippians 3:10). For it is by carrying our own cross daily and laying down our natural soul-life that we willingly become weak in our own natural strength, so that the power of Christ can become strong in us (2 Corinthians 4:7-12; 12:9-10).

Therefore, true spiritual authority is derived from the quality of our personal relationship and real submission to Jesus Christ. The degree to which the cross has done its work in our lives, so that we are submitted to our Lord Jesus and intimately know Him, is the measure of which Jesus can speak through us with His authority to the rest of the body, either through our life's example or by our words. The elders' words can only have weight to the extent that the saints give it to them. The elders deserve honor, but that respect has to be earned. When an elder or any other leader in the church is consistently living by the Spirit in this manner, they have a spiritual authority which is authentic, powerful and persuasive, but when they are habitually living by the flesh (governed by their unconverted and unbroken soul-life), their authority lacks spiritual power, persuasiveness and credibility.

Another safeguard the Lord has installed to protect His church from the abuse of authority is the New Covenant leadership system of plurality of elders. The popular single-pastor or senior-pastor system of our day would have been regarded as strange and worldly-minded to the churches in the first century. Although there is a recognized divine order based on differences in ministry roles and levels of spiritual maturity, there is no carnal religious rank in the New Covenant church. Some Christians might ask, "What about 1 Corinthians 12:28 where Paul says, "God has appointed in the church, first apostles, second prophets, third teachers, then workers of miracles....?" Paul is not talking about religious rank in this passage; he is simply stating the strategic order of God-appointed ministries in building the house of God, the body of Christ. For example, apostles and prophets (such as Paul and Silas) first establish the church's foundation, and teachers and other gifted ministries (such as Apollos, Aquila and Priscilla) then build upon that foundation (1 Corinthians 3:10-11; Ephesians 2:20). Therefore, just as the elders themselves are members of the priesthood of believers and not above them in religious rank, the New Covenant church does not have any "head elder" or "senior pastor" who is designated above the other elders in position or rank. The modern-day church office of "senior pastor" or "head elder" simply did not exist in the first century church. Although the New Testament records that God sometimes used different elders to be temporary "spokesmen" in specific situations, He never designated any elder to occupy an office of permanent, formal supremacy above the other elders. This kind of a "top dog" author-ity structure is a carnal concept of leadership that is an invention of man and a "necessary evil" for secular and worldly institutions to be able to effectively function in this sinful Fallen world. However, under the divine provisions of the New Covenant, the senior-pastor system only becomes necessary in church government when God's people have rejected Christ's spiritual authority over their lives. Instead of submitting to Jesus Christ as their chief shepherd and sovereign head, they want to have a man (often a carnal man) appointed as their senior pastor and head of their church. For example, the Bible records that because the people of Israel rejected God as their king, they then wanted to have a man (Saul) appointed as their king to rule over them, just like all the heathen nations also had a king (1 Samuel 8:4-7). In God's New Covenant church, there is no "top dog" senior leader apart from Jesus Christ Himself: all the elders are co-equal with each other in their shared leadership function and must depend upon one another to collectively seek the mind of Christ for His flock. The elders may have different spiritual gifts and roles, such as teaching, prophesying, evangelism, counseling or administration, but no single elder has positional authority or power over the other elders. God has designed this checks and balances system in the New Covenant church to safeguard His flock and prevent anyone with a charming, manipulative and ambitious personality (no matter how spiritually gifted they are) from gaining a position of carnal power and dominance over the priesthood of believers.

Some modern-day pastors who support the contemporary, unBiblical "senior-pastor" system argue that James (the brother of Jesus) was designated the senior pastor in the church at Jerusalem. Therefore, they think the church at Jerusalem should be the enduring model for how church government should work. However, the Bible never calls James the senior pastor of the church at Jerusalem. It is true that James was prominently recognized among the leaders in the church at Jerusalem (Acts 15:13; 21:18), just as Peter was also recognized as a prominent leader in that same church (Acts 2:14, 37; 15:7), but there was no senior-pastor system established in any of the first century churches, as evidenced that Peter, John and James were equally recognized by Paul as pillars of the church at Jerusalem (Galatians 2:9). Moreover, within just a decade or so, the church at Jerusalem ceased to be a good model of how a New Covenant church should function. What happened to the church at Jerusalem? A large number of former Pharisee priests joined the church at Jerusalem and allied themselves with James' leadership (Acts 6:7; 15:5; Galatians 2:12). These former Pharisees brought with them a religious zeal for obeying the Mosaic Law in order to establish their righteousness before God, but they did not have a true knowledge and understanding of New Covenant grace and truth, and how to practice the righteousness that comes only from living by faith in Jesus Christ and His completed work on the cross.

In their case, the words of Paul are appropriate: "They have a zeal for God but not in accordance with knowledge. For not knowing about God's righteousness and seeking to establish their own, they did not subject themselves to the righteousness of God. For Christ is the end of the Law, so there may be righteousness for everyone who believes (Romans 10:2-5)." These former Pharisees had such a strong influence on the other Jewish believers in the church at Jerusalem that, within just a few short years, they could boast that many of their church members zealously obeyed the Mosaic Law and its customs and ceremonies (Acts 21:20-24). But if the church at Jerusalem had been living in the truth and grace of the New Covenant, their boast would have been: "See how many of our members have been freed from bondage to the Mosaic Law to serve God in newness of the Spirit (Romans 7:6)." The church at Jerusalem recklessly disregarded Jesus' warning to "beware of the leaven of the Pharisees, which is hypocrisy (Luke 12:1)," and also ignored Paul's reminder that "a little leaven leavens the whole lump of dough (Galatians 5:9)." These former Pharisees then tried to compel the Gentile churches in Asia Minor (now the nation of Turkey) to obey the Mosaic Law and its customs and ceremonies, in order to be righteous before God (Acts 15:1-5; Galatians 2:4, 12-16). The efforts of these former Pharisees to subjugate the Gentile believers to the Mosaic Law was strongly rebuked by Paul who called these Pharisee infiltrators "false brethren" (Galatians 2:4). Paul warned, "It was for freedom that Christ set us free. Stand firm, therefore, and do not subject yourselves again to a yoke of slavery (Galatians 5:1)."

History then records that, in A.D. 62, James (the brother of Jesus) was martyred by Herod Agrippa, the grandson of Herod the Great, and shortly thereafter the church at Jerusalem relocated across the Jordan River to the mostly Gentile city of Pella on the West Bank to escape further persecution. Later, the Jewish church at Pella is reported to have split into two Jewish congregations on the West Bank, with one church holding to the belief that only Jewish Christians must obey the Mosaic Law and its religious customs and ceremonies, while the other church insisted that the Gentile Christians must also do the same. Over time, these Jewish churches on the West Bank found themselves increasingly left behind the mainstream of Christianity, which by then consisted primarily of Gentile churches, and these isolated Jewish churches eventually faded out from church history. With the destruction of the Temple in Jerusalem in A.D. 70, and the rapidly declining influence of these Jewish churches, the model for New Covenant church beliefs and practices became the church at Antioch, and other Gentile churches like it. All of these Gentile churches had a clearly recognizable plurality of leadership among the more mature, elder brethren; and none of these churches functioned with a designated senior-pastor or head-elder system.

On the basis of Paul's establishment of the Gentile churches in the first century, we see that God had wisely ordained that several elders together share the oversight and shepherding of the church so that no one individual can treat the church as his own personal property and indelibly stamp his own personality upon the church, and thereby gain an overriding carnal influence. This plurality of co-equal elders also helps protect and check a well-meaning, particularly gifted brother, who might naturally assume the ascendancy and primacy among the elders, from overstepping his authority. A careful review of the Scriptures and church history should convince anyone with an open mind that to have a co-equal plurality of pastors (elders) in a local church is Biblical, but the modern day single-pastor or senior-pastor system is not Biblical. Nowhere in the New Testament does Paul or Peter or John address their church letters to Pastor What's His Name, and yet if you ask many Christians today where they go to church, they will say they go to Pastor What's His Name's church.

When men are appointed as co-elders (shepherds) in the body of Christ, it is a sacred trust, to which they are held accountable to God. No saint should have to submit to an elder who is self-willed, lawless, abusive and clearly not submitted to Christ's headship. Once again, if any elder violates this trust and abuses and exceeds their authority with the other elders and the priesthood of believers, Christ has established a mechanism for the other elders and the local church to effectively discipline, and, if necessary, remove that dominating and overbearing elder – the same mechanism that can be used to discipline or remove any member who is unrepentantly quarrelsome, rebellious and lawless. Some Christians think a co-equal plurality of elders who share collegial leadership in the church is unworkable. As a comparison, they argue that Moses was the head of the Hebrew elders under the Old Covenant. However, the Old Covenant was only a shadow and copy of the spiritual pattern of things to come. In the New Covenant, the reality is fulfilled in Jesus Christ (Colossians 2:17). Under the Old Covenant, Moses was appointed a prophet in God's house and his brother Aaron was appointed as high priest. However, Jesus is far greater than Moses or Aaron; therefore God has appointed Jesus as the Apostle, Prophet, and High Priest over His house, the church (Hebrews 3:1-6). Consequently, under the New Covenant, no man can stand in the place of Christ as the Chief Shepherd and Head of God's church (Colossians 1:18; 1 Peter 5:4).

Some Christians argue that "the business world could never work without a head boss, so how could Christ's church ever function this way?" That is precisely the problem with the false church; it is modeled after the world's example and it is run like a business, instead of a spiritual body with a spiritual head boss, Jesus Christ, whom every saint freely submits to in love. Others contend that the institution of marriage (where the husband is the head of the wife) shows how the church should function with a senior pastor who is the head of the elders and head of the church. Once again, this is not a proper analogy. The only comparison the Bible makes to the marriage covenant (where the two become one flesh) is to Jesus Christ and His church (where Jesus is the head of the church and the two become spiritually joined into one). Using the precious and holy example of the marriage covenant to justify having a senior pastor who spiritually rules over the church is illogical and unBiblical. It is twisted and faulty reasoning to compare the unique, intimate relationship between husband and wife with the relationship between a pastor and the members of a church. This is why the Bible says that every man is the head of his own home, and Christ is the head of every man (1 Corinthians 11:3). Thus the Bible declares that Jesus Christ (not some pastor) is the only head of the church (Colossians 1:18). Once again, this is why no man can ever stand in the place of Christ as the spiritual head of the priesthood of believers.

The Bible says that every fact is to be confirmed by the testimony of at least two witnesses (Deuteronomy 19:15; 2 Corinthians 13:1). There are two witnesses that confirm the divine truth of the co-equal plurality of elders in the church. One witness is God's Word which records the New Covenant pattern of plurality of elders in the Book of Acts as well as in the Epistles (Scripture citations have already been given). From these Scriptural accounts, two facts are established whenever elders are mentioned: 1) Each local church had a plurality of elders; and 2) There is never a head elder or senior pastor designated in any local church. The other witness is the heavenly pattern revealed by the Spirit in the Book of Revelation. The Holy Spirit revealed to the apostle John that a plurality of elders (twenty-four to be exact) are seated around God's throne (Revelation 4:4). The Holy Spirit showed John this plurality of elders a dozen times, and there is not a head elder or senior pastor among them. In fact, the only

Chief Shepherd ever mentioned in John's vision is Jesus Christ, the Lamb of God, who is in the center of God's throne (Revelation 5:6-14). These two witnesses (the Word and the Spirit) confirm the New Covenant pattern of co-equal plurality of elders.

To sum up, the New Covenant church is not an autocracy carnally ruled by one man or even a few men, nor is it a democracy in which every member has an equal vote; it is a divine theocracy – a spiritual body sovereignly governed by its head, Jesus Christ, to whom every member freely submits their self-will and soul-life, and with whom every member has a direct and living connection. If the priesthood of believers stays connected to their head Jesus Christ and hear and obey His voice, they will have Christ's resurrection life and spiritual unity, and the kingdom of God will be advanced through them. However, if the priesthood of believers does not hear and obey their head Jesus Christ, there will be selfish ambition, strife and disorder and the kingdom of God will not be advanced. The Bible warns: "For where jealousy and selfish ambition exist, there is disorder and every evil thing (James 3:16)." We may then ask, "How does corporate decision-making practically work in a New Covenant church?" Through what we might call Spirit-directed, elder-led, congregational consensus. Consensus does not mean the same as unanimous, which means that every person in the church completely agrees to a decision. Consensus also does not mean the same as a majority, which means that more than fifty percent of the church members vote to agree on a decision. Instead, consensus means that there is general agreement reached within the church to go forward with a decision. Of course, some church members may be in more perfect agreement with the final decision than others, but all members agree to go forward with the decision. This is what is called consensus.

Thus, in the New Covenant church, major decisions are not made behind closed doors by the elders, who then impose their will and direct the members of the church to implement their decision. Instead, major decisions are deliberated and concurred in by the whole church (remember that, by God's design, house churches are small in size, which makes this more workable). On the other hand, large institutional churches, which are not God's design, need a command and control hierarchal structure to function. Of course, this is spiritually unhealthy in many ways not only for the saints, but also for the pastor who must carnally lead the church as the director of a large organization, and not as God's shepherd who knows each person in the flock personally. Within God's New Covenant church, the elders/shepherds can facilitate the process to help the church reach consensus by providing sound advice and Scriptural teaching that is pertinent to the issue, and can try to persuade the rest of the saints on the merits of a decision. However, the elders do not unilaterally make major decisions, nor can they force their decisions upon the church. Reaching consensus is a deliberative process of discussion and persuasion that aims to build unity, resulting in the general agreement and concurrence of the whole church. As Paul taught, "I appeal to you, brothers, in the name of our Lord Jesus Christ, that all of you agree with one another so that there may be no divisions among you so that you may be of one mind and judgment (1 Corinthians 1:10)."

In the beginning of this book, we said the New Testament Greek word for "church" is *ekklesia,* which means an assembly or congregation (Matthew 16:18), and whose root meaning is "called out from." Therefore, the church consists of all people who have been called out from the world to gather together in name of the Lord. However, in the Greek culture of the time, the word *ekklesia* also had a more precise meaning; it meant a congregation of people who assemble together for the purpose of making collective decisions. Therefore, the *ekklesia* or church is not just the gathering together of the saints of God. It is also what happens when the saints gather together. Of course, most of the time, the saints' purpose in meeting together is to share the "Lord's Supper" with one another as a full fellowship meal; minister to the Lord and to one another; and intercede corporately in prayer for others. However, there are occasions when the saints will also meet together to discuss and decide important issues, such as church direction and discipline. In doing so, the saints fulfill one of God's intentions for His New Covenant church: to be a body of citizens of His kingdom who have authority and responsibility in Christ to deliberate and settle church matters and pass judgments, when necessary. This corporate decision-making is part of God's divine preparation of the bride of Christ for the age to come when the saints will rule the nations with their King, our Lord Jesus Christ. For if we cannot properly manage our own church affairs here on earth, how can we responsibly manage the nations in the age to come?

Building consensus in the body of Christ takes time, communication, love, gentleness, self-control, humility, patience, and mutual respect; in other words, the labor of faith and the fruit that comes from abiding in the Spirit. Much of the process of building consensus does not take place during an actual church meeting; instead, it is an on-going process that takes place during our fellowship with one another during the week. As someone has said, "Consensus is built on the experience of Christian community. It requires strong relationships able to tolerate struggling through issues together. It requires mutual love and respect to hear each other when there is disagreement. Consensus also requires a commitment to know and understand each other more than a desire to convince or railroad others." In this regard, the process can be just as important as the end decision in the working out of true *koinonia* among the saints. Thus there is a divine balance between the elders' leadership and congregational consensus. The elders are instrumental to building consensus, but ultimately the church must concur with that consensus. This is how God has designed the body of Christ to work under Christ's headship and the Holy Spirit's direction. We might use the metaphor of the trusty old Swiss clock. Before the age of electronic clocks, the invention of the Swiss clock was known through-out the world as a masterpiece of intricate and complex machinery that accurately kept precise time. All of the clock's gears, springs, pendulums and weights were carefully designed to harmoniously interact with one another in order to operate this trusted and classic timepiece. Each of the clock's internal components had a specific purpose, which was essential to the clock's overall effectiveness. If any of the individual parts did not func-tion properly, it could lead to increased friction between the parts, and the clock would eventually break down and not work. But when all the parts functioned properly according to the clock master's design and purpose, the clock worked perfectly. In the same way, God has designed every member of the His New Covenant church to function according to His divine pur-pose, and to interact harmoniously and effectively with the other members of His body. One final comment on this metaphor: just as all the parts of the clock needed to be regularly lubricated with oil in order for the clock to function smoothly and effectively, the members of the New Covenant church need to be continually filled with the oil of the Holy Spirit in order to function together in a harmonious and effective manner. The Bible says, "Behold, how good and pleasant it is for brothers to live together in unity. It is like the precious oil poured upon the head, running down on the beard, even Aaron's beard, coming down upon the edge of his robes. It is like the dew of Hermon coming down upon Mount Zion. For there the Lord bestows His blessing - even life forevermore (Psalm 133)."

What do we do in the case where there is no agreement among the elders or no consensus among the church members whether to proceed on a major decision? Then it is wiser to not proceed until a consensus can be reached through continued prayer and further discussion. In this regard, the New Covenant church is more elder-led than elder-ruled. Of course, there are excep-tions to this principle when the elders must take immediate decisive action; for example, to deal with someone who is demonically disruptive in a church meeting. In the process of reaching consensus, there may be occasions when someone in the fellowship can never be persuaded. In this situation, the dissenter should consider compromising and yielding to the wisdom of the elders and the prevailing congregational consensus. Of course, no one should ever yield to anyone if the action proposed is unBiblical, unethical, immoral or illegal. Although elder-led, congregational decision-making may not be the most efficient or speedy form of church government, it is better than the alternative since it helps protect the New Covenant church from falling into either authoritarianism or anarchy. It also helps encourage the church's reliance upon the Holy Spirit to "get things done," as well as the saints' love, gentleness, self-control and patience with one another, which is the spiritual fruit of practicing the righteousness that comes from abiding (staying united by faith) in Christ.

We can see an example of Holy Spirit-directed, elder-led, congregational consensus in the Book of Acts, Chapter 15, when the church at Jerusalem met to settle the controversial issue of whether the Gentiles, who had become Christians, needed to religiously follow the Mosaic Law and its customs in order to be righteous. The New Testament indicates the whole church discussed this issue and that, initially at least, there were differing opinions (verse 4-5). The apostles and elders then deliberated the issue (verse 6). During this debate, Peter voiced his opinion that the Gentiles should not have to follow the unbearable yoke of the Mosaic Law; instead they are saved by the grace of the Lord Jesus Christ alone (verse 10). Paul and Barnabas, who were of the same mind as Peter, confirmed how God was miraculously working among the Gentiles even though they were not following the Mosaic Law (verse 7-12). James then summarized to the whole church the Scriptural basis and reasoning why the Gentiles should not have to follow the Mosaic Law (verse 13-21). The whole church then agreed and concurred with this judgment, which would impact the future of Christianity. And Luke recorded their collective decision with the following note: "It seemed good to the apostles and the elders, with the concurrence of the whole church… *(and)* it seemed good to the Holy Spirit and to us (Acts 15:22, 28)." Note that Luke did not say that the elders made this decision unilaterally and privately without the whole church's input, or that the whole church blindly and passively submitted to the elders' decision without any deliberation or concurrence on the merits of the issue.

Let me repeat my earlier exhortation: although this is God's design and was the practice of the first century church, this New Covenant form of local church leadership and congregational consensus only works if the elders (indeed all the saints) are truly submitted to Christ their head and to one another in the humility of the Holy Spirit (1 Peter 5:5). And this is only possible if a church knows how to overcome sin by faith in the truth of the cross of Christ. The saints must know how (by the power of the Spirit) to carry their own cross and "put to death" their soulish attitudes and behavior, in order to walk in Christ's resurrection life and bear His spiritual fruit. This daily process of sanctification must be a true, working reality in the lives of all the saints who desire to submit to Christ's sovereignty in the New Covenant church. Their working faith must be based on the Biblical truth of Christ's completed work on the cross (not the false church's erroneous and superficial teaching on co-crucifixion that mistakenly maintains born again believers still have a sinful nature). Otherwise, zealous Christians will try in vain to lay down their naturally soulish, selfish lives for one another without possessing an accurate and complete knowledge of the cross of Christ that would enable them to truly "die to self" by the power of the Spirit. This is why much of the house church movement of the 1970s and 1980s "died on the vine" and failed to bear lasting fruit. It is also the reason why the present house church movement is also destined to spiritually fail if its members do not come by faith into an accurate knowledge and practical application of the Biblical truth of the cross. This daily working out of the correct Biblical truth of the cross in our lives is absolutely central and crucial if we desire to achieve God's divine purpose for His church – to be Christ's holy bride; otherwise, all the New Covenant church principles and protections, and checks and balances that Jesus Christ has given us will fail.

THE DIFFERENT ROLES OF MEN AND WOMEN IN THE NEW COVENANT CHURCH

17   In God's eyes, there is no question that men and women are equal. The Bible says that men and women were both created "in the image of God (Genesis 1:27)." And the New Testament confirms this equality of the sexes: "There is neither male nor female, for you are all one in Christ Jesus (Galatians 3:28)." Indeed, women have proven themselves to be equally as gifted, talented and intelligent as their male counterparts in secular fields such as medicine, science, engineering, education, business, architecture, the arts, etc. The issue, therefore, is not one of gender equality, but rather of role and function. For when it comes to the family and the church, the Bible prescribes that men and women should have different roles. The man's leading role and the woman's support role is made clear by God at the very beginning of their divine creation. The Bible says that God made woman to be a helpmate for man (Genesis 2:18). Paul confirms that the leadership role of man continues under the New Covenant: "Now I want you to understand that Christ is the head of every man, and the man is the head of the woman (1 Corinthians 11:3)." Therefore, God has appointed the husband to be the head of the family. Ephesians 5:23 clarifies this divine truth: "The husband is the head of the wife even as Christ is the head of the church." And Colossians 3:18 instructs: "Wives, submit to your husbands

as is fitting in the Lord." And Peter counsels, "Wives, be submissive to your husbands (1 Peter 3:1)." Some people argue that a wife's submission to her husband is a consequence of the Fall, when God told Eve that Adam would rule over her (Genesis 3:16). However, this divine order in the family, with the husband as the servant leader and the wife as the support helper, was established at God's creation, which occurred before the Fall.

The New Testament also confirms this divine order: "For man did not originate from woman, but woman from man; for indeed man was not created for woman's sake, but the woman for man's sake (1 Corinthians 11:8-9)." However, this divine order between men and women does not detract from their equality. For example, the following Scripture highlights the interdependent relationship between men and women: "In the Lord, however, a woman is not independent of man, nor is a man independent of woman. For as the woman originates from man *(Adam's rib),* so also the man is born of woman, and all things originate from God (1 Corinthians 11:11)." This Scripture confirms that a husband and wife are to have an equal and mutual ministry to one another. And Ephesians 5:21 declares: "Submit to one another out of reverence for Christ." Therefore, a wife's submission to her husband for the purpose of divine order in the family does not confer inferiority; it only prescribes a difference in function. For example, there is perfect equality within the Trinity of God; yet Jesus was in full submission to His Father's will (John 5:30; 12:49; Philippians 2:5-8).

We recognize that, throughout history, men have often unjustly and cruelly dominated and humiliated women, and treated them as inferior subjects. Even men who called themselves "Christians" have misused their "headship" position to bully, subjugate, and even abuse their wives. All of these men will be held accountable by God and face His judgment and vengeance. This historical injustice against women is one of the reasons why the modern-day "feminist" movement aggressively champions equal rights and protections for women. In true Christianity, women are considered equal with men, and worthy of all respect and honor. The Bible instructs Christian men to treat younger women with respect as sisters and honor older women as mothers (1 Timothy 5:1-2). Husbands are commanded to cherish their wives and treat them with "honor as a fellow heir of the grace of life" (1 Peter 3:7; and Ephesians 5:29). The Bible teaches: "Husbands, love your wives, just as Christ loved the church and gave Himself up for her... so husbands should love their wives as their own bodies, for he who loves his wife loves himself (Ephesians 5:25, 28)." God will not hear the prayers of any man who mistreats his wife, or any other women, for that matter (1 Peter 3:7).

How then should decision-making work in a Christian family? Decisions that affect their joint household should be mutually discussed and agreed upon by both husband and wife. Even though he is the head of the household, the husband does not unilaterally decide a matter and then impose his will to make his wife comply with his decision. This kind of bullish attitude and demeaning behavior does not honor and respect a wife as an equal partner in the marriage and the kingdom of God. Or, if the wife wants to do something that would impact the household, the husband cannot simply "veto" her initiative. Once again, the issue must be discussed and prayed about together to find God's will, and a joint decision should then be made by both husband and wife, showing mutual respect for each other's opinions. Going through this process of mutual deliberation and collaborative decision-making is as important to the marriage as is the outcome of their decision. On issues of lesser concern, it may be wiser to defer to the other spouse's desires whenever possible, in a spirit of compromise. On issues of greater impact, such as the household budget, it would be best to hold off on any action until mutual agreement can be reached through prayer and further discussion, in keeping with the Bible's command to be mutually submitted to one another (Ephesians 5:21). An exception to this joint decision-making process might occur in the event of an emergency or imminent danger when the husband, as head of the household, must act decisively with speed to protect his family. However, this would be the exception, and not the household rule. When a husband treats his wife each day with genuine respect and kindness, joint decision-making in their marriage becomes easier, but if a husband subjects his wife daily to a "thousand cuts" of disrespect and even small unkindnesses, then the trust required to engage in genuine joint decision-making will be absent. If a husband desires to spiritually lead his family into greater sanctification and maturity in Christ, then treating his wife with fairness, respect and kindness in all matters is a prerequisite. If any man lacks compassion and understanding on this kind of marriage partnership, let him simply ask himself, "What if God had reversed the roles, and the husband had to submit to his wife, as the head of the household?" Would he not want his wife to treat him as a full equal with all fairness and respect? Does not the Bible teach us to treat others as we would want to be treated? It is also essential that such a self-willed husband hears the convicting voice of the Holy Spirit within him, and repents and begins a life of love and serving his wife, which all those in Christ Jesus are now capable of because they are dead to sin.

There are two temptations that both husband and wife must not yield to when "working out" their marriage relationship. Although not all marriages will face these particular challenges, they are not uncommon. The husband may be carnally tempted to choose "efficiency" over joint decision-making in his marriage. The temptation to take advantage of and simply "lord it over" his wife and make unilateral decisions can be great, especially if his wife is a quiet, compliant and deeply submissive female. The husband may rationalize to himself that it is important to run the household efficiently and "get the job done" quickly, with the least amount of troublesome debate and delay. However, if he overrules his wife's feelings and opinions too often, there will be resentment and trouble brewing in their marriage, even if it is not immediately evident. On the other hand, the wife may be carnally tempted to quietly submit to this kind of "alpha male" dominating and condescending leadership, when instead she should "speak the truth in love" to him (Ephesians 4:25). If she does not speak truthfully to him, she may be allowing her husband to develop into a stubborn, domineering bully for the sake of maintaining "peace" in their household. And if she has young children, this temptation will be even greater, since she will feel a need to protect the sanctity of her home. Although the Bible instructs wives to submit to a carnal-minded husband and "win them" over without a word (of course, not in the case of abuse), there is a godly way to submit to a carnal man without losing one's spiritual authority and self-respect. God's way is to be submitted first and foremost to the Lord Jesus, and then actively "fight the good fight of faith" by trusting in God's intervention and taking every difficulty in the marriage to Him in prayer. The Bible teaches that this kind of "submitting" finds favor with God, and God answers the prayers of such a righteous woman (1 Peter 3:1-6). Unfortunately, the wife may have to endure years of emotional suffering under an immature, carnal-minded husband before she sees the answer to her prayers, but she should always remind herself that "God works all things together for the good to those who love God, and are called according to His purpose (Romans 8:28)."

In closing, a marriage based on mutual respect and equality and joint decision-making may not be the most efficient way to run a household in terms of quick action, but it is the best way to honor God and keep the sacred trust of the marriage partnership and the dignity of both husband and wife. Of course, this kind of Christian marriage partnership is only possible when both husband and wife are equally submitted to their head, Jesus Christ, and both know the power and freedom that the Lord's sacrifice on the cross has provided them. Both husband and wife need to deeply and devotedly give themselves over to true submission to God, and believe they are new creations in Christ and no longer have sinful natures. This is the Biblical truth that enables them to resist capitulating to fear or sin in any form, and be yoked together in the highest purpose of the marriage union that God has designed.

God has ordained that the same divine order that exists in the family is also to exist in the church, which is His heavenly family. Just as God has appointed men be the leaders of their households, He has appointed men to be the leaders (elders) of the church, which is His household. For example, 1 Timothy 3:1 states: "Now, an overseer *(an elder)* must be above reproach, the husband of one wife." And Paul instructs Titus: "The reason I left you in Crete was that you would set in order what was unfinished and appoint elders in every city as I directed you. An elder must be blameless, the husband of one wife (Titus 1:5-6)." Once again, it is not a question of equality; for both men and women are equally water baptized into God's New Covenant community (Acts 5:14; 8:12; 1 Corinthians 12:13), and both men and women are equally baptized into God's Spirit (Acts 2:17-18; 8:12-17). And both men and women are equally made members of God's royal priesthood (1 Peter 2:9; Revelation 1:5-6), and both men and women are equally given spiritual gifts so they can do the work of ministry together (Romans 12:5-8; 1 Peter 4:10).

Thus, in Christ, there is complete equality between men and women; but with different ministry roles and functions in the home and in the church (Romans 12:4). For example, in the sphere of Christian ministry, women have the freedom to witness for Christ; share a word of encouragement, wisdom or knowledge; share a testimony; share a psalm or spiritual song; speak in tongues and interpret tongues; prophesy; show mercy and hospitality to the saints; pray for those in need; teach other women; and perform a variety of other valuable ministries in the body of Christ. However, the Bible says that women may not usurp men's authority to lead the church and teach Biblical doctrine to the church. This clearly excludes women from ministering in the leadership role of an apostle or elder/pastor. In this regard, Paul specifically instructs that women are "not permitted to teach or to have authority over a man (1 Timothy 2:11-12)." The Greek word for "teach" used here is *didache,* which in its Scriptural context specifically means to instruct the church in theological doctrine (see also 1 Timothy 5:17; Titus 1:9).

Some Christians might ask, "Why are women allowed to prophesy in church but not allowed to teach the church?" The Bible clearly states that women can prophesy in church. For example, after the 120 men and women in the upper room were baptized in the Holy Spirit, Peter says, "This is what was spoken by the prophet Joel, 'It will be the last days,' God says, 'That I will pour out My Spirit on all people. Your sons and *your daughters will prophesy*' (Acts 2:16-17; Joel 28-30)." And Paul also specifically permits women to prophesy in church (1 Corinthians 11:5). Further, an example in the New Testament of women who prophesied are the four daughters of Philip the evangelist, each of whom exercised the Holy Spirit's gift of prophecy (Acts 21:8-9). What then is the distinction between a woman teaching in church and prophesying in church? By Biblical definition, the gift of prophecy is given for the "edification, exhortation and consolation" of the church (1 Corinthians 14:3). However, prophecy is not given for instructing the church in Biblical doctrine, which is the role of the elders and other spiritually mature brothers.

The Bible consistently links teaching Biblical doctrine with the man's leadership role in the church. For example, the Bible says that an elder must be able to teach (1 Timothy 3:2). And 1 Timothy 5:17 states: "The elders who rule well are to be considered worthy of double honor, especially those who work hard at preaching and teaching." And Titus 1:5-9 also lists the ability to teach doctrine as one of the qualifications of an elder: "He must be able to exhort others in sound doctrine and refute those who contradict it." That is why there are examples of men in the New Testament who are called "teachers" in the church, such as Paul, Manaen, and Apollos (Acts 13:1; 18:24-2), and although there are examples of women who prophesy in the church (Acts 21:8-9), there are no examples of women who teach Biblical doctrine to the church. The Bible does state, however, that older Christian women can "train the younger women to love their husbands and children, to be self-controlled and pure, to be homemakers, to be kind, and to be subject to their husbands, so that the Word of God will not be dishonored (Titus 2:3-5)." Of course, it is impossible for spiritually mature women to train younger Christian women how to lead a submissive and godly life without also teaching them the basic Biblical doctrine of our sanctification and co-crucifixion with Christ. However, this kind of woman-to-woman teaching and counseling would naturally occur outside of the normal church meeting, just as women teaching other women the basic Biblical doctrine of salvation would naturally occur outside the normal church meeting. Note that there is a difference between the situation where a Christian sister shares a personal testimony in church or where a Christian sister privately explains the practical application of a divine truth to someone outside of church, and the case of an elder Christian brother who systemically and authoritatively teaches Biblical doctrine to the church.

Some Christians might ask, "What about the example of those women in our day who successfully plant churches and pastor churches?" The problem is that we cannot look to others for our example of what is "successful." We can only measure what is truly "successful" by the exacting plumbline of the Word of God. How does the Bible define what is "successful?" The Bible says that we are only "successful" in God's eyes when we obey His exact commands. Jesus said, "So that the world may know that I love the Father, I do *exactly* as the Father commanded Me (John 14:31)." For example, although some individuals in the Old Testament practiced polygamy, it is evident starting with the Book of Genesis and the Mosaic Law in the Old Testament, and also from Christ's commands and the apostles' teachings in the New Testament, that polygamy was never God's intention for the sacredness of the marriage union, and that polygamy was neither endorsed nor approved by God (Genesis 2:24; Deuteronomy 17:17; Matthew 19:3-10; Ephesians 5:31-32; 1 Timothy 3:2, 12; Titus 1:5). Therefore, we cannot use the dubious example of those who seemed to "successfully" practice polygamy to justify a practice that violates God's revealed will and command. In the same way, the Scriptures are abundantly clear that, in the family as well as in the church, God's design is for men to have the designated leadership role. Although this divine order goes against the tide of the women's liberation movement and feminist teaching on equality of gender roles in our modern culture, our model for the family and the church cannot be what the "politically correct" world demands, but what God commands. From a Biblical perspective, it is not a matter of whether some Christian sisters are not capable of leading or teaching the New Covenant church better than some Christian brothers could; it is whether this is wise and permissible in God's eyes. Although this may be a bitter pill to swallow for many professing Christian women who have been raised in our upside-down, lawless contemporary culture, and who are not truly submitted to the headship of Jesus Christ and to the headship of their husbands (if they are married); this is God's divine order and spiritual protection for godly women, which produces the peaceful fruit of righteousness in their lives and finds favor with God. These distinctions in gender roles are based on God's divine design at creation.

This does not mean that women have to wear head coverings in our day as a sign of submissiveness before they can pray or prophesy in church (1 Corinthians 11:2-5); however, it does mean that women should be submitted to Jesus Christ, the head of the church, and to the men who are leading the church, so that they can function in church with a humble and submissive spirit using all their God-given spiritual gifts and ministries (Acts 2:17-18; 1 Peter 3:3-4; 1 Corinthians 14:34-35). Note that men also should be submitted to Jesus Christ and to the elders in the church if they want to properly function in church. The Bible exhorts all believers to "obey your leaders and submit to their authority, for they keep watch over your souls as men who will give an account (Hebrews 13:17)." And Peter said, "You younger men, in the same way, be submissive to your elders (1 Peter 5:5)." Paul also wrote, "Now we ask you, brothers, to respect those who diligently labor among you, and have charge over you in the Lord and give you instruction, and that you hold them in high esteem because of their work (1 Thessalonians 5:12-13)." There is a great difference, however, between how a woman submits to her husband, and how the saints (both men and women) submit to their elders in the church. A wife's submission to her husband is sacred and unique in God, and obviously much more intimate, personal and private (Ephesians 5:22-33). Further, no man or woman should ever obey any so-called elder who instructs them to do something illegal, immoral, unethical, and against God's commands. In this situation, the words of Peter prevail today: "We must obey God rather than men (Acts 5:29)."

Peter instructed Christian women in the first century church: "Your beauty should not come from outward adornment... instead it should be from your inner self, the unfading beauty of a gentle and quiet spirit, which is of great worth in God's sight. For this is the way the holy women of the past who put their hope in God used to adorn themselves (1 Peter 3:3-5)." Many Christian women would say that it is impossible for any modern woman to submit herself to a man (especially a selfish and unjust man) without having hidden resentment. They are right! It is impossible unless a woman is first truly submitted to the headship of Jesus Christ. It is really a question of identity. If a woman's identity is completely in Christ, then true submission is not humiliating and is very possible in the Spirit. However, if a woman's identity is still wedded to her natural (and unconverted) soul-life, then she will find true submission humiliating and impossible. She may even outwardly appear to submit, but inwardly she will become resentful and manipulative. How can a Christian woman lose her soulish worldly identity and find her true spiritual identity in Christ? The Bible says she must believe and act on the divine truth that when she was born again, Christ removed her sinful nature (which was the core of her worldly identity) and replaced it with His divine nature (which is the basis for her new identity in Christ). The Bible says, "Therefore, if anyone is in Christ, they are a new person; their old being has gone and their new life has begun (2 Corinthians 5:17; see also Romans 6:6-7; Colossians 2:11-12)."

There are many wise and godly women mentioned in the Bible who are inspiring examples of faithful obedience and service to God. For example, in the New Testament, Paul commends three women - Phoebe, Euodia and Syntyche – as faithful co-workers who greatly helped him and others in the cause of the gospel (Romans 16:1-2; Philippians 4:2-3). Another good example in the New Testament of a submissive woman greatly used of the Lord is Priscilla, the wife of Aquila, the tentmaker. Paul stayed with Aquila and Priscilla in Corinth where he planted a church that later met regularly in their house (1 Corinthians 16:19). From there, Priscilla and Aquila traveled with Paul to Ephesus (Acts 18:18). Once in Ephesus, Priscilla and Aquila met Apollos, an itinerant teacher of God's Word, and together they explained the Christian faith more accurately to Apollos (Acts 18:26). Note that Priscilla ministered together with her husband Aquila to privately counsel Apollos on the particulars of the faith (she did not minister to Apollos alone; she did not publically teach Biblical doctrine to Apollos and others; nor did she question or challenge Apollos in public). When Aquila and Priscilla later relocated to Rome, a church once again regularly met in their house (Romans 16:5). Because of their service to the Lord, Paul held this couple in such high regard that he called them: "fellow workers in Christ Jesus," and said that "they risked their lives for me. Not only do I give thanks, but all the churches of the Gentiles are grateful to them (Romans 16:3-4)." These churches recognized that Priscilla had a true spiritual partnership with her husband in advancing the gospel and establishing Christ's church, just as the mother has an equal and indispensable, vital role as the father in establishing a healthy and functioning family. Priscilla and Aquila are an inspiring example of God's highest purpose for the marriage union between husband and wife: a divine partnership in the gospel. Priscilla's ministry and knowledge of the Lord was invaluable to Aquila, and

Aquila's ministry and knowledge of the Lord was invaluable to Priscilla. Thus their union in marriage was a God-appointed equal partnership in advancing the gospel of Christ. A woman's godly influence on her husband and family and the church can be profound in the eyes of God. There are many wives, mothers and homemakers who will be given a far greater reward and responsibility in the heavenly age to come than many men who have had publically-acclaimed ministries here on earth. As Jesus said, "Many who are first will be last, and the last will be first (Mark 10:31)."

A woman's supporting role in the family does not mean that she cannot have a business or career or ministry outside of the home (especially if her children are older). However, a wife's first priority is always to her family, as should also be her husband's priority, but only in a different role. For example, the "virtuous woman" of Proverbs 31 is called "a wife of noble character." The Bible describes her as a trustworthy, industrious, charitable, wise woman who feared the Lord and was a great helpmate to her husband. She taught her family and household servants the goodness of the Lord. And she had a business outside the home buying and developing property, and making and selling clothing. The Bible says her husband was one of the respected elders in the city. Note that it was her husband (and not her) who was one of the elders. Finally, the Bible says "her children rise up and bless her; her husband also praises her, saying: 'Many women have done nobly, but you excel them all' (Proverbs 31:28-29)." And yet how many women in our modern society hold in high esteem the godly role of a wife, mother and homemaker? How many women born and raised in our feminist culture fear God and are submitted to the authority and leadership of Jesus Christ?

It is popular today to dismiss Biblical teaching on the different roles of men and women (in the family and in the church) as no longer culturally relevant since women are more educated and society is more "enlightened."

However, our instruction on how men and women in our day should function in the home and in the church must come from the "operating manual" itself (which is the Bible) and from the author of the operating manual (who is God Himself). The Bible's instruction on this issue originates with the creation order and designated gender roles of God's own design. Since men and women are descended from Adam and Eve, this divine order is a timeless truth that transcends all cultures and societies. When the women in a society abandon their God-given purpose and role as a helpmate and partner to their husband in order to satisfy their own self-identity and fulfill their own self-ambition, it leads to the breakdown of the family and the church, which are the foundation of a society, and the Bible says where "selfish ambition exists, there is disorder and every evil thing (James 3:16)."

Once again, the service of our sisters in Christ in the church is of immeasurable worth. Their participation in building up the body of Christ and advancing the gospel of Christ is invaluable. Women can minister to the body through prophecy, testimony, singing, praying; words of wisdom, encouragement and knowledge; teaching other women, as well as many other spiritual gifts that God has given them; but they may not function as overseers in the church. However, if the men in a church are spiritually ignorant, spiritually immature or simply lazy, it is naturally tempting for the more gifted, vocal and active women in the church to take the ascendancy and assume leadership. This may sometimes be overtly done, but more often than not, it is covertly done behind the scenes. Yet, without exception, whenever a woman violates God's divine mandate and usurps and undermines the leadership and teaching function of the Christian brothers, it opens a woman up to deception, which can have a disastrous outcome not only in her life and ministry, but also for her household and the church of God. These destructive consequences may not be readily seen to the undiscerning eye, but if they run their sinful course, they will produce bad fruit unless that woman repents with a sincere change of heart and behavior. The Bible says, "For it was Adam who was first created and then Eve. And it was not Adam who was deceived; it was the woman who was deceived and became a sinner. But women will be saved *(restored)* through childbearing *(being a wife, mother and homemaker)* if they continue in faith, love and holiness with propriety (1 Timothy 2:13-15)." It was Eve who was deceived, not Adam. Adam sinned knowingly and willfully; therefore God held Adam fully accountable for his disobedience and its disastrous effect on the human race (Romans 5:17-19). However, Eve sinned first when she usurped Adam's leadership and acted on her own initiative to eat fruit from the tree of the knowledge of good and evil (Genesis 3:1-6).

When a woman steps outside of her lawful God-given role and authority, and assumes the leadership role of men in the home or in the church, her lawless attitude does not adorn her with godly beauty and holy propriety. On the contrary, when a Christian woman dominates a Christian man, she becomes spiritually discordant like a "noisy gong or clanging cymbal" (1 Corinthians 13:1). As a result of the "women's liberation" onslaught on the minds of both men and women, there are many women (who profess to be Christians) who are not in true submission to either Jesus Christ or to their husbands (if they are married). As a consequence, their lack of submissiveness can emerge in the weekly gatherings of the saints and produce confusion and disorder. A woman who is not submitted to God's divine order may try to usurp God's appointed leadership in the meetings and may even try to disrupt the meetings. For example, she may try to publically question or challenge the teaching or authority of the elders, or she may try to publically instruct the men in the fellowship, or she may underhandedly try to encourage other women to function outside of their God-given roles (both in the home and in the church). The lawless attitude of a rebellious woman is a "Jezebel spirit" that can infect the whole church (Revelation 2:20-23).

The negative influence of a woman who is not submitted to the headship of Jesus Christ can be very insidious since a woman can outwardly appear very submissive, but inwardly still be very rebellious, to both the Lord and her husband. Whenever a woman tries to usurp the authority of her husband or the church elders, she can bring sin and disorder into her family and the church. Note that many men who profess to be Christians in our day are also not truly submitted to the headship of Jesus Christ and can also bring a lawless spirit and disorder into Christ's church. Unfortunately, this can happen because we live in a day when the lawless spirit of the world has greatly influenced the attitudes and behavior of both men and women. It is the godly role of elders to instruct and protect the flock from these destructive influences. If there is proper Biblical instruction and godly discipline in a church, those who are lawless (both men and women) will generally not seek to find a home in a church that corrects and disciplines those who are rebellious, and those who are lawfully submitted to our Lord Jesus Christ will find spiritual peace and safety in that church.

The recurring problem of women usurping men's leadership role in the family and in the church is a direct consequence of the Fall when sin entered into the human race. During the time of the Old Covenant, the prophet Isaiah declared God's judgement and calamity upon the people because they had abandoned the Lord and His ways. As part of this judgement, God said, "I will make mere lads their princes, and capricious children will govern them... and women rule over them (Isaiah 3:4, 12)." In other words, one of the consequences that occurs when a people stop following God and obeying Him is that God will allow the women to rule over the men. This fruit of sin is already a prominent feature of our secular lawless society, and the lie that women can and should govern and instruct the men in church is now spreading throughout the contemporary church. Women ruling over men will thus be one of the marks that distinguishes the false church of Satan from the true church of God (for only the true church will continue to follow God's New Covenant commands and instructions concerning the divine order between men and women and their different roles in the home and in the church).

By His death on the cross, Jesus Christ has done away with the curse of the Fall and redeemed us from sin's deception and destruction; thereby making it possible for men and women to live in God's divine order and harmony in the freedom and power of the New Covenant. The only way that godly men and women can walk in Christ's abundant resurrection life and function in proper Biblical order and respect for one another is to be truly submitted to Christ's headship, believing and acting on the Biblical truth that they are dead to sin, but alive to God in Christ (because they no longer have a sin nature and Christ's divine nature now indwells them). This is the only way that true Biblical submission to one another and to godly appointed authority in the church is possible for both men and women.

How The New Covenant Church Handles Finances

18 Most Christians today accept without any question the idea that pastors should receive an annual salary from their local church. However, they may be surprised to learn that there is no Scriptural or historical evidence that the elders who pastored the local churches in the first century were given a full-time salary to meet all their financial needs and family obligations. The elders were not full-time Christian workers; they were simply elder brothers in the local church who had a responsibility to shepherd the flock, but still earned their living by working in a trade or profession like any other brother in the church. Some Christians might ask, "But what about when Jesus sent out His disciples?" It is true that when

Jesus commissioned His disciples to go out and preach the gospel, He told them, "The worker is worthy of his wages (Luke 10:7)." And Paul also wrote: "The Lord directed those who proclaim the gospel to get their living from the gospel (1 Corinthians 9:14)." The question then is not whether it is right for someone to get their living from proclaiming the gospel, but which workers were Jesus and Paul specifically referring to, and what exactly did they mean by this? To answer this question, we must carefully examine the intent and meaning of both Jesus' and Paul's statements. From its Scriptural context, we see that Jesus was referring to the workers whom He had personally called, trained, and sent out to preach His gospel from city to city. This is the only calling, training and sending that counts in God's eyes. It does not matter if you have been called by your church, trained by your denominational seminary, and sent out by your mission board. If you have not been personally called, trained, and sent out by God to preach His gospel, then you are not worthy of God's support through God's people.

Jesus told His itinerant preachers of the gospel that they were to stay in the homes of those they ministered to and share in their meals. Jesus told them, "Stay in the house *(that receives you)*, eating and drinking whatever they give you; for the laborer is worthy of his wages (Luke 10:7)." Having their basic needs of food and lodging supplied is clearly what Jesus meant by "wages." He did not say His ministers could have a fixed annual salary. He did not say they could ask other Christians to pledge them money each month. He did not say they could make public appeals for money to meet their financial needs. He did not say they could collect tithes and offerings every Sunday morning to support their ministries. Instead, Jesus said their support would consist simply of any food and lodging voluntarily provided to them by those to whom they ministered. This is the same kind of support that Paul described in his statement in 1 Corinthians 9:14. The New Testament Greek word for "living" used in this verse is *zao*, which means *a way of subsistence or sustenance*. In other words, Paul said that those who preach the gospel have a right to have their basic needs of sustenance met. These basic subsistence needs consist of food, drink, lodging and clothing. This is confirmed by Paul's prior question in verse four of this passage: "Do we not have a right to eat and drink?" This is also consistent with Paul's instruction to Timothy: "If we have food and clothing, with these we will be content (1 Timothy 6:8)." Paul's teaching on this subject supports Jesus' instruction on this matter: those whom God has sent out to proclaim His gospel can depend on God's people to provide them with their basic sustenance needs of food, lodging and clothing. Furthermore, Jesus and Paul were both specifically referring to those workers whom God had "sent out" as apostles in a traveling ministry when they said their basic subsistence needs would be met by staying in the homes of those they were ministering to (Luke 10:7; 1 Corinthians 9:5-6). Limiting material support for those in a traveling ministry to their basic needs also helps protect God's flock from greedy ministers who would devour and live off the sheep. These ravenous wolves in sheep's clothing will then look in other places for easy prey.

What about the elders who shepherd the local church? Since they are not commissioned by God to have a traveling ministry to the body of Christ, they are expected to work a regular secular job to provide for their material needs. The primary difference between the work of an elder (who is not supported by the church) and the work of an apostle (whose basic needs may be supplied by the church) is that the apostle travels from location to location to proclaim the gospel and, consequently, requires food and lodging in each location; whereas the elder remains in one location where he has his own home and is able to provide for his own basic necessities by working a secular job, and where he is able to share the responsibility of shepherding and teaching duties with the other co-elders in the local church. In short, the ministry of elders is local; the ministry of apostles is extra-local. This extra-local distinction can also cover the ministry of traveling prophets, evangelists and teachers since their field of work is geographically broader and more mobile than the elders who shepherd a local congregation (Titus

3:13). In our day, however, the need for traveling ministries is not nearly as great as it was two thousand years ago. Although there is no ideal substitute for face-to-face personal ministry, a significant amount of apostolic, evangelistic and teaching work can now be done through advanced technology such as the worldwide web, video conferencing, podcasts, skyping, live streaming, eBooks and smart phone technology.

Since the local elders all work regular jobs like the rest of the brethren, this helps prevent a clergy-laity dichotomy and mindset from developing in the church. Also, since the local elders earn their own living and do not have to be financially supported, this allows the local church to help any members of the body who are truly poor and suffering. As Paul said, "At the present time, your abundance will supply what they need, so that in turn their abundance will supply what you need, so that there may be equality, as it is written: 'He who gathered much did not have too much, and he who gathered little did not lack' (2 Corinthians 8:14-15)." The only Biblical instruction on collecting money in church every Sunday is found in 1 Corinthians 16:1-2. In this passage, Paul directs the Corinthian church to take up a weekly "collection for the saints" for the sole purpose of helping those saints who are suffering and in need. Note that Paul does not direct the church to take up a "collection for the pastor's salary or for the building program." Nor does Paul direct the church to take up a weekly collection of the members' tithes; instead, he encourages each member of the church to help meet the material needs of the suffering saints in keeping with their own individual financial ability. This was the New Testament way for Sunday collections, which has now been abandoned by the false church system. A careful review of Scriptures clearly reveals the New Covenant house churches in the first-century had no weekly collection of the Old Covenant tithe tax to pay for a pastor's salary or a building program. Consequently, since money should not be a major issue or concern to the functioning of the local New Covenant church, the saints can simply meet together in homes as the family of God and use their resources to advance the gospel, and practically care for one another's needs; they also do not need to officially "incorporate" themselves as a recognized, religious organization in order to seek State-sanctioned approval to operate as a licensed and regulated tax-exempt institution under the eyes of the government.

When a traveling apostle (or prophet, evangelist or teacher) returns home for a length of time, he might then once again become one of the elders in his local church just as Peter and John did in the church at Jerusalem (1 Peter 5:1; 2 John 1; 3 John 1). However, note that neither Peter nor John then became the "head elder" or "senior pastor." As Peter himself said, "To the elders among you, I appeal to you *as a fellow elder* (1 Peter 5:1)." This unique situation of a traveling apostle or teacher, who is back home again and is now functioning as an elder in his local church for a time, may be the case where Paul seems to allow a food and lodging provision for an elder who is called to full-time preaching and teaching: "The elders who oversee the church well are worthy of double honor, especially those who work hard at preaching and teaching, for the Scripture says, 'Do not muzzle the ox while he is threshing,' and 'The worker is worthy of his wages.' (1 Timothy 5:17-18)." Based on the whole of Paul's instruction, this unusual situation where an elder needs to be devoted full-time to the interests of a local house church is clearly the exception and not the general rule. In fact, many Bible teachers think this particular Scripture does not address financially supporting those elders who teach, but instead exhorts the church to especially honor those elders who work hard at their shepherding and teaching. The prevailing thought here is about providing elders the honor they deserve; it is not about providing them with a salary. And even if Paul was referring to giving material support, then based on all the other Scriptural guidance on this subject, Paul's statement, "the worker is worthy of his wages," means food or lodging only; it does not mean a full-time salary with fringe benefits. This is consistent with Paul's advice to the church at Galatia: "The one who is taught the Word should share all good things with the one who teaches him (Galatians 6:6)." Once again, based on the entirety of Jesus' and Paul's instruction, sharing all "good things" means sharing food, lodging, clothing, and perhaps giving an occasional monetary gift to help cover the traveling costs for those full-time servants of God's Word who are in extra-local itinerant ministry. However, this verse cannot be misconstrued to mean that all the local elders (shepherds) who teach in their church are to be paid a tax-free, full-time salary with a housing allowance, a car allowance, a travel allowance, a library or book allowance, a medical insurance plan, a retirement plan, a college fund plan for their children, and provided with a full-time secretary and office space. Elders in the first century church were mature and trustworthy brothers – self-supporting family men with secular jobs. They were not paid clergy who considered the ministry a job or professional career.

Unfortunately, many pastors in our day will not even consider shepherding a local church if their expected total compensation package is not "adequate." This reveals a hireling or mercenary mentality rather than a true shepherd's heart for God's flock. This certainly is not what Jesus envisioned when He sent His disciples out to go from city to city and proclaim the gospel (Matthew 10:5-11; Luke 9:1-6; 10:1-9). Jesus would be outraged by today's concept of a salaried clergy living an affluent lifestyle off the tithes of God's flock. Jesus certainly did not intend that any of His workers would become rich off His gospel and grow fat off His sheep. When Paul gave instructions to the elders of the church at Ephesus, he told them not to be greedy for money, but to earn a living by their own hands in order to meet their own needs and also the needs of others (Acts 20:33-34). Paul said that by doing this, they honored Jesus' teaching that "it is more blessed to give than to receive (Acts 20:35)." Paul's further guidance to the saints (including the elder-shepherds) was that "if anyone is not willing to work, then he is not to eat either... if anyone does not provide for his relatives, and especially for his immediate family, he has denied the faith and is worse than an unbeliever (2 Thessalonians 3:10; 1 Timothy 5:8)."

Based on Jesus' and Paul's teaching on this subject, anyone who believes they are called into the ministry should ask themselves: Am I called, trained and sent out by God? Am I preaching the true and complete gospel that Paul preached? Am I willing to not receive a salary from others? Am I willing to not ask others for money to meet my financial needs? Am I called to a traveling, extra-local ministry to the body of Christ? Am I willing to stay in believers' homes and share their meals while I am ministering? Am I willing to work a regular job, if necessary, to proclaim the gospel free of charge? If your answer to all of these questions is yes, then you might be worthy of God's people supporting your basic sustenance needs. But if this basic needs test does not satisfy your financial comfort level, then you should not be in Christ's ministry. God has His ways and means of providing for His work and His workers, and His ways are very different than man's ways and means.

How someone in "Christian ministry" deals with the question of finances reveals very clearly and practically the quality of their faith (or lack thereof), and whether they are called of God and sent by God. Instead of appealing to men publically to financially support their ministry, they should appeal to God privately. Jesus said, "Pray to your Father who is in secret, and your Father who sees what is done in secret will reward you (Matthew 6:6)." For whomever God calls and sends, He also supplies. Remember that God was able to miraculously send ravens to provide food for the prophet Elijah in his time of need (1 Kings 17:5-6). And what if God does not miraculously supply your needs? Then God may choose to supply your needs by telling you to get a regular wage earning job. You may even find that working an everyday secular job is character-building and faith-building. How a church deals with the question of finances also clearly reveals whether that church is abiding in Christ's truth and has His resurrection life or not.

Some Christians will complain that this is not how it is done in today's church. That is true, but we cannot look at today's false church as a Biblical model; we can only look at the Scriptures to be our guide in this question of finances. When Jesus sent His disciples out to proclaim the gospel, He told them, "Freely you have received, so freely give (Matthew 10:8)." It is unthinkable to imagine Matthew, Mark, Luke or John selling copies of their gospel scrolls in the Jerusalem marketplace to raise money for their ministry and personal household needs. We could never imagine Peter promoting discounted copies of his epistles or Paul hawking replicas of his "healing handkerchiefs," to fund their apostolic ministries. If a divine revelation or teaching was freely given to them from God, these servants of Christ knew it was wrong to charge the body of Christ and personally gain any profit from it. If they had marketed their ministries for personal financial gain, they would have corrupted the purity of the gospel of Christ. The entire history of the Christian church would have taken a wrong turn shortly after its birth. Yet, this shocking and scandalous behavior is precisely what many false ministers are doing today. Because most Christians do not know (and believe to the point of acting on) the truth of the gospel that they have been crucified with Christ to the world, the church's ability to discern good from evil in the area of finances has been severely compromised.

We now live in a day that rivals the medieval age for the most financially corrupt time in church history. In those days, the Catholic church, in order to raise money to complete the construction of Saint Peter's Basilica in Rome, sold "tickets" called indulgences, which would forgive the buyer of all their sins and permit them to go to heaven. Of course, that was outrageous; yet in terms of the sheer amount of money being fraudulently collected under the pretense of promoting the gospel message, our age holds the dubious distinction of having no rival. In our generation, false apostles, prophets, evangelists, pastors and teachers are "merchandising the anointing" by making an obscene amount of money off their "Christian" ministries. In pitiful contrast to Paul's example, false ministers, like ravenous wolves in sheep's clothing, are devouring God's sheep and turning God's house into a den of thieves. False shepherds with hearts of greed are fleecing the flock of God by constantly extorting God's sheep to give them ten percent or more of their income. We use the term "extorting" instead of "exhorting" because they are scaring God's sheep into tithing by telling them they are robbing God and under a curse if they do not give at least ten percent of their income to them. However, the truth is that any minister who uses emotional blackmail to get tithes out of God's sheep is robbing God and under a curse for preying on His flock.

In this age of moral compromise, some of the world's best-known preachers have resorted to publicly begging for money to keep their ministries afloat. And false shepherds are shamelessly charging their congregations for copies of their sermons and for counseling sessions. These greedy clergy have made the church a profitable business, and the ministry a comfortable and lucrative career. Instead of the strong rebuke they deserve, they receive fame, fortune and adulation from the world of Churchianity. No wonder so many ambitious and opportunistic carnal-minded young men are eager to get into the ministry! If more churches followed Jesus' and Paul's instructions on the question of finances, it would protect God's sheep from being fleeced by unethical, covetous and lazy ministers who just want to "feed off the flock." Jude called these charlatans "shepherds who feed only themselves" (Jude 19).

In dramatic contrast to these false ministers stands our brother Paul. Even though Paul, as a traveling apostle, had a right to support from the churches, he did not make use of this right (1 Corinthians 9:12, 15; 2 Corinthians 11:7-8). Instead, he established a pattern of not asking for support for himself from the churches that he served. In Corinth, Paul supported himself as a blue-collar worker (a tent maker) to meet his own needs and the needs of those traveling with him (Acts 18:2-3; 1 Corinthians 4:12). In Thessalonica, he did the same (2 Thessalonians 3:7-8). Paul said, "For you recall, brothers, our labor and hardship: how we worked night and day in order not to be a burden to anyone while we proclaimed the gospel of God to you (1 Thessalonians 2:9)." And in Ephesus, Paul also did the same (Acts 20:34). Paul worked to support both himself and others in order to be a model for the rest of those in ministry. Paul said, "For you yourselves know how you ought to follow our example. We were not idle when we were with you, nor did we eat anyone's food without paying for it. On the contrary, we worked night and day so that we would not be a burden to any of you. We did this, not because we did not have a right to such support, but in order to make ourselves a model for you so that you would follow our example (2 Thessalonians 3:7-9)."

Paul had several reasons for doing this. First, Paul said, "I have a stewardship entrusted to me. What then is my reward? That when I preach the gospel, I may offer the gospel free of charge, and not make use of my right to the gospel (1 Corinthians 9:5-6)." In other words, Paul said that if he received free lodging and food from the churches as payments-in-kind in exchange for his preaching the gospel to them, he would only be compensated for doing his job since it was his heavenly commission to proclaim the gospel (Acts 26:15-19). However, Paul knew that if he voluntarily gave up his right to food and lodging by reimbursing the local church for his daily sustenance, he could then share the gospel free of charge to them, and he would then receive an even greater reward from God (1 Corinthians 9:12-17). Therefore, Paul worked as a tent maker to supply his own subsistence needs, as well as supply the daily needs of those traveling in ministry with him. Second, Paul said he did not want to be a household burden to any of his brothers and sisters; therefore, he worked a regular job to supply his own needs and others' needs (Acts 20:34; 2 Thessalonians 3:8). Third, Paul said wanted his brothers and sisters in Christ to know his motive in ministering to them was out of love and not because he wanted their money or goods (Acts 20:33-35). Paul said, "I am not seeking my own profit, but the profit of many, so that they may be saved (1 Corinthians 10:33)." Fourth, Paul said he wanted to make sure he personally caused no hindrance or stumbling block to the gospel of Christ (1 Corinthians 9:12). Even in Paul's day, there were many false ministers peddling the gospel for personal profit and out of selfish ambition, and by their behavior bringing shame on the church (2 Corinthians 2:17; Philippians 1:17). Therefore Paul said, "We give no cause for offense in anything, so that our ministry will not be discredited (2 Corinthians 6:3)."

And finally, Paul said because he offered the gospel without charge, he was under financial obligation to no man (1 Corinthians 9:19). He could then share the truth of the whole gospel without any personal conflict of interest. Paul knew if your own livelihood and your family's financial needs depended on people supporting your ministry, it would be difficult to share the whole counsel of God with them since you could easily offend those who support you. This creates a conflict of interest that very few salaried clergy have been able to overcome. Therefore, they find themselves under constant temptation to compromise the truth of God's Word and share what people want to hear rather than what they need to hear. Sadly, when God's people are fed a compromised gospel, they stop walking in Christ's truth, holiness and power. They then become spiritually weak and sick and easy prey for the enemy. Thus Paul, in the interest of doing everything he possibly could for the sake of advancing the gospel of Christ, voluntarily gave up his right to basic support from the churches in order to avoid all appearance of any conflict of interest. When it comes to finances, all of God's servants must strive to be resolutely independent lest they try to please men. As Paul said, "Am I now seeking the favor of men, or of God? Or, am I trying to please men? If I were still trying to please men, I would not be a bondservant of Christ... Therefore, I declare to you today that I am innocent of the blood of all men. For I did not shrink from proclaiming to you the whole purpose of God (Acts 20:26-27; Galatians 1:10)."

Jesus declared, "Greater love has no one than this, that one lay down his life for his friends (John 15:13)." John also affirmed, "We know love by this, that He laid down his life for us; and we ought to lay down our lives for the brethren (1 John 3:16)." One of the tangible ways Paul laid down his life and showed his love for the body of Christ was by working a regular job to supply for his needs and the needs of others, so that he could offer the gospel free of charge to the body of Christ. In view of the present darkness of our time and the disgraceful conduct of multitudes of self-profiteering clergy in the false church who are discrediting the gospel, every true minister of Christ should prayerfully consider following Paul's example of a bondservant and begin to offer the gospel free of charge and, if necessary, start working a regular job like the rest of the brethren. As Peter exhorted, "Be shepherds of God's flock that is under your care... voluntarily according to the will of God; and not for personal profit, but with eagerness... proving to be examples to the flock (1 Peter 5:2-3)." And as Paul himself called out, "Brethren, join in following my example, and observe those who walk according to the pattern you have in us (Philippians 3:17)."

THE NEW COVENANT CHURCH IS DESTINED TO SUFFER FOR CHRIST'S SAKE

19 Many Christians believe God is infinitely happy and that He also wants us to be happy. They believe the idea of sorrow and suffering is negative thinking that should be avoided at all costs. However,

this is a false gospel. It ignores the whole counsel of God as revealed by His Word. Many Christians mistakenly believe the pursuit of happiness is God's purpose for their lives and is their God-given right and entitlement. However, this directly contradicts the Bible, which declares the pursuit of holiness is our God-given purpose and obligation. Multitudes are now reaping the godless fruit of pursuing temporal, earthly happiness and pleasure instead of the righteousness, peace and joy of God that comes by faith; and the church has been severely compromised by buying into this false gospel. The Bible is also clear we cannot pursue the holiness of God without suffering here on earth. In contrast to the false gospel of happiness, the Bible says Christ was "a man of sorrows and familiar with suffering (Isaiah 53:3)." Even though He was the Son of God, God perfected Jesus as the Son of Man, the author of our salvation, through many sufferings (Hebrews 2:10; also 5:8). Jesus Himself said, "The Son of Man must suffer many things (Mark 8:31)." Jesus Christ could not have redeemed His bride without suffering, even to the point of suffering death on the cross. Similarly, the bride of Christ cannot be prepared for eternal union and co-regency with Christ without also suffering. The Bible says, "If we suffer, we shall also reign with Him (2 Timothy 2:12)." Jesus told His disciples they could expect to drink from His cup of suffering (Matthew 20:22-23). Peter said, "For you have been called for this purpose, since Christ also suffered for you, leaving you an example for you to follow in His steps (1 Peter 2:21)." And Paul said, "We must go through many hardships to enter the kingdom of God (Acts 14:22)." This hardship and suffering refers not to our initial salvation, but to the suffering that is associated with the process of our daily sanctification and our growing spiritual maturity.

What does it mean to suffer for Christ and His kingdom? It means we are willing to suffer the pain of disapproval, rejection, alienation and persecution that we can expect to receive from the world for Christ's sake. The Bible says, "Everyone who wants to live a godly life in Christ Jesus will be persecuted (2 Timothy 3:1)." It means we are willing to suffer the loss of our own self-sovereignty every time we refuse to indulge our selfish natural desires for the sake of Christ's kingdom. Jesus said, "Whoever wants to save his self-life will lose it, but whoever loses his self-life for My sake will save it (Luke 9:24)." However, we must always remember that what we gain in return is far greater than any pain or loss we suffer. What we gain is the Lord Jesus Christ Himself. Anytime we underestimate the worth of Jesus Christ and overestimate the value of what we lose, we will feel sorry for ourselves whenever we suffer rejection from the world or deny ourselves the pleasures of the world for Christ's sake. However, gaining Jesus Christ is worth far more than everything we have to lose. Knowing Jesus Christ is worth far beyond anything we have to suffer. This was Paul's personal testimony: "Whatever things were gain to me, those things I have counted as loss for the sake of Christ. More than that, I count all things to be loss in view of the surpassing value of knowing Christ Jesus my Lord, for whom I have suffered the loss of all things, and count them but rubbish so that I might gain Christ (Philippians 3:7-8)."

We are destined to suffer because we cannot possess our spiritual inheritance in Christ if we do not suffer for Christ's sake (Romans 8:17). The Bible says, "For to you it has been granted for Christ's sake, not only to believe in Him, but also to suffer for His sake… for you yourselves know that we have been destined for this… we kept telling you in advance that we were going to suffer affliction (Philippians 1:29; 1 Thessalonians 3:3-4)." We are destined to suffer because we cannot know Jesus Christ without suffering for His sake. As Paul said, "I want to know Christ… and the fellowship of sharing in His sufferings (Philippians 3:10)." We are destined to suffer because we cannot overcome sin and put to death the carnal desires of our unconverted, natural soul-life without suffering emotionally and physically. The Bible says, "Therefore since Christ has suffered in the flesh *(in body and soul)*, arm yourselves with the same purpose, because he who has suffered in the flesh *(in body and soul)* has ceased from sin, so as to live the rest of his time in the flesh no longer for the lusts of men, but for the will of God (1 Peter 4:1-2)." We are destined to suffer because we cannot be God's legitimate sons if we are not willing to suffer the pain of His divine discipline (Hebrews 12:5-10). We are destined to suffer because we cannot bear God's spiritual fruit if we are not willing to suffer the pain of His divine pruning (John 15:2). We are destined to suffer because we cannot be God's soldiers if we are not willing to suffer the hardship of His divine training (2 Timothy 2:3).

We are destined to suffer for Christ's sake because suffering produces empathy within us so that we are able to comfort others who are also suffering. The Bible says, "Blessed be the God and Father of our Lord Jesus Christ, the Father of compassion and God of all comfort, who comforts us in all our troubles, so that we can comfort those who are in any trouble with the comfort that we ourselves have received from God. For just as the sufferings of Christ are ours in abundance, so also our comfort is abundant through Christ (2 Corinthian 1:3-5)." We are destined to suffer for Christ's sake because suffering produces Christian character and spiritual maturity in us (Romans 5:3-4; James 1:2-4). Therefore, when we ask God to help us grow in Christ, we should not be surprised when we encounter hardship and suffering (1 Peter 4:12-13). God is Sovereign and God is Love. When we suffer as a devout Christian, it is not some random accident without any purpose or meaning; God is able to divinely weave our suffering into His master plan and purpose for our lives. Although we may never fully understand the reason why we suffer during our time on earth, God allows suffering to come into our lives (according to His infinite knowledge of our spiritual need and for our eternal good). The Bible reassures us, "We know that God causes all things to work together for good to those who love God, to those who are called according to His purpose (Romans 8:28)." What then is the mystery or reason for our suffering? Paul said, "We do not want you to be unaware, brethren, of our affliction... that we were burdened excessively, beyond our strength, so that we despaired even of life; indeed, in our hearts we felt the sentence of death. But this happened so that we would not rely on ourselves, but in God (2 Corinthians 1:8-9)." The Greek word for affliction is thlipsis. It is also translated as tribulation and simply means pressure. God has designed that suffering would apply pressure on us until we are pressed far beyond our natural ability. When we finally come to the end of our own strength and yet continue to trust in God, God will reveal to us how we can only spiritually live by depending on the power of Christ's Spirit in us. Ultimately, this is the divine revelation that (when we were born again) God included us in His Son's death so that His resurrected Son might sovereignly and powerfully live in us (Romans 6:3-11; Colossians 1:27). It is from this heavenly viewpoint that Jesus Christ told Paul: "My power is perfected in your weakness," and Paul responded: "Therefore, I will boast all the more gladly in my weaknesses, so that Christ's power may dwell in me. This is why, for Christ's sake, I delight in weaknesses, in insults, in hardships, in persecutions, in difficulties; for when I am weak, then I am strong (2 Corinthians 12:9-10)."

If we try to deny ourselves the pleasures of this world and suffer the loss of all things by applying our natural strength and self-discipline to live an ascetic religious lifestyle, we will be the most miserable of souls. There is only one way to suffer the loss of all things in the joy and power of the Holy Spirit, and that is to believe and act on the truth of the cross that we no longer live, but Christ lives in us. As Paul testified, "I *(my old man of sin)* have been crucified with Christ and I *(my sinful nature)* no longer live, but Christ lives in me; and the life I now live, I live by faith in the Son of God (Galatians 2:20)." Since the Son of God died in our place; He now wants to live in our place. God has made this exchanged life possible by using Christ's death on the cross to remove our sinful nature and replace it with His Son's holy nature when we were born again. This divine exchange is the secret to the overcoming Christian life, and to enduring difficult and painful trials through the joy of the Lord. God has designed suffering to reveal and continually reinforce this vital Biblical truth of the cross within us: I am dead to the world because I no longer have a sinful nature, and Christ's Spirit now lives in me. It is this joy of knowing Jesus Christ (who lives in you) that enables you to endure suffering for His sake. As the Bible says, "The joy of the Lord is your strength (Nehemiah 8:10)."

As we said earlier, many Christians believe they are entitled to happiness rather than destined to suffer for Christ' sake. This is a false gospel that will cause many to fall away from the faith during the coming tribulation and persecution. God has not called us to happiness, but He has called us to holiness (1 Thessalonians 4:3-8; 1 Peter 1:14-16). There is no exception to this call for a Christian. Our reaction to affliction will determine whether our suffering produces God's divine objective – the deep spiritual joy and surpassing inner peace that comes from knowing Jesus Christ and being progressively conformed to His glorious image. The Bible says, "Our present sufferings are not worth comparing with the glory to be revealed in us... for momentary, light affliction is producing for us an eternal weight of glory far beyond comparison (Romans 8:18; 2 Corinthians 4:17)." Yielding to self-pity, anger, resentment and bitterness is a waste of our suffering. We should always remind ourselves of the divine truth that we are giving up the fleeting happiness of earthly pleasures for the greater joy of laying hold of God's eternal glory.

If we understand God's divine purpose in our suffering, we can by faith then accept our affliction and sorrow, and trust in a wise and loving Almighty God, who will turn our suffering into our good for His glory. The Bible says, "So then, those who suffer according to God's will should entrust their souls to their faithful Creator in doing what is right (1 Peter 5:19)." When we patiently endure suffering by faith in Christ in this way, we will gain the deep spiritual joy that comes from doing what is right and pleasing to God. Jesus Himself endured the physical suffering and shame of the cross by fixing His eyes on the eternal joy that awaited Him with the Father (Hebrews 12:2). And as King David declared of God, "You have turned my mourning into dancing; you have removed my sackcloth and clothed me with gladness (Psalm 3:11)." With this in mind, James wrote to the saints, "Count it all joy, my brothers, when you encounter various trials, because you know that the testing of your faith produces perseverance. And perseverance will have its perfect result, that you may be mature and complete, not lacking anything (James 1:2-4)."

The prophet Malachi foretold that the Messiah would purify His chosen people as a refiner purifies gold and silver: "But who can endure the day of His coming? And who can stand when He appears? For He is like a refiner's fire... He will purify the sons of Levi and refine them like gold and silver, so they may present to the Lord offerings in righteousness (Malachi 3:2-3)." Zechariah also prophesied that the Lord would purify the surviving remnant of His people like gold and silver are refined: "And I will bring the third part through the fire, refine them as silver is refined, and test them as gold is tested (Zechariah 13:9)." And in the Book of Proverbs, King Solomon describes the Lord as the refiner of His people: "The melting pot is for silver and the crucible is for gold, but it is the Lord who tests the hearts of men (Proverbs 17:3)." In Biblical times, when the metal smith or refiner wanted to purify gold or silver, he would put the precious metals in a refining pot called a crucible. He would then build a fiery furnace under the crucible. When the gold or silver had melted in the crucible, the refiner would skim off the dross or impurities that rose to the surface. The refiner would then repeat this process until he could see his own image reflected in the molten surface of the crucible.

Trials, afflictions and persecutions are the crucible that Christ uses to purify His people until He sees His image fully reflected in us like precious gold or silver. As the Lord said, "Behold, I have refined you, but not as silver; I have tested you in the furnace of affliction (Isaiah 48:10)." Gold or silver that passed the test of the furnace was called "refined" and had precious value. The Bible says, "Take away the dross from the silver and there comes out a vessel for the smith (Proverbs 25:4)." Those metals that failed to pass the test were "rejected." In Jeremiah 6:29-30, God calls the people of Israel "rejected silver" because He tried in vain to refine them, but they stubbornly rejected His discipline and resisted His attempts to train them in righteousness. This crucible of suffering that refines our faith is also called the baptism of fire by John the Baptist (Luke 3:16). Thus God has designed His crucible of suffering to humble us and reveal the fullness of His Son in us, like precious gold that is refined by fire. Affliction, loneliness, heartbreak and persecution are all intended to bring us to the end of ourselves and into Christ's fullness. For as long as we think we have any spiritual life or strength in ourselves, Christ's life cannot be fully revealed in us. Jesus told the church of Laodicea that they must buy gold from Him that has been refined by fire (Revelation 3:18). This means there is a price that the church must pay if she wants to become as purified gold for Christ's sake. What will it cost the church to purchase this "pure gold" from our Lord? Through the centuries, God has never changed the price: the cost is always our natural self-life or soul-life, which we must give up by faith in Christ's completed work on the cross. Jesus said, "He who has found his soul-life will lose it, and he who has lost his soul-life for My sake will find it (Matthew 10:39)."

Remember that God does not want to destroy our soul; however, He wants to purify and transform our soul into His Son's image, if we allow His crucible of suffering to accomplish His divine purpose in us. Paul said, "We also rejoice in our sufferings, because we know that suffering produces perseverance, and perseverance, proven character (Romans 5:3-4)." The Greek word used here for character is dokimē, whose root meaning is "proven and tested," just as gold and silver has been tested and purified in the crucible. In other words, God uses affliction and suffering to test our faith and purify our soul, and form the character of Christ in us, like pure gold that has been tested and proven through fire. With this in mind, Peter wrote, "In this you greatly rejoice, though now for a little while you may have had to suffer grief in all kinds of trials. These have come so that your faith – of greater worth than gold, which perishes even though refined by fire – may be proved genuine and may result in praise, glory and honor when Jesus Christ is revealed (1 Peter 1:6-7)."

The Bible says that when we saved, we received an initial "deposit" of this gold – when God sent the Holy Spirit into our hearts (2 Corinthians 1:2: 5:5; Galatians 4:6). This deposit is like a divine seed of God that is planted within us. The Bible says, "No one who is born of God will continue to practice sin, because God's seed abides in him (1 John 3:9; see also Galatians 3:16)." This divine seed contains the full growth potential of Christ's resurrection life. The Bible says, "Of His fullness we have all received" (John 1:16; see also Ephesians 1:22-23). However, for the seed of Christ to grow and fully mature in our lives, it must reside in "good soil" - in what the Bible calls a "good and honest" heart of persevering faith (Luke 8:15). And the Bible says the only way for us to have this kind of persevering or enduring faith is for our faith to be tested (Romans 5:3; James 1:2-4). It may surprise some Christians that the testing of our faith can come through two different kinds of trials. Jesus illustrated these two kinds of tests in His parable of the sower and the seed. Jesus described the responses of four groups of people to hearing the gospel of the kingdom (Matthew 13:3-8, 18-23; Mark 4:3-8, 13-20; Luke 8:4-15). The seed that fell beside the road represented those people who never received the gospel of the kingdom (the good seed of Christ) into their hearts because the devil snatched the gospel away from them before it could have any affect in their lives. The seed that fell into the good ground represented those people who received the gospel of the kingdom

(Christ's seed) into their hearts and, by holding firmly onto this seed with persevering faith; they produced the fullness of Christ's resurrection life, and lasting spiritual fruit in their lives (Luke 8:15). However, Jesus also described two other kinds of people who initially received God's seed of the kingdom with joy, but then failed to produce any lasting spiritual fruit. The people in these two groups encountered two different kinds of trials that tested their faith. Jesus described the first kind of trial in Matthew 13:21; Mark 4:17; and Luke 8:13. The testing in these Christians' lives was trouble, affliction and persecution; in other words, the sufferings of adversity. When these Christians were faced with adversity, their faith failed and they produced no lasting spiritual fruit. Jesus described the second kind of trial in Matthew 13:22; Mark 4:19; and Luke 8:14. The testing in these Christians' lives was the deceitfulness of riches and the pleasures of this life; in other words, the comforts of prosperity. When these Christians were faced with prosperity, their faith also failed and they produced no lasting spiritual fruit. These two different types of tests represent the trials and temptations that all Christians can expect to face. The first test comes when we encounter prolonged sufferings and hardships. The second test comes when we encounter the riches and pleasures of the world's so-called "good life."

Speaking of Jesus, John the Baptist declared, "His winnowing fork is in His hand, and He will thoroughly clear His threshing floor, and He will gather His wheat into His barn, and He will burn up the chaff with unquenchable fire (Matthew 3:12)." The winnowing fork is the tool that farmers in Biblical times used to sift out the chaff from the wheat. In the same way, God uses trials and temptations as a divine winnowing fork to sift our attitudes and motives, and reveal the purity of our faith. For example, even though it was Satan who inspired wicked men to crucify Him, Jesus said that He accepted the shame and suffering of the cross as from "His Father's cup" (Acts 2:22-23; John 18:11). Another Biblical example of this principle is the case of Joseph in the Old Testament. After suffering thirteen years of imprisonment and hardship because his brothers had betrayed him and sold him into slavery, Joseph told them, "You meant evil against me, but God meant it for good in order to bring about this present result, to preserve many people alive (Genesis 50:20)." Even though Joseph's hardship and suffering was carried out by malicious men undoubtedly inspired by Satan, God used Joseph's suffering to purify his faith, prove his character, and prepare him to save a remnant of God's people from the coming great famine (Genesis 45:5-8). Yet another example of this type of testing of our faith can be found in the New Testament when Satan tempted Peter to deny the Lord. Jesus told Simon Peter: "Simon, Simon, I tell you Satan has asked to sift you like wheat. But I have prayed for you, that your faith may not fail. And when you have turned back, strengthen your brothers (Luke 22:31-32)."

In our nearly fifty years of Christian experience, we have seen many more Christians fall away from the faith (and never come back) because they were seduced by the world's so-called "good life," than because they suffered hardship. Remember that God uses both these tests of prosperity and adversity to reveal what attitudes and motives are in our hearts, and prove whether our faith will endure or fail when it is tested under fire. Also remember that God's way of escape for us to endure and overcome all trials and temptations is for us to believe and act on the Biblical truth that we have died with Christ and our life is now hidden with Christ (1 Corinthians 10:13; Colossians 3:1-4). This powerful truth of the cross of Christ is our spiritual hiding place during all times of trouble and temptation (Psalm 32:7). The Bible says, "Therefore, do not throw away your confidence, which has a great reward. For you have need of endurance, so that when you have done the will of God, you will receive what He promised (Hebrews 10:35-36)." If we hold firmly onto God's seed planted within us with a persevering faith through both these tests, Christ's Spirit will grow within us until the kingdom of God takes over our entire life. As Jesus said, "The kingdom of heaven is like a mustard seed, which a man took and planted in his field. And though it is smaller than all the other seeds, when it is fully grown, it is the largest of the garden plants and becomes a tree (Matthew 13:31-32)."

To sum up, although we may be surprised when we encounter trials and temptations that try our souls, Peter assures us this testing is essential in order to purify and prove our faith in Christ, and reveal God's glory to us and in us: "Dear friends, do not be surprised at the fiery ordeal you are suffering, as though something strange were happening to you. But rejoice that you participate in the sufferings of Christ, so that you may be overjoyed when His glory is revealed (1 Peter 4:12-13)." The Bible records that Job (whom God called the most righteous man alive on earth at that time) endured this fiery crucible of testing, and emerged with an overcoming faith when he declared, "Though He slay me, yet will I trust in Him... when He has tested me, I will come forth as gold (Job 13:15; 23:10)." The Bible says that God's end-time church will also endure a great trial of suffering. And when God's crucible of fire has removed the dross of unbelief from His church in the coming tribulation and persecution, she will be dressed as the precious bride of Christ in proven faith that is like pure gold. This is the heavenly vision our Lord gave to the apostle John: "And I saw the holy city, the new Jerusalem, coming down out of heaven, beautifully adorned for her husband... and the city was like pure gold (Revelation 21:2, 18)."

THE CONFLICT BETWEEN TWO KINGDOMS

20 From a heavenly perspective, the history of mankind is the story of the conflict between two kingdoms. In the beginning, there was only one kingdom – the kingdom of God. However,

an archangel named Lucifer led a rebellion against God and persuaded one-third of the angels to join him (Isaiah 14:12-15; Ezekiel 28:12-17; Revelation 12:3-4). Lucifer, who is now called Satan (Revelation 12:9; 20:2), and also called the devil (Luke 4:2; John 8:44; Revelation 12:12) was defeated by God and His army of loyal angels. The devil and his rebellious angels, now called demons or evil spirits (Luke 9:1), were cast out of heaven (Revelation 12:7-9). The devil then set up his own spiritual kingdom over the earth, which he rules with his army of demons. Consequently, the Bible says the devil is "the ruler of demons," "the ruler of this world," "the ruler of the power of the air," and "the god of this world" (Matthew 12:24; John 12:31; Ephesians 2:2; 2 Corinthians 4:4). The Bible says that Satan deceives and leads the whole world astray with his sorcery, so that all the nations of the earth are under his influence and domain (Revelation 12:9; 18:23). Whereas God is the spiritual embodiment of holiness (Isaiah 6:3), and His kingdom is the dominion of light; the devil is the embodiment of evil (Matthew 13:19), and his kingdom is the dominion of darkness (Colossians 1:13). And whereas God's kingdom is called the new Jerusalem (Hebrews 12:22-23; Revelation 21:2, 10); Satan's kingdom is called Babylon (Revelation 11:15; 17:5, 18).

Before we go any further, let us quickly jump to the end of the story of this conflict between two kingdoms. At the close of this age, there will once again only be one kingdom - the kingdom of God; for Jesus Christ, the Son of God and the King of kings, will have judged and condemned Satan to eternal punishment and torment (Revelation 11:15; 12:10; 20:10). The Bible clearly foretells this final triumph of good over evil, and the certainty of Satan's downfall and doom. The outcome is never in doubt, no matter how tumultuous the world's events may appear, or whatever crises and challenges we may face in our own lives. The Bible assures us "the God of peace will soon crush Satan under your feet (Romans 16:20)."

Let us now return to the present conflict between the two kingdoms. To reclaim the world from Satan's control, God created Adam and Eve, the first humans, to populate the earth and rule over the world. As long as Adam and Eve obeyed God, they would have dominion over the earth (Genesis 1:26-28). But instead of preserving their friendship and obedience to God, Adam and Eve sinned against God and fell under Satan's domain. As a consequence, sin entered into the entire human race and all mankind inherited Adam's sinful nature (Romans 5:19). Since then, Satan has been able to influence and control men and women through their sinful nature, which is now at work in the hearts and minds of everyone who is not born again of the Spirit (Ephesians 2:2; 2 Timothy 2:26). As a result, the history of humanity has been tragically marred by mankind's continual rebellion against God the Creator, and the earth has been plagued with greed, poverty, selfish ambition, warfare, disease, genocide, and an endless series of calamities that naturally occur in a sinful, fallen world.

Yet despite humanity's fall into sin, God did not change His divine plan. At the right time, God sent His Son, born as a man, to destroy Satan's power and restore mankind to Himself and to His eternal purpose. Jesus Christ came to earth with one overriding mission - to live a sinless life in obedience to God, and die on the cross in order to rescue us from Satan's rule and reconcile us to God (John 3:16; Colossians 1:13, 19-20). What Adam had lost through his disobedience, Christ then regained for us by His obedience, even to the point of death on the cross (Romans 5:18-19). How did God accomplish this victory over Satan and sin through His Son's death? The Bible says that through Christ's death on the cross, God delivered us from the curse of the Fall. God not only freed us from the penalty of sin, by forgiving our sins through Christ's sacrifice on the cross; He also freed us from the power of sin, by removing our sinful nature through Christ's victory on the cross (Romans

6:6; Colossians 2:11). The crucifixion of Jesus Christ is, therefore, the most momentous strategic event in human history and the triumph of the ages.

Because Jesus Christ willingly sacrificed Himself to save mankind from Satan's rule, the Bible says that God the Father appointed Christ as King to reign over His kingdom, and rule in the lives of everyone who belongs to His kingdom (Philippians 2:5-11). The Bible says the prophets heralded this coming of Christ the King (Isaiah 9:6-7; Daniel 7:13-14). When Jesus was born, the wise men hailed His birth as King (Matthew 2:2). Jesus Himself said, "I am a King... for this reason I have come into the world (John 18:37)." Christ's Kingship over heaven and earth is the fulfillment of the ages. The first century disciples declared that Jesus was King (John 1:49; Luke 19:38). The angels in heaven worship Jesus as the King of kings (Revelation 17:14). By His sacrificial death at Calvary, Jesus proved He is a King worthy of our devotion and obedience (Revelation 5:12). The kingdom of God was at the heart of Jesus' ministry (Mark 1:14-15). Jesus told His disciples to seek His kingdom, pray for His kingdom, and proclaim His kingdom (Matthew 6:10, 6:33; 24:14). The Kingship of Christ and the kingdom of God are inseparable. When Jesus was on earth, He was the personification of the kingdom of God. Since God the Father has appointed Jesus as King, the kingdom of God is the realm of Christ's sovereign rule, and is manifested in the lives of all those who submit to His rule (Ephesians 1:22).

How do you enter into the kingdom of God and come under Christ's Kingship? Jesus said you must be born again of the Holy Spirit to enter the kingdom of God (John 3:3-7). And how can you be born again? The Bible says you must declare your wholehearted allegiance to Jesus Christ, the risen King (Romans 10:9). When you receive Christ as your King and are born again, God removes your sinful nature, through which Satan was able to control you, and replaces it with His Holy Spirit, which makes you a child of God and a citizen of His kingdom (John 1:12; Romans 6:4-6). As a result, you no longer have the spirit of this world's kingdom indwelling you; instead, the Spirit of Christ the King now dwells in you (1 Corinthians 2:12; Romans 8:9). This is the miracle of our new birth: you are now a member of Christ's body, which is His church, the manifestation of His kingdom here on earth. The New Testament Greek word for church is *ekklesia,* which means assembly or congregation, and whose root meaning simply is "called out from." Therefore, the New Covenant church comprises all those people whom God has called out from the kingdom of this world to gather together in the name of the true and righteous King, Jesus Christ (Matthew 18:26).

The Bible uses several terms to describe Christ's church; for example, the city of God, the temple of the Spirit, and the body of Christ. However, the "bride of Christ" may best describe the divine relationship God desires the church to have with His Son and King. The Bible says that, as a husband loves his wife, Christ loved the church and gave His life for her, so that He might rescue her from the kingdom of darkness and "present to Himself a glorious church, having no spot or wrinkle or any such thing; but that she would be holy and blameless (Ephesians 5:25-7)." Jesus Christ is God the Savior King who came not only to die for His kingdom, but to reign over His kingdom (Philippians 2:8-11). And the Bible says the citizens of His kingdom are joint-heirs of the kingdom with the King Himself (Romans 8:17). Even more, Jesus Christ the King calls every faithful subject of His kingdom into a close personal friendship with Him. Jesus said, "You are My friends if you do what I command you. No longer do I call you servants, because a servant does not know his master's business. Instead, I have called you friends, for everything that I have learned from My Father I have made known to you (John 15:14-15)." Thus the Bible compares the spiritual union and intimate friendship that we are able to have with Christ our King to that of a marriage union between husband and wife (Ephesians 5:31-32).

Whereas everyone who is born of God belongs to His kingdom of light; everyone who is not born of God is still under Satan's rule and belongs to his kingdom of darkness (Ephesians 5:8). Jesus said those who are not born of God are children of the devil and are controlled by the devil (John 8:44). The Bible says, "Whoever practices sin is of the devil because the devil has sinned from the beginning. The Son of God appeared for this purpose, to destroy the devil's work (1 John 3:8)." Therefore, everyone who is not born of God already belongs to Babylon, but every Christian who is still governed by his natural *(psyche)* soul-life (instead of by the Holy Spirit) remains captive to Babylon. The Bible says that Babylon is a dwelling place for every kind of demonic spirit (Revelation 18:2). You may be born again, but if your soulish-life *(psychikos)* is not submitted to Christ's rule, it then becomes a psychic gateway to demonic deception, and you will be easily deceived and snared by Babylon's dark forces. And if you habitually seek comfort, companionship and fulfillment in Babylon, you are hostile to God's kingdom. James warned, "You adulterous people, don't you know that friendship with the world is hatred toward God? Anyone who chooses to be a friend of the world becomes an enemy of God (James 4:4)." The Bible says that if you do not act like a true citizen of the kingdom of heaven, then you are an enemy of the cross of Christ (Philippians 3:18-20). And Paul declared, "I warn you, as I did before, that those who live like this will not inherit the kingdom of God (Galatians 5:21)." Therefore, every child of God must choose whom they will serve – the new Jerusalem or the old Babylon!

Salvation is only the beginning and not the end of God's eternal purpose for His people. The power of Christ's gospel is intended to not only save us from Babylon; it is intended keep us (sanctify us) from ever returning to Babylon. On the eve of His crucifixion, Jesus prayed to His heavenly Father on behalf of His disciples, "I do not ask you to take them out of the world, but to keep them from the evil one. They are not of world, even as I am not of this world. Sanctify them in the truth; Your word is truth (John 17:15-17)." James warned God's people to keep themselves "unpolluted by the world (James 1:27)." John further wrote, "Do not love the world nor the things in the world. If anyone loves the world, the love of the Father is not in him. For all that is in the world, the lust of the flesh and the lust of the eyes and the boastful pride of life, is not from the Father, but is from the world (John 2:15-16)." And Paul exhorted, "No soldier in active service entangles himself in the affairs of everyday life, so that he may please his commanding officer (2 Timothy 2:4)." Many professing Christians say they want to avoid getting the mark of the Beast on their body, but tragically they already have the mark of Babylon on their soul.

Therefore, the bride of Christ comprises the new Jerusalem, the holy city of God, and the kingdom of God. In dark contrast, Babylon is the abominable city of Satan, the mother of harlots, and the kingdom of this world (Revelation 17 & 18). Jesus said, "Where your treasure is, there your heart will be also (Matthew 6:21)." Your heart cannot be divided between two cities – the new Jerusalem and the old Babylon. Jesus said, "Either you will hate the one and love the other, or you will be devoted to the one and despise the other (Matthew 6:21-24)." Yet many of God's people are not only doing business in Babylon, they are living in Babylon and loving Babylon. This is appalling, since God's intention was, by His Son's death, to rescue us from the kingdom of darkness and bring us into the kingdom of His beloved Son (Colossians 1:13). After we are saved, the Bible says that if we do not come completely out of Babylon, we will be judged with Babylon. The Bible foretells God's judgment of Babylon and those in Babylon: "Fallen, fallen is Babylon the great! She has become a dwelling place of demons and a prison of every unclean spirit... Come out of her, my people, so that you will not share in her sins and receive her plagues (Revelation 18:2-4)."

How can you escape the tentacles of Babylon and God's wrath to come? If you are a born again Christian, begin to believe and act on what Christ has accomplished for you on the cross. Only the cross of Christ can save you and deliver you from the kingdom of Babylon. The Bible says that when Christ was crucified, your sinful nature was not only crucified with Him; it was removed from you, so that Christ might sovereignly live in you (Romans 6:3-11; Galatians 2:20; Colossians 2:11-12). Therefore, the cross of Christ has fully delivered you from the power of Babylon. Since you no longer have a sinful nature, Babylon should no longer have any spiritual foothold in you. As Paul testified, "May I never boast except in the cross of the Lord Jesus Christ, through which the world has been crucified to me and I to the world (Galatians 6:14)." Babylon rules and corrupts every realm and sector of this world – politics, economics, culture and religion (Revelation 18:3). John said, "The whole world is under the control of the evil one (1 John 5:19)." Many Christians can see how the economics of greed, the national politics of ambition, and the secular culture of immorality are evil and belong to the kingdom of Babylon. But Satan, the god of this world, has blinded the minds of many Christians and prevented them from seeing how the false security of counterfeit Christianity (also known as Churchianity) is also evil and belongs to Babylon (2 Timothy 3:5). When Christians trust in their economic investments to save them, they are trusting in Babylon to save them. When Christians trust in their national politics to save them, they are trusting in Babylon to save them. And when Christians trust in their false church to save them, they are trusting in Babylon to save them. Whereas the true church is the faithful bride of Christ, the false church is the adulterous harlot of Satan. This is why every child of God must come out of the false church before God's judgment falls upon Babylon. "'Therefore, come out from their midst and be separate,' says the Lord... 'And I will be a Father to you, and you shall be sons and daughters to me (2 Corinthians 6:17-18).'"

The Bible says, "Our struggle is not against flesh and blood, but against the rulers, against the authorities, against the powers of this world darkness, against the spiritual forces of evil in the heavenly realms (Ephesians 6:11-12)." In other words, our struggle against the sin of this world is ultimately a spiritual battle of faith against the devil and his demonic forces. True spiritual warfare begins the day we are born again. Before we were saved, there was no need for the devil to wage spiritual warfare against us since we were already enslaved to him by our sinful nature. However, after we have been saved and freed from sin, the devil will wage full-on warfare to bring us back into captivity to sin and darkness. Motivated by his age old jealousy and hatred of God, the devil is engaged in a worldwide spiritual struggle to defeat God's divine purpose for His church, the bride of Christ. The Bible warns us: "Be on the alert. Your adversary, the devil, prowls around like a roaring lion seeking someone to devour. But resist him, standing firm in your faith (1 Peter 5:8-9)."

Satan's objective is to keep the billions of people on earth who are enslaved to sin from ever being freed by the gospel of Jesus Christ. Therefore, in his war against the saints, Satan's aim is to stop the church from fulfilling God's divine purpose as the bride of Christ, and thereby thwart the church from reaching the lost with the gospel of Christ. To achieve his goal, Satan pursues a three-pronged strategy: 1) The devil incites the unrighteous nations to persecute the church, with the aim of preventing the saints from fulfilling God's purpose (Matthew 24:9; Revelation 12:17; 13:7); 2) The devil entices Christians to become consumed with worldly political affairs, economic pursuits and cultural crusades, with the aim of distracting the saints from true obedience and single-minded devotion to our King and Lord, Jesus Christ (Luke 8:14; 1 John 2:15-17); and 3) The devil infiltrates the church with as many false Christians as possible, with the aim of compromising the church and seducing the saints into following a false and powerless gospel (Matthew 13:37-43; 1 John 2:18; Jude v. 4).

Since Satan can no longer control the saints who are born of God through their sinful nature (since it is now dead and gone), he has switched his tactics - the battleground is now our mind. The devil will try to attack our thought-life in order to ensnare us in unbelief and sin. How is it possible for us to resist the devil, that supernatural evil one, who seeks to deceive and destroy us with sin? The Bible says we cannot use natural weapons or our natural strength to overcome Satan and sin. Paul taught, "The weapons of our warfare are not natural, but divinely powerful to demolish strongholds. We cast down vain imaginations and every barrier of pride that exalts itself against the knowledge of God, and we take every thought captive to the obedience of Christ (2 Corinthians 10:4-5)." In other words, our mind needs to be continually renewed and fortified by the truth of God's Word, so that we are able to aggressively resist the devil and forcefully reject all sinful attitudes and fantasies that would try to ensnare us in sin. As John exhorted: "I write to you, young men, because you are strong, and the Word of God abides in you, and you have overcome the evil one (1 John 2:14)."

Jesus said, "Apart from Me you can do nothing (John 15:5)," and this includes overcoming our adversary, the devil. If overcoming Satan depended upon our own willpower, strength, self-discipline and religious methods, we would surely be defeated. Therefore, we must put no confidence in our own natural ability to overcome the enemy; instead, we must put our faith and confidence solely in our King, Jesus Christ, and His complete victory on the cross, which is the only basis upon which we can overcome the devil and the darkness and deception of sin (Galatians 3:3; 6:14; Philippians 3:3). Thank God that He has given us all the spiritual weapons we need to overcome the devil (2 Corinthians 6:7; 10:4). And thank God that He has given us guardian angels to assist and protect us in our spiritual struggle against the devil (Psalm 34:7; Hebrews 1:14).

In his battle plan to capture our minds, the devil usually employs three weapons: 1) Temptation (Matthew 4:3; 1 Thessalonians 3:5); 2) Deception (2 Corinthians 11:3; 2 Timothy 2:26); and 3) Accusation (1 Timothy 4:6; Revelation 12:10). However, the primary "weapon of mass destruction," which our enemy, the devil, will use against us in this spiritual battle of the mind is a combination of all three called the "Big Lie." What is the Big Lie? The Big Lie is the devil's constant, lying, slanderous accusation against the saints of God that they are still have a sinful nature and are hopelessly chronic sinners (John 8:44; Romans 8:33-34; Revelation 12:10). The New Testament Greek word for "the devil" means the slanderer or false accuser. What could be more slanderous than falsely accusing born again Christians that they still have an ungodly sinful nature within them that causes them to sin? In effect, the devil is slandering and falsely accusing God that His Son's sacrifice on the cross was not sufficient to free those who were captive to sin. The devil repeatedly uses this Big Lie to try to deceive, tempt and entrap us in sin. The devil also uses this Big Lie to accuse, discourage and condemn us after he has ensnared us in sin. As soon as you swallow this Big Lie, and come under the accusing lie and incessant condemnation that you are just a hopelessly chronic sinner, the devil has critically undermined your faith in the power of the blood of Christ. And if the devil can undermine your faith in Christ's triumph on the cross, he can then try to undermine your faith in Christ the King Himself. But thank God that Jesus Christ has given us the victory over the devil and sin. The Bible says, "Everyone who is born of God overcomes the world and this is the victory that has overcome the world – our faith. Who is the one who overcomes the world? The one who believes that Jesus is the Son of God (1 John 5:4-5)." As Paul wrote: "Thanks be to God, who gives us the victory through our

Lord Jesus Christ... thanks be to God, who always leads us in triumph in Christ... we overwhelmingly conquer through Him who loved us... (1 Corinthians 15:57; 2 Corinthians 2:14; Romans 8:37)."

Remember that our faith in Christ and His triumph on the cross must have corresponding action to be effective (James 2:18-26). Faith is not passive; if we want to overcome Satan and sin, our faith must be active and even forceful. Jesus said, "The kingdom of God is forcefully advancing, and forceful men take hold of it (Matthew 11:12)." Another Bible translation uses even stronger language: "The kingdom of God suffers violence, and violent men take it by force." It is not enough to just hear God's Word, but then not act on it. Jesus said, "Why do you call Me, Lord, Lord," and do not do what I say?... My brothers are those who hear God's Word and act on it (Luke 6:46-49; 8:21)." We must believe and forcefully act on God's Word; otherwise it will have no power in our lives. The Bible says, "For we also have had the gospel preached to us, just as they did; but the Word they heard was of no value to them, because those who heard it did not combine it with faith (Hebrew 4:2)."

It is by trusting in Christ our Commander and King that we are able to successfully battle and defeat our enemy, the devil. A picture of this kind of warfare can be found in the Old Testament. In 445 B.C., the prophet Nehemiah led God's people to rebuild the ruined walls of Jerusalem and restore the holy city (Nehemiah Chapters 1-4). However, the enemies of God tried to prevent them from rebuilding the holy city, by harassing the workers and threatening to attack them day and night. Consequently, Nehemiah gave the workers specific instructions that they should work with construction tools in one hand and weapons in the other, so they would be ready to battle their enemies whenever they were attacked. Nehemiah wrote, "From that time on, half of my men carried on the work, while the other half were equipped with spears, shields, bows, and armor... those who carried materials did their work with one hand and held a weapon in the other, and each of the builders wore his sword at his side as he worked (Nehemiah 4:16-18)." During this time of rebuilding, Nehemiah encouraged his co-workers with these words: "Our God will fight for us (Nehemiah 4:20)." What was the result? Nehemiah and his co-workers succeeded in rebuilding the city's walls and restoring the true worship of God to Jerusalem.

It should be the heart's desire of every Christian to rebuild God's city, His church. However, if we are serious about restoring the new Jerusalem, we must recognize our mission requires not just building the city of God, but also battling the enemies of God, those demonic forces that would try to stop the New Covenant church from being restored to God's glory and fulfill His divine purpose. Therefore, as soldiers of the cross in the army of God, we need to be spiritually vigilant and put on the armor of God, so that we can employ His shield of faith (the cross of Christ) and His sword of the Spirit (the Word of God) to repel the enemy's spiritual attacks against us and against our brothers and sisters in Christ (Ephesians 6:11-19; 1 John 2:14). As Paul instructed, "Put on the full armor of God so that you will be able to stand firm against the schemes of the devil… the night is nearly over; the day is almost here. So let us put aside the deeds of darkness and put on the armor of light ((Ephesian 6:11; Romans 13:12)." By putting on God's armor, every Christian can triumph over the devil and his kingdom of darkness and sin. However, in order for God's armor to protect us in battle, two actions are necessary. The first action required of us is to *repent*. Every soldier of Christ must repent from any deeds of darkness. The Bible warns us, "Do not give the devil a foothold (Ephesians 4:27)." Any Christian who continues to practice sin will have chinks or holes in his armor, and the enemy will use these openings to snare and defeat him. Peter warned, "Be on the alert. Your enemy the devil prowls around like a roaring lion looking around for someone to devour (1 Peter 5:8)."

Some Christians think they can practice sin every day but then quickly grab their armor when the spiritual battle gets intense. But if you have a habit of practicing sin, you will not be defensively ready when the enemy attacks you, and you will not then be able to take the spiritual offensive against the devil to free his prisoners who are held captive to sin. You will not have the faith to put on God's armor to protect and empower you during your time of greatest need in spiritual combat. We must practice righteousness every day by faith in the truth of the cross of Christ, so that we can wear God's armor and use His spiritual weapons to wage spiritual warfare. If we cannot defeat sin in our own daily life, how can we hope to rescue others held captive in sin by Satan? Carrying our cross daily is, therefore, our basic training for spiritual combat. John wrote, "God is light... if we walk in the light as He Himself is in the light... the blood of Jesus His Son purifies us from all sin (1 John 1:5-7)." The second action required of us as soldiers of Christ is to *believe*. Every Christian soldier must have complete faith in His Commander Jesus Christ who enlisted him into His service and given him His marching orders. Therefore, it is crucial for us to believe that God, through Jesus Christ, has already totally defeated the devil, the lord of darkness. The Bible says Christ completely disarmed Satan's forces of darkness and conquered sin and death when He triumphed over them through the cross (Colossians 2:16). The Bible says, "So that by His death, He (Christ) might destroy him who holds the power of death - that is, the devil – and free those who all their lives were held in slavery by their fear of death (Hebrews 2:14-15)." Therefore, when we wear God's armor of light, the devil cannot spiritual harm us and we do not have to fear any demonic power (Psalm 23; 1 John 5:18). As Paul instructed, "The Lord is faithful, and He will strengthen and protect you from the evil one (2 Thessalonians 3:3)." And the Bible assures us: "No weapon formed against you will succeed (Isaiah 54:17)."

All of the devil's weapons (temptation, deception, accusation, and the Big Lie) are feeble compared to the most powerful weapon in God's heavenly arsenal - the blood of Christ. The Bible says, "They *(the saints)* overcame him *(the devil)* by the blood of the Lamb and by the word of their testimony (Revelation 12:11)." The blood speaks of the totality of Christ's triumph on the cross, by which He completely destroyed Satan's power over us (Colossians 2:15; Hebrews 2:14; 1 John 3:8). Even though Satan still rules this world of sin, he has already been defeated and rendered powerless in the heavenly realm by Christ's death and resurrection. Jesus said, "The ruler of this world has already been judged and condemned (John 16:11)." Therefore, the blood of the Lamb is the basis for Babylon's defeat. For by His blood, Jesus Christ not only freed us from the penalty of sin, by forgiving us our sins (Ephesians 1:7; 1 John 1:7-9), He also freed us from the power of sin, by removing our sin nature (Romans 6:6-7; Colossians 2:11). Thus, by Christ's blood shed on the cross, God has decisively freed us from enslavement to sin and destroyed the devil's hold over us (Colossian 2:15; 1 John 3:8; Hebrews 2:14). By His death and resurrection, Jesus Christ has already conquered Satan, and stripped him of his authority and power. The Bible says, "When He (Jesus) had disarmed the rulers and authorities, He made a public spectacle of them, having triumphed over them through the cross (Colossians 2:15)." Consequently, after Jesus had risen from the dead, He declared, "*All authority* has been given to Me, in heaven and on earth (Matthew 18:28).

Jesus specifically instructed His disciples on the tactics of spiritual warfare: "If I cast our demons by the Spirit of God, then the kingdom of God has come upon you. Or how can anyone enter the strong man's house and carry off his possessions unless he first binds up the strong man? (Matthew 12:28)." There is a similar teaching by Jesus in Luke 11:20-23: "But if I cast our demons by the finger of God, then the kingdom of God has come upon you. When a strong man, fully armed, guards his own house, his possessions are secure. But when someone stronger than he attacks him and overpowers, he takes away from him all his armor on which he had relied and divides up his plunder. He who is not with Me is against Me; and he who does not gather with Me, scatters." In this parable, Satan is the armed strong man who closely guards all the souls who are his prisoners to sin. But Jesus, who is the One stronger than Satan, disarmed and defeated Satan by His death on the cross, so that those souls who were once held captive to sin can now be freed by the gospel of Christ. The Bible says, "Greater is He *(Christ)* who is in you, than he *(the devil)* who is in the world (1 John 4:4)." Jesus declared there is no neutral ground in the conflict between the kingdom of light and the kingdom of darkness. From the moment we are born again, we must choose whether to be on Christ's side, or on Satan's side. We either overcome Satan and sin by our faith in the cross of Christ, or we are overcome by Satan and sin as a result of our unbelief and disobedience to Christ the King.

Jesus further taught His disciples on spiritual warfare: "I will give you the keys of the kingdom of heaven; and whatever you bind on earth shall have been bound in heaven, and whatever you loose on earth shall have been loosed in heaven (Matthew 16:19)." What does this mean? This means that, by His triumph on the cross and His resurrection over death, Jesus Christ has already completely bound Satan's power in the heavenly realm, and He has now given His overcoming church the keys of the kingdom of heaven, so that they can exercise His authority on earth to bind the demonic forces of darkness and set captive souls free (see Luke 4:18 for Christ's mission and our commission). When we bind the enemy and set souls free who were captive to sin, it does not take away their individual free will to receive or reject Christ as Lord; however, it does set them free for a time from Satan's blinding deception and power, so they can have a God-appointed window of opportunity to freely make this life and death spiritual choice. By bringing God's heavenly rule into our earthly realm in this way through our Spirit-directed prayers, the New Covenant church fulfills Jesus' instruction on prayer: "Our Father who is in heaven, hallowed be Your name. Your kingdom come, your will be done, on earth as it is in heaven (Matthew 6:9-10)." John further taught on prayer: "This is the confidence which we have before Him, that if we ask anything according to His will, He hears us. And if we know that He hears us in whatever we ask, we know that we have the requests which we have asked from Him (1 John 4:14-15)." Therefore, when we pray Spirit-empowered prayers, the outcome is certain because we are praying according to God's will and power. Even if we do not see immediate outward results when we bind the devil and loose the souls of those who were held captive by him, we can have confidence in God's Word that our prayers have been answered. Paul exhorted, "With prayer and petition pray at all times in the Spirit. With this in mind, be on the alert and always keep on praying for all the saints (Ephesians 6:18)." When we obey Christ's command to wage persistent and aggressive intercessory prayer warfare on behalf of God's elect, we fulfill our divine destiny as knights in Christ's kingdom - priestly prayer warriors who execute His will on earth. For the Bible says, "He *(Christ)* has freed us from our sins by His blood and has made us to be a kingdom of priests to serve His God and Father (Revelation 1:5-6)."

The Bible says that when God crowned Jesus Christ with glory and honor and power, He put all things under Christ's feet (Hebrews 2:7-8; see also 2 Corinthians 15:25). Concerning Christ's absolute authority over Satan and his forces of darkness, Paul wrote, "God raised Christ from the dead and seated Him at His right hand in the heavenly realm, far above all rule and authority and power and dominion, and every name that is named, not only in the present age but in the age to come. And God put all things in subjection under His feet, and appointed Him to be the head over everything in the church (Ephesians 1:20-22)." Yet, the Bible also says, "At the present time, we do not see all things put under His feet (Hebrews 2:8)." Once again, this means that Christ has already put Satan under His feet by His triumph on the cross, and it is now up to the New Covenant church, His bride, to exercise Christ's authority and crush the devil's demonic forces under our feet. Jesus told His disciples: "I saw Satan fall like lightening from heaven. I have given you authority to tread on *(put under your feet)* snakes and scorpions *(demonic spirits),* and to overcome all the power of the enemy, and nothing will harm you (Luke 10:18-19)." Just as Jesus Christ defeated the devil during the trial in the wilderness by testifying to the truth of God's Word (Luke 4:1-14), we can also "fight the good fight of faith (1 Timothy 6:12)" to overcome the devil's attacks by testifying to the truth of God's Word, and also reminding our fellow saints of this truth. And this is that divine truth: through the cross of Christ, God removed our sinful nature when we were saved, so that His Son's Spirit of truth, holiness and power would dwell in us, and enable us by faith to overcome Satan and sin (Romans 6:1-11; Galatians 2:20; 4:6; Colossians 2:11; 2 Timothy 1:7). Therefore, when we carry our own cross daily and "put down" all sinful thoughts and passions that would try to stop us from accomplishing God's will, we "put under our feet" the enemies of God. This is why learning to overcome all compromising sins in our lives by faith in the cross of Christ is essential training in spiritual warfare. When we overcome Satan and sin in our individual lives in this way, and then help free others who have been held captive to sin, we take possession of the Promised Land - the kingdom of God, which is our divine inheritance, purchased for us by the blood of Christ. When we walk in the fullness of Christ's power and authority, the kingdom of God will be openly manifested in this world as we heal the sick and deliver those oppressed by the devil (Acts 10:38). For Jesus gave His disciples "power and authority to drive out all demons and heal diseases, and He sent them out to proclaim the kingdom of God and to heal the sick (Luke 9:1-2)."

In closing, the bride of Christ who crushes Satan under her feet wears the full armor of God under her wedding dress (Ephesians 6:10-17). When

Christ's warrior bride uses the power of the blood in spiritual warfare, she goes "nuclear" against Satan. When Satan accuses Christ's bride of failing God (Revelation 12:10), she stops his lies with the shield of faith and proclaims she is under no condemnation because of the blood of Christ (Romans 8:1; 33-34). When Satan tempts Christ's bride to love (and not lose) her natural soul-life (John 12:25), she uses the sword of the Spirit to make him flee and proclaims she has died to the world because of the blood of Christ (Galatians 6:14). The bride who overcomes Satan believes and acts on the divine truth that she has died with Christ and no longer has a sinful nature, and she is full of the Spirit and testimony of Jesus Christ, her Bridegroom (Matthew 25:1-13).

In the final spiritual conflict of this age, a great persecution will come upon the church. The Bible says the bride of overcomers who triumph over Satan during this time of intense spiritual warfare will have one distinguishing mark: "They loved not their lives" when faced with death (Revelation 12:11). This indicates true Christians will die in this final conflict between the two kingdoms rather than forsake their bold testimony of Christ. It also indicates the final test of our faith in this end-time persecution will be our willingness to lose our lives for Christ our King's sake. This is the bride who will conquer Satan by the blood of the Lamb and the word of her testimony, who does not love her natural life, even when faced with death. Jesus gave this prophetic promise to His overcoming bride: "I am coming soon. Hold on to what you have so that no one will take your crown. He who overcomes, I will make a pillar in the temple of My God and he will never leave it. I will write on him the name of My God, and the name of the city of My God, the new Jerusalem which is coming down out of heaven from My God (Revelation 3:11-12)." At the end of this age, we will see the final victory of God over evil when Jesus Christ returns as the King of kings on His white war horse, with His conquering bride and avenging army of angels, and casts Satan and his demonic forces into the eternal lake of fire (Revelation 19:11-21; 20:10). The apostle John heralded the certainty of this crowning triumph of Christ: "Now have come the salvation and the power and the kingdom of our God, and the authority of His Christ. For the accuser of our brothers, who accuses them before God day and night, has been thrown down... the kingdom of this world has become the kingdom of our Lord and His Christ, and He will reign forever and ever (Revelation 12:10; 11:15)."

How to Walk in True Holiness

21 Many Christians confuse legalism with any Bible teaching that emphasizes holiness, which simply means obedience to Christ. However, this is only true if the obedience that is taught is the obedience of the flesh; that is, the obedience that comes from trying to act moral by our own natural willpower and self-discipline. Biblical obedience, on the other hand, is the obedience which comes from acting solely by faith in God's grace. Paul declared that the gospel of grace was intended to bring us into "the obedience of faith" (Romans 1:5; 16:19). The New Testament contains dozens of verses which clearly address our obligation to obey God. For example, John the Baptist said, "He who does not obey the Son will not see life, but the wrath of God abides on him (John 3:34)." Jesus Himself said, "If anyone loves Me, he will obey My teaching... he who does not love Me will not obey My teaching (John 14:23; see also John 3:36; Romans 6:16; 2 Corinthians 10:5; Hebrews 5:9; 1 Peter 1:22)." We need to re-member that God never intended that His New Covenant grace would be used as an excuse for disobedience and sin. Paul exhorted, "What shall we

say then? Are we to continue in sin so that grace may increase? May it never be! (Romans 6:1-2)." God never intended that His New Covenant grace would nullify His requirement for us to live holy and obedient lives.

Therefore, if we do not preach and practice holiness, we are not fulfilling the whole purpose of God. If we reject holiness, we reject the apostle Paul's instruction: "Let us purify ourselves from everything that contaminates body and spirit, perfecting holiness in the fear of God (2 Corinthians 7:1)." If we reject holiness, we reject the apostle Peter's teaching: "Like the Holy One who called you, be holy yourselves in all your behavior (1 Peter 1:15)." If we reject holiness, we reject the apostle John's instruction: "No one who abides in Him keeps on sinning. No one who continues to sin has either seen Him or knows Him (1 John 3:6)." If we reject holiness, we reject God Himself. The Bible says, "God did not call us to be impure, but to live a holy life. Therefore, he who rejects this instruction does not reject man but God, who gives you His Holy Spirit (1 Thessalonians 4:7-8)."

The Bible commands us to "pursue... holiness, for without holiness no one will see the Lord (Hebrews 12:14)." However, most Christians who zealously pursue holiness lack a sound Biblical knowledge of how to practice holiness. In the words of Paul: "I testify of them that they have a zeal for God, but their zeal is not based on knowledge. Since they do not know about the righteousness that comes from God and are seeking to establish their own, they did not submit themselves to the righteousness of God (Romans 10:2-3)." A common error of many Christians is to practice some form of religious legalism, but mistake it for the practice of righteousness. Since legalism is performance-based and not faith-based, it is only natural that when you perform well (according to your standard of righteousness) you will feel good or righteous; but when you perform badly, you will feel bad or unrighteous. It is also natural that you will feel resentful and angry towards other Christians who are not trying as hard to perform and behave according to your standard of righteousness.

Before we go on, we need to better define legalism. Legalism is the systematic attempt to please God by your own works rather than relying by faith solely on what Jesus Christ accomplished on the cross. The practice of legalism (in its many forms) may not only rely on self-effort to be justified and saved; it can also rely on self-effort to walk in sanctification and live holy. For example, a person may be rightly saved by faith, but then wrongly practice legalism to live the Christian life (Galatians 3:3). We might also call the practice of legalism "moralism," since it produces an outward "moral" behavior, instead of a heart that has been inwardly and authentically transformed by faith. Whenever Christians practice legalism or moralism instead of faith, they cut themselves off from God's grace (Galatians 5:4). Since legalism or moralism is not of faith, it is sin (Romans 14:23). In fact, legalism or moralism can be a religious cloak for lawlessness. That is why Jesus exposed the Pharisees, who practiced moralism, for their lawlessness. "So you, too, outwardly appear righteous to men, but inwardly you are full of hypocrisy and lawlessness (Matthew 23:28)." Just as the Pharisees practiced a counterfeit Judaism; whenever professing "Christians" practice moralism, they are practicing a counterfeit Christianity.

Legalism and grace are in direct opposition to one another. Legalism means you must do something to obtain God's righteousness; whereas grace means God did something to impute righteousness to you, which you then receive by faith. Therefore, God's righteousness (based on grace) depends on our faith in Christ's completed work on the cross; whereas man's righteousness (based on legalism) depends on our natural willpower and self-effort. Legalism and grace are mutually exclusive. You cannot be under grace and practice legalism at the same time. If you are practicing legalism, then you are not under grace. Paul warned, "Are you so foolish? After beginning by the Spirit, are you now trying to attain your goal by your human effort?... You have been severed from Christ... you have fallen from grace (Galatians 3:3; 5:4)."

Legalism is also the erroneous belief that if you follow religious rules and regulations, you will be righteous in God's eyes. Paul warned believers against the futility of religious legalism in Colossians 2:20-23: "Since you died with Christ to the basic principles of the world... why do you submit to its rules?... Such practices have the appearance of wisdom with their self-imposed religion, false humility and ascetic discipline, but they have no value in restraining sinful desires." For example, legalism is the false belief that if you follow certain rules (such as attending church twice a week and tithing ten percent of your income to the church), you will be righteous in God's eyes. Or, if you are a more serious-minded Christian who is concerned about practicing inward holiness and not just outwardly following so-called "Christian" rules, then legalism is trying your best to practice a strict "moral" lifestyle and devoting yourself to following Christian disciplines, such as Bible reading, witnessing, prayer and fasting, and acts of service. Thus, legalism is the religion of "always trying harder."

Some Christians also mistakenly believe that the way to overcome sin is to immerse yourself in ministry activities. Their rationale is that if you are busily employed doing the work of ministry, you are unavailable for the devil's work. Under this misguided philosophy, the more you are tempted by sin, the more time and energy you should devote to ministry. However, this is religious legalism since it depends on your work (instead of your faith in Christ's completed work on the cross) to walk in holiness. Using "ministry" in this carnal way to overcome sin is guaranteed to produce spiritual self-deception and either self-pride or spiritual burn-out. In other words, all of your man-made religious attempts at trying harder to live a holy Christian life cannot stop you from practicing sin. Since these religious practices and disciplines (however well-intended) do not spring from faith in the truth of the cross and the sanctifying work of the Holy Spirit, they are a complete waste of effort, spiritually worthless, and even spiritually dangerous. God's righteousness is never credited to anyone based on rule-keeping and outward religious moralism. Ultimately, the root of legalism is self-righteousness. It is the sin of pride to think "I have the moral ability to successfully live the Christian life and please God, whereas other Christians who cannot are morally inferior."

Yet, God does expect us to live holy lives that are set apart and wholly devoted to Him so that we might truly know Him (2 Timothy 2:21; Hebrews 12:14), and so that we might shine as lights in this world (Philippians 2:15). However, many Christians have been "burned" by legalistic teaching that exhorts them to live holy lives by using more will-power and trying harder (read your Bible more, pray more, go to church more, get involved in ministry more, etc.). In spite of these bad experiences and erroneous teachings, we must be very careful not to reject the truth concerning holiness. If you have been "burned" by this kind of false teaching on holiness, the soulish tendency is to either reject God's standard of holiness and succumb to worldliness (the lust of the flesh, the lust of the eyes and the boastful pride of life) because holiness seems impossible or, perhaps even worse, inwardly continue to practice lawlessness, but become more and more outwardly religious and ministry-minded.

Jesus condemned religious legalism and warned that people who practiced it "trusted in their own righteousness and regarded others with contempt (Luke 18:9; see also Romans 14:10)." If we continue down the spiritually suffocating path of legalism and are honest with ourselves, we will eventually "look in the mirror" and face the awful realization that we have become an uptight and miserable Christian. At this point, we may have the following reaction: we may "let go" of trying so hard to be holy and yet continue going to church, but settle for a much lower (and carnal) standard of holiness, which is often expressed as: "we are all sinners like everyone else, the only difference is that we are forgiven." In effect, we may give up trying to be holy since holiness seems impossible. But then, does God really expect us to stop practicing sin and be holy? Most certainly! Did not Jesus say, "Go and sin no more (John 5:17; 8:11)?" And did not Paul say, "Come back to your senses as you should, and stop sinning (1 Corinthians 15:34)?" And did not Peter say, "Like the Holy One who called you, be holy in all your behavior (1 Peter 1:15)?"

Many professing Christians who practice legalism or moralism may outwardly appear to be more "perfect" than Christians who practice true faith. However, God does not judge according to men's outward appearances of "morality," but according to the motives and attitudes of men's hearts (John 7:24; 2 Corinthians 5:12; Hebrews 4:12-13). Jesus said, "You are those who justify yourselves in the sight of men, but God knows your hearts; for that which is highly esteemed among men is detestable in the sight of God (Luke 16:15)." In the New Testament, the Greek word for "perfect" is *teleios,* which does not mean faultless behavior; instead, it means complete or fully mature. With this in mind, Paul wrote, "We proclaim Him, admonishing and teaching everyone with all wisdom, so that we may present everyone perfect *(fully mature)* in Christ (Colossians 1:28)." In other words, God does not expect us to be perfect in the sense of flawless or sinless; however, God does expect us to practice a pattern (the Greek word is *typos*) or lifestyle of faith that progressively leads to spiritual maturity (Philippians 4:9; 2 Peter 1:10). Theologically, this is called "progressive sanctification." To this end, Paul exhorted, "Brethren, join in following my example and observe those who walk according to the pattern *(typos)* you have in us (Philippians 3:17)." Practicing a pattern or lifestyle of faith is what the Bible also calls practicing the righteousness that is by faith (Roman 1:17). John taught, "You know that everyone who practices righteousness is born of Him (1 John 2:29)." In God's eyes, it is better to have an authentic but "imperfect" life based on a small amount of true faith (Matthew 17:20) than to have the appearance of an outwardly "perfect" life based on a great amount of willpower and natural self-discipline (Matthew 23:27-28). The Bible says, "We have this treasure in jars of clay to show that this all-surpassing power is from God and not from us (2 Corinthians 4:7)."

If our life is based on faith in Christ's work on the cross, our deeds will be credited to us as righteousness and we will have God's approval. However, if our life is based on our natural willpower, our deeds will not be credited to us as righteousness and we will not have God's approval. When we practice legalism or moralism, Christianity becomes just a Biblical behavioral code that we try to follow by our best efforts rather than believing that Jesus Christ can live His life in us. The true child of God hates legalism because he sees it as an endless row of unscalable mountains that he must try to climb in vain; whereas the self-righteous person loves legalism because he sees it as a daily opportunity to take pride in his efforts to climb the "mountains of morality." The antidote to sin is not to redouble our self-efforts to live godly. The only true antidote to sin is to repent from unbelief and then believe and act on Christ's completed work on the cross. The fruit of legalism is secret pride, religious hypocrisy, and further bondage to sin; whereas the fruit of faithful obedience to Christ is humility, true holiness, and freedom from sin. If we are practicing legalism or moralism, we are still slaves to sin and cut off from God's grace. However, if we are practicing the righteousness that comes solely by faith in the cross of Christ, we have been freed from sin and will receive the eternal riches of our inheritance in Him (Romans 6:22). This is the difference between practicing the God-given righteousness that comes only from faith, and practicing the man-made religious legalism and false "morality" that comes from natural willpower and self-effort. The former is true Christianity, whereas the latter is a counterfeit Christianity, which is appropriately called Churchianity because it is not centered on true faith in Christ.

There are actually two wayward extremes that every Christian should avoid in trying to live an authentic Christian life, which above all is a holy life. We have already discussed religious legalism, which is the first extreme. The second extreme is licentiousness. Both extremes are carnal in nature and both stem from ignorance and unbelief about what Jesus Christ has accomplished for us by His death on the cross. Licentiousness is a lack of godly self-control, which leads to unrestrained worldly excess. The word licentiousness is derived from the same Greek root word for license. In other words, licentiousness misuses God's grace as a license to practice sin. As Paul warned, "Shall we sin because we are not under law but under grace? May it never be!... Do not use your freedom as a license to gratify sinful desires... for the grace of God that brings salvation has appeared to all men, training us to deny ungodliness and worldly passions and to live sober-minded, upright and godly lives in this present age (Romans 6:15; Galatians 5:13; Titus 2:11-12)." Although licentiousness is often associated with sexual immorality, it can also mean the excessive pursuit of any worldly pleasures. Any Christian who continues to misuse God's grace as a license to sin will inevitably fall into some form of licentiousness.

The Bible uses the term "dissipation" to describe the fruit of licentiousness (see Luke 21:34; Ephesians 5:18; 1 Peter 4:3-4; Titus 1:6). From a Biblical perspective, dissipation means squandering and wasting your life on worthless worldly things (such as accumulating riches and indulging in sinful and sensual pleasures); things which the world sometimes perversely calls the "good life." Jesus warned His disciples about the danger of falling into licentiousness: "These are the ones who have heard (the Word of God), and as they go on their way they are choked with worries and riches and pleasures of this life, and bring no fruit to maturity (Luke 8:14)." The Bible says that people who live for earthly pleasure are "spiritually dead," even though they are still physically alive (1 Timothy 5:6). Christians who practice licentiousness usually have a false concept of grace. They believe that God's grace is inexhaustible and covers all their present and future sinful actions, even if they live a life of faithlessness and routinely practice sin in its various forms. This is dead wrong! This is "cheap grace," which is not God's grace at all! The Bible warns us to beware of "ungodly persons who turn the grace of our God into licentiousness (Jude 4)."

The problem of legalism and licentiousness is not new. Back in the first century, the Galatian church fell into legalism and the Corinthian church fell into licentiousness. Both churches had to be rebuked and exhorted to turn back to the straight and narrow path of devoted obedience to the Lord Jesus Christ (Galatians 1:6-9; 5:4-11; 2 Corinthians 11:1-4; 12:20-21)." Since both legalism and licentiousness stem from unbelief and disobedience to God's truth, both are an expression of ungodly lawlessness (legalism is lawlessness with a religious mask). Of course, not all Christians wander so far down the path of legalism or licentiousness that they become spiritually crippled by the rigid straitjacket of legalism or morally bankrupted by the worldly pleasures of licentiousness. Yet the tragic reality is that many sincere Christians spend their lives wandering back and forth between varying degrees of legalism and licentiousness (to what degree depends on their natural inclinations) without ever finding the way of true holiness in Jesus Christ. As one sad believer on this frustrating journey lamented, "Am I condemned to living a life of no victory over sin?"

Now that we have examined the problem of legalism and licentiousness, let us look at God's remedy for dealing with the true root of our dilemma, which is sin-sickness. The only antidote for sin-sickness is the cross of Christ. According to the gospel, Christ not only died to free us from the *penalty* of sin, He also died to free us from the *power* of sin. When we were saved, God spiritually immersed us into Christ's death to remove our sinful nature so that we would no longer be captive to sin. Paul taught, "Do you not know that all of us who have been baptized *(immersed)* into Christ Jesus have been baptized *(immersed)* into His death?... For we know that our old self was crucified with Him, in order that our body of sin *(our sinful nature)* might be done away with, so that we would no longer be slaves to sin. For he who has died has been freed from sin (Romans 6:3, 6-7; see also Colossians 2:11-12)." Thus, when we were born again, God removed our sinful nature, so that Christ could sovereignly live in us (Colossians 1:27). But after we have experienced this great salvation and freedom from sin, we must be careful to avoid the extremes of either legalism or licentiousness as we pursue God's path of righteousness and holiness.

Why is it so common for many sincere Christians to fall into thinking (after Jesus has saved them) that they need to try hard to sanctify themselves and live a holy life? One reason is that we still have an unrenewed mind after we are saved. Although we no longer have an Adam sinful nature (because God removed it when we were born again), we still have an old Adam way of thinking (an unrenewed mind). Our unrenewed mind needs to be transformed according to the truth of God's Word, particularly the truth that we no longer have a sinful nature and Christ now lives in us (Romans 6:1-7; 2 Corinthians 13:5). Until our faith is firmly established in this divine truth, we will fall into the same old sinful patterns of thinking and acting. Because of our unrenewed mind, we can have a natural, ingrained tendency to erroneously believe that we are capable of living a sanctified or holy life if we only apply more natural self-discipline and try harder. Even after the Holy Spirit gives us divine revelation that only faith in Christ's death on the cross can possibly grant us freedom from the power of sin, our natural habit (especially when we are tired, tempted, stressed, sick, or in pain) can be to fall back on our own strength to try to overcome sin. However, that is precisely the time for us to resist this natural urge and the temptation to use our willpower to try harder to resist sin. Instead, we can (and should) overcome the sins that easily entangled us in the past by standing firm on the sure foundation of faith that we are "dead to sin but alive to God in Christ Jesus (Romans 6:11)." This is how (inch-by-inch and day-by-day) we overcome the "giants" of sin that would stop us from taking God's Promised Land, which is our spiritual inheritance in Christ.

The work of God never changes – it is always the work of faith. Jesus said, "This is the work of God – that you believe in Him whom He has sent (John 6:29)." Since Christ has already delivered us from our sinful nature and sin's domination over us, our "work of faith" is to keep our eyes fixed each day on Jesus Christ and His finished work on the cross. Whenever we step out of God's work of faith and enter into our own self-effort, we take the burden for our sanctification out of God's hands and put it in our own hands. This act of unbelief prevents God from doing the sanctifying work of the Spirit in us that comes only from believing and acting on the divine truth that we no longer have a sinful nature and Christ now lives in us (Galatians 2:20). It also produces ungodly anxiety and stress since we have decided (in unbelief) that the work of God now depends on our own work instead of Christ working in us. This yoke of unbelief is an awful burden to bear. The Bible calls it "the yoke of slavery." As Paul exhorted, "It was for freedom that Christ has set us free. Stand firm, then, and do not let yourselves be burdened again by a yoke of slavery (Galatians 5:1)." This oppressive yoke of unbelief and legalism is in marked contrast to Jesus' yoke of faith and discipleship. For Jesus said, "Come to Me, all who are weary and heavy-laden, and I will give you rest. Take My yoke upon you… My yoke is easy and My burden is light (Matthew 11:28-30)."

It is important to remember that faith is always active – not passive. As Paul said, "Fight the good fight of faith (1 Timothy 6:12)." We cannot just forget about what Jesus has done on the cross and then expect God to transform us. Many Christians have drifted away from the faith and into licentiousness because they unwisely practiced this kind of "passive faith," which is really not faith at all. True faith believes and acts on the divine facts. Jesus said, "My brothers are those who hear God's Word and act on it (Luke 8:21)." If we never acted on our belief that Jesus Christ, the Son of God, died on the cross for our sins, we would never be saved. In the same way, if we do not act on our belief that God, through Christ's death on the cross, has removed our sinful nature to free us from sin's bondage, we will never experience true freedom from chronic, entangling sins.

It is also important to remember that God wants us to have His joy as we pursue a life of holiness in Him. The Bible says that in God we can have the fullness of His joy (Psalm 16:11). And Jesus said, "These things I have spoken to you so that My joy may be in you, and that your joy may be made full (John 15:11)." Indeed, the Bible contains over 450 Scriptural references to joy (and its various forms - joyful, joyous, rejoice etc.). If God can make the sunrise and sunset shout for joy, and the mountains and the trees sing for joy, surely He can fill us – His children - with His joy (Psalm 65:8; 96:12; 98:8; John 16:22). However, in order for us to have the joy of the Lord, we need to stand firm by faith in the spiritual freedom that Jesus Christ has purchased for us by His death on the cross. What greater joy can there be than for us to know (after we are born again) that God has removed our sinful nature and replaced it with His Son's nature, so we might truly know Him and serve Him? Whenever we find that we have lost the joy of the Lord, it is a red flag warning us we have stepped out of this place of faith. Whenever we find ourselves afraid and overcome by sin, it is a sure sign that we have wandered off the path of true holiness and spiritual joy found only in Christ. Whenever we are overwhelmed by a sense of failure, it reveals we are trying to sanctify ourselves in our own strength instead of fixing our eyes on Jesus Christ and the freedom from sin that He has given us by His death on the cross.

Whenever we become angry and merciless with ourselves and with others, it is an indication that we have come under the heavy yoke of legalism and stepped out of the yoke of faith and joy and rest in Christ. Christ's yoke of discipleship is easy if we are really living by faith, and where the Spirit of the Lord is, there is spiritual liberty and joy and mercy; not legalism and carnal severity. "Now the Lord is the Spirit, and where the Spirit of the Lord is, there is liberty (2 Corinthians 3:17)." We cannot sanctify ourselves apart from faith in the cross of Christ, nor can we sanctify others; only Christ can accomplish His sanctification by living in us through His Spirit. Therefore, we must remember to always stand firm by faith in Christ and His completed work on the cross, by which He has given us His joy and liberty. This is the spiritual joy and true freedom (from legalism and licentiousness) that comes from wholeheartedly submitting to Christ's Lordship and the truth of His Word (see John 8:31-36).

What do we do if we find we have taken a wrong turn off the road to holiness and wandered down the path of legalism or licentiousness? There is no condemnation for those who belong to Jesus Christ. We simply turn around (repent), ask God to restore the joy of our salvation, and go back to fixing our eyes on Jesus Christ and what He has done for us on the cross. As we abide (remain united by faith) in Christ and His Word, the truth of the cross will light the way of holiness for us (Psalm 119:105). And this is that truth: Christ died for us and included us in His death (to remove our sinful nature), so that He could sovereignly live in us. If we believe and act on this divine truth, we will walk on God's straight and narrow way of holiness, and we will avoid falling into the ditch of either legalism or licentiousness. By faith in Christ's triumph on the cross, we will walk on God's holy road that leads to eternal life

(Romans 6:22), and experience God's righteousness and joy in this present life. "For the kingdom of God is... righteousness and peace and joy in the Holy Spirit (Romans 14:17)."

WHO IS THE FAMILY OF GOD?

22 The desire to belong to a family is a deep need in every person. When we are born again of the Spirit, this desire and expectation is intensified now that we belong to the family of God. Unfortunately, for many sincere Christians, their yearning to have fellowship with a loving and godly church family will not be met, and some will even have their hopes completely devastated. Why does this happen? It will help if we understand what the Bible says about Christian fellowship. The New Testament Greek the word for fellowship is *koinonia,* which also means communion or community. Within its Biblical context, *koinonia* fellowship means more than our just having a form of *social* community with other Christians, it also means our having *spiritual* communion with other Christians, based on our mutual spiritual communion with Christ. To this end, the apostle John said, "We proclaim to you what we have seen and heard, so that you also may have *fellowship* with us. And our *fellowship* is with the Father and with His Son, Jesus Christ... God is light, and in Him there is no darkness at all. If we claim to have *fellowship* with Him yet walk in the darkness, we lie and do not live by the truth. But if we walk in the light as He is in the light, we have *fellowship* with one another (1 John 1:3, 5-7)."

Some Christians mistakenly think that you can have spiritual fellowship with any person who is saved and has God's Spirit indwelling them. But the Bible says that is only true if that person is practicing righteousness that is based on faith. If that Christian is practicing unrighteousness (unrepentant sin), then they are walking in darkness and rebellion to God's Spirit, and it not possible to have spiritual fellowship with them (1 Corinthians 5:11). The Bible is clear that we can only have spiritual fellowship with other Christians who practice righteousness and do not practice sin. John wrote, "No one who abides in Him keeps on sinning. No one who continues to sin has seen Him or knows Him... by this the children of God and the children of the devil are obvious: anyone who does not practice righteousness is not of God (1 John 3:6, 10)." Of course, none of us should expect to find a perfect church of sinless Christians with whom we can have fellowship, but we should expect to belong to an authentic church that is growing in the grace and truth of our Lord Jesus Christ, the love of God, and the fellowship of the Holy Spirit.

Since only those Christians who practice righteousness are genuine believers with whom we can experience true spiritual fellowship, we must examine ourselves: "How can we practice righteousness that comes by faith so that we can have fellowship with God and with His people who also practice this kind righteousness?" Once again, the Bible is clear: we can only practice righteousness if we have been freed from sin's power (Romans 6:18). And how can we be freed from sin's power? The Bible says we were freed from sin's power when we died to sin (Romans 6:7). But when did we die to sin? The Bible says we died to sin when we were born again and our sinful nature died and was removed from us (Romans 6:6; Colossians 2:11). Therefore, if you believe and act on this Biblical truth, you are able to practice the righteousness that is based on faith, and have spiritual fellowship with other Christians of the same faith (Philippians 3:9).

Just as there is only one door to enter into salvation, there is only one door to walk in the way of sanctification and righteousness: believing in the Lord Jesus Christ and His finished work on the cross. There is no other way to practice righteousness that is based on faith. Anyone who tries to practice righteousness by any other way is unbelieving and disobedient to the Word of God. Instead of submitting themselves to God's righteousness, they are practicing a false righteousness and a counterfeit Christianity. They may outwardly appear righteous to men, but they are lawless and full of hypocrisy on the inside. They have a different faith (really a false faith), a different gospel, a different spirit, and a different Jesus. Is it any wonder that when true Christians try to fellowship with unbelieving "Christians," they may be attacked by Satan? Of such unbelieving "Christians," the Bible warns: "Do not be yoked together with unbelievers, for what partnership has righteousness with lawlessness or what fellowship can light have with darkness? Or what harmony has Christ with the devil?" (2 Corinthians 6:14-15) This is why true Christians will often encounter rejection, hostility and persecution if they try to fellowship with false Christians who do not practice true righteousness based on faith in the cross of Christ.

Jesus said that in the Day of Judgment there would be many people who claim to be Christians and profess that He is their Lord, but God will not allow them into His family because they did not practice God's righteousness that is based on faith (Matthew 7:21-23). The Bible says that in these last days many people will practice an outward form of Christianity, but their lives will deny the power of Christ's crucifixion and resurrection. The Bible warns us not to try to have any fellowship with such people (2 Timothy 3:5). When a church is filled with this kind of false Christians, it is a false church. It does not matter whether you belong to a house church or a mega church, if it is filled with false Christians, it is a false church and you must get out! Jesus said, "When the Son of Man comes, will He find faith on the earth? (Luke 18:8)." This would indicate, that when Jesus returns, there will be very few real Christians who are actually practicing

God's righteousness that is based on faith in the truth of the cross of Christ, compared to the multitudes of imposters who are practicing a different kind of faith, which really is not faith at all.

In closing, who is the family of God? Who are our true brothers and sisters in Christ? The Bible says, "Both He *(Jesus)* who makes men holy and those who are made holy are of the same family. So Jesus is not ashamed to call them brothers (Hebrews 2:11." And Jesus said, "Whoever does the will of My Father in heaven is My brother and sister (Matthew 12:48)." Although God has called many to salvation, it is only those few who, after being saved, do the will of God and practice true righteousness and holiness based on faith who are chosen worthy to belong to His heavenly family (Matthew 22:14; 1 John 2:15-17). In these last days, it is far better to go outside the camp of counterfeit Christians and suffer loneliness and reproach with Christ, than to belong to a false church and have fake fellowship with fake Christians (Hebrews 13:5). And if our heart's desire for true *koinonia* fellowship with the family of God is not met until the age to come, we can be more than content today with our fellowship with the Father and with His Son Jesus Christ. The Bible says, "How great is the love the Father has lavished on us, that we would be called children of God! And that is who we are!" (1 John 3:1)

THE COMING TRIBULATION

23 May 14th, 1948 was an extraordinary date in terms of fulfilling end-time Bible prophecy. On that day, the house of Israel was reborn as a sovereign nation after nearly two thousand years of exile from their homeland. The rebirth and resettlement of Israel as a nation was the

realization of a remarkable vision that God gave the prophet Ezekiel over twenty-six centuries ago around 571 B.C. (Ezekiel Chapters 34-37). God's vision to Ezekiel actually contained two distinct provisions. God first showed Ezekiel that Israel would be restored to her land: "I will bring them out from the nations and gather them from the countries, and I will bring them into their own land... I will take the sons of Israel and from among the nations where they have gone, and I will gather them from all around and bring them back into their own land. I will make them one nation in the land... and they will no longer be two nations (*Judah and Ephraim*) and no longer be divided into two kingdoms (Ezekiel 34:13; 37:21-22)." However, God also showed Ezekiel that Israel would be restored to her God and Messiah: "I will give you a new heart and put a new spirit within you; and I will remove the heart of stone from you and give you a heart of flesh. I will put My Spirit within you and cause you to walk in My statutes, and you will be careful to obey My laws... I will save them from all their sinful backsliding and I will cleanse them. They will be My people, and I will be their God. My servant David will be king over them, and they will all have one shepherd (Ezekiel 36:26-27; 37:23-24)." In this Old Testament Scripture, David's kingship prophetically foreshadowed the reign of Jesus the Messiah King, who is David's descendent. In the same way, the old city of Jerusalem was a shadow and symbol of the heavenly Jerusalem and Christ's kingdom. Jerusalem was called the city of David since within its walls were the throne of David and the tabernacle of David. For King David not only made Jerusalem the royal city from which he ruled; he also made it the holy city by installing God's Ark of the Covenant on Mount Zion in Jerusalem. The Bible says that Jesus the Messiah King is the fulfillment of God's covenant with David (Isaiah 9:7; Luke 1:31-33). For the throne of David foreshadowed Christ's Sovereignty over His church and the tabernacle of David foreshadowed Christ's Presence in His church. The Bible says, "God placed all things under His (*Christ's*) feet and appointed

Him to be head over everything for the church, which is His body, the fullness of Him who fills all in all (Ephesians 1:22-23).

The first fulfillment of Ezekiel's vision occurred on May 14, 1948 with the physical restoration of the Jewish people back to their land as a sovereign nation for the first time since A.D. 70; and as a united nation for the first time since 961 B.C. when Israel was divided into two kingdoms - Ephraim and Judah. However, the second fulfillment of Ezekiel's vision (the spiritual restoration of the Jewish people to God and His Messiah) has still to occur. Yet this will undoubtedly happen. God once again made His Covenant promise very clear to Ezekiel: "From that day forward the house of Israel will know that I am the Lord their God. And the nations will know that the people of Israel went into exile for their sin, because they were unfaithful to Me. So I hid My face from them and handed them over to their enemies, and they all fell by the sword. I dealt with them according to their uncleanness and their offenses, and I hid My face from them. Therefore this is what the Lord God says, 'I will now bring Jacob back from captivity and will have compassion on all the people of Israel, and I will be zealous for My holy name. They will forget their shame and all the unfaithfulness they showed toward Me when they lived in safety in their land with no one to make them afraid. When I have brought them back from the nations and have gathered them from the countries of their enemies, I will show Myself holy through them in the sight of many nations. Then they will know that I am the Lord their God, for though I sent them into exile among the nations, I will gather them to their own land, not leaving any behind. I will no longer hide My face from them, for I will pour out My Spirit on the house of Israel,' declares the Lord God (Ezekiel 39:22-29).'" The apostle Paul also confirmed God's covenant promise to the Jews when he quoted the prophets Isaiah and Jeremiah: "The Deliverer will come from Zion; He will remove ungodliness from Jacob. This is My covenant with them, when I take away their sins (Romans 11:26-27)." Thus both the Old

Testament and the New Testament confirm that God has not forgotten His divine election of the Jews and that, at the right time, He will bring a multitude ("all Israel will be saved") into His kingdom (Romans 11:25-29).

Although God has brought the Jewish people back to their Land, the Jewish people have yet to come back in great numbers to their God. For in A.D. 30, the nation of Israel (except for a very small remnant) rejected Jesus as their Messiah (Yeshua ha'Mashiah). As a result of their rejection of the Messiah, God not only dispersed the Jews to many foreign lands in A.D. 70; He then opened the door for the Gentiles to come into the kingdom of God (Romans 10:21-11:11). This marked the beginning of what the Bible calls "the times of the Gentiles" in terms of God's spiritual dispensation. At the end of His earthly ministry, Jesus foresaw that the "times of the Gentiles" was to begin. When Jesus' disciples told Him that Greeks (Gentiles) were seeking Him, Jesus knew this was a prophetic "signpost" indicating that God's gospel would soon be given to the Gentiles. Jesus then announced that His time to die had come, so that He might birth His church, and bear much fruit by bringing many sons and daughters (both Jews and Gentiles) into glory (John 12:20-25; Hebrews 2:10). Jesus knew that through His death and resurrection, God would bring all the Gentiles who are appointed for salvation into His kingdom. With this in view, Jesus said, "I have other sheep *(the Gentiles),* which are not of this fold; I must bring them also, and they will hear My voice; and they will become one flock with one shepherd (John 10:16)."

Thus, over twenty-six centuries ago, God through His prophet Ezekiel declared the Jewish people would be restored first to their land and then to their God through His New Covenant in Christ Jesus. Then, six centuries after Ezekiel's prophecy, God through the apostle Paul declared the restoration of the Jewish people to God and their Messiah would occur when the "fullness of the Gentiles" had come into the kingdom of God (Romans

11:25). How will we know when that time comes? Jesus Himself gave us the answer when He said "the times of the Gentiles" would be fulfilled when Jerusalem was no longer under the control of the Gentile nations (Luke 21:28). This remarkable prophetic event was fulfilled during the Arab-Israeli Six-Day War on June 7th 1967, when Israel regained sovereignty over the old city of Jerusalem for the first time in nineteen centuries. This historic watershed event signaled the beginning of the end of "the time of the Gentiles" as Jesus declared. We are now in a time of transition at the end of this age. The time for the restoration of all things is at hand before the return of Christ (Acts 3:20-21). Although many more Gentiles will continue to come into the kingdom of God, particularly in the last great worldwide outpouring of the Holy Spirit, we are also on the verge of the day when a multitude of Jews will also come into the kingdom of God through Jesus Christ. These are the Jews whom God has declared are "children of the promise," and not "children of the flesh" according to Romans 9:8 and Galatians 4:21-31.

The restoration of Israel (those who are "children of the promise") to God will help usher in the Messianic Age (also called the Millennium) when Jesus the Messiah King (Melekh ha'Mashiah) will return and rule the nations of the earth from His throne in Jerusalem for a thousand years (Revelation Chapter 20). The Bible describes a number of events that will occur before Christ returns to establish the Messianic Age. It is not our intent here to describe these events in detail or to establish an end-time timeline. We realize that many sincere Christians have differing opinions about the meaning and timing of these prophetic events. We are also keenly aware of our Lord's instruction: "But of that day and hour no one knows, not even the angels of heaven, nor the Son, but the Father alone (Matthew 24:36)." However in the same passage, Jesus said, "Now learn the parable from the fig tree: when its branch has already become tender and puts forth its leaves, you know that summer is near; so you too, when you see all these things, recognize that He is near, right at the door (Matthew 24:32-33)." And Paul wrote, "Now as to the times and the epochs, brethren, you have no need of anything to be written to you. For you yourselves know full well that the day of the Lord will come like a thief in the night. While they are saying, 'Peace and safety!' then destruction will come upon them suddenly like labor pains upon a woman with child, and they will not escape. But you, brethren, are not in darkness, that the day would overtake you like a thief; for you are all sons of light and sons of day (1 Thessalonians 5:1-5)." Although we may not know the exact day or hour, we can clearly see the leaves on the fig tree and discern the seasons and signs of the times (Matthew 16:3). With this in mind, we offer the following general roadmap of end-time events based on our interpretation of Biblical prophecy. These events may not necessarily occur in the following order and some of them may overlap.

- What Jesus called "the great tribulation" will come upon the whole world (Daniel 12:1; Zephaniah 1:14-17; Matthew 24:21; Mark 13:19; Luke 21:35). This will be an unprecedented time of worldwide calamity and distress, which God will use to judge the unrighteous and godless nations. The church will also have to endure this tribulation as part of God's divine plan to purify and prepare the bride of Christ for her eternal union with His Son (Matthew 24:22; Revelation 7:14). This is the time of great suffering and labor pains on the earth leading to Christ's return and the birth of the Messianic Age (Matthew 24:8; 29-31).

- Christ's eternal gospel will be restored to the church and preached to all the nations (Matthew 24:14; Revelation 10:7; 14:6), thus fulfilling Christ' great commission to the church and marking His imminent return (Matthew 28:18; Mark 16:15; Revelation 14:6-7).

This eternal gospel is the message of the Cross and Kingship of Christ (Matthew 4:23; 13:19-23; 24:14; Acts 17:7; 1 Corinthians 1:17-18; Galatians 6:14).

- The Holy Spirit will be poured out upon the whole earth with unprecedented scope and there will be a great harvest of souls (both Jew and Gentile) among all the nations (Joel 2:28-29; Zechariah 12:10; Revelation 7:9-14; 14:14-16). This last great worldwide outpouring of the Holy Spirit is what the Bible prophetically calls the "latter rain," since the first great outpouring of the Holy Spirit ("the early rain") upon the earth occurred in the first century when the New Covenant church was birthed (Jeremiah 5:23-24; Joel 2:23; Zechariah 10:1; James 5:7). However, before this spiritual "latter rain" (also called the spring rain) can fall upon the earth, the spiritual winter (the great tribulation) must first come upon the whole earth to prepare the spiritual "ground" in the hearts of God's elect to receive the outpouring of the Holy Spirit, and prepare the way for the last great harvest of souls into God's kingdom. During this great world-wide outpouring of the Holy Spirit, God will raise up His end-time church as a powerful witness before Jesus Christ's return; and prepare His New Covenant church for the Messianic Age to come.

- The Antichrist ("the man of lawlessness") will come to power with a message of peace and prosperity for the nations, and deceive and control humanity (Daniel 7:25; 8:9-14; 9:27; Matthew 24:15; 1 Thessalonians 5:3; 2 Thessalonians 2:1-12; Revelation 13:1-18). In time, he also persecute, imprison and kill the true saints of God (Daniel 7:21, 25; 11:33; 12:7; Matthew 24:9; Luke 21:16-17; Revelation 12:17; 13:7).

- The church will experience a great apostasy when many professing Christians will fall away from the faith and betray even their fellow Christians who remain faithful to Christ (Matthew 24:10; 2 Thessalonians 2:1-3; 1 Timothy 4:1; 2 Timothy 2:18; Revelation 11:2; 13:7). The present day false church is paving the way for this great apostasy to occur.

- The Lord will have an overcoming remnant of devoted followers, many of whom will die as martyrs for their faith (Daniel 11:32-33; Matthew 24:9; Luke 21:16; Revelation 7:13-14; 11:7; 12:11; 14:4, 12-13; 15:2). The crucible of these trying end-time events will purify the faith of these true believers whom God has called to be the bride of Christ (Revelation 19:7; 21:2).

- Israel will be attacked by her enemies and threatened with imminent destruction (Ezekiel 38:15-16; Zechariah 12:2-3). This is the culmination of the great tribulation for Israel, which the Bible prophetically calls the "time of Jacob's trouble" (Jeremiah 30:7).

- The nations of the world will experience God's wrath and judgment (Isaiah 63:1-7; Zechariah 12:8-9; Romans 2:5; Revelation 6:15-17; 14:7-11; 17-20; Chapters 16-18; 19:11-16).

- Jesus Christ, who first came as the Lamb of God, will now return as the Lion of Judah and King of Kings to crush Satan, judge the nations and establish the thousand year Messianic Age on earth (Isaiah 2:2-3; 9:6-7; Jeremiah 33:14-22; Ezekiel 34:23-24; Daniel 7:27; Micah 4:1-3; Zechariah 2:10-12; 8:3; 12:10-14; 14:3-19; Matthew 24:29-31; 1 Thessalonians 4:16-17; 2 Thessalonians 1:7-10; Jude 14-15; Revelation 11:15; 20:4-6).

We believe the rebirth of the nation of Israel on May 14th 1948, and Israel's regaining sovereignty over the city of Jerusalem on June 6, 1967, signaled the beginning of these end-time climactic events. We are presently living in the perilous "last hours" of the last days when the earth is in great spiritual darkness and deception (Isaiah 60:1-2). The world is godless, lawless and loveless. The nations of the world are filled with corruption and ripe for judgment (Genesis 6:11-12). Israel's many enemies are encircling her like hungry vultures gathering around a corpse (Matthew 24:28). Millions of people who call themselves Christians are lovers of self, lovers of money and lovers of pleasure rather than lovers of God. The publically-recognized institutional church has fallen into apostasy and multitudes are practicing a counterfeit form of "Christianity." Millions of people profess to be Christians, but their attitudes, affections and actions deny the reality of Jesus Christ and the power of His death and resurrection because they are not submitted to Christ's sovereignty (2 Timothy 3:1-5). The stage is now set for the Bible's final end-time prophecies to be fulfilled.

The next significant prophetic event likely to occur will be the great tribulation (Revelation 14:6-7). But some Christians might say, "What about 2 Thessalonians 2:1-8? Does not the apostasy (when the church falls away from the faith) have to happen first? And does not the man of lawlessness first have to take his place in the temple of God? And before this can happen, does not the Islamic Dome of the Rock first need to be demolished so that the Jewish Temple can be rebuilt in its place?" Remember, however, that ever since Jesus died and rose from the dead, the true temple of God is no longer a physical building located in the city of Jerusalem; it is now the living church of God's people (John 4:20-24; Ephesians 2:19-22; 1 Peter 2:5). Consequently, the Dome of the Rock does not have to be demolished and the Jewish Temple does not have to be rebuilt in order for this prophecy to be fulfilled. The present day reality is that the publically-recognized, institutional church has already fallen away from true faith in Christ, and the spirit of the antichrist and lawlessness is now the dominating presence in this temple of apostasy. However, God has preserved a remnant of faithful saints who dwell in the Ark of His Eternal Covenant, which is the Ark of His Presence. These are the true saints who have died to the sin of the world, and whose lives are hidden with Christ in God (Colossians 3:3). These true saints dwell in God's Most Holy Place, the Holy of Holies, where they are protected from the deception and destruction of the "man of lawlessness." Those in the apostate church dwell in the outer court, where they will be overcome by the spirit of the antichrist during the great tribulation and persecution, as we see them being overcome even now (2 Thessalonians 2:8-12; Revelation 11:1-2).

Therefore, God will use the great tribulation to righteously judge and punish the godless nations; to scourge, discipline and purify His church; and to prepare the hearts of all those destined for His kingdom to receive the restored, complete gospel of Jesus Christ and the last great outpouring and harvest of the Holy Spirit. We are presently in the calm before the storm - on the eve of the great tribulation. The onset of the great tribulation will sound the "final hour" of God's prophetic clock. Just like the days of Noah before the great flood covered the earth and just like the days of Lot before the fiery destruction of Sodom and Gomorrah, people today are buying and selling, building and planting, eating and drinking, and marrying and giving in marriage until that hour when the great tribulation covers the face of the earth like a giant avalanche or tidal wave (Matthew 24:36-39; Luke 17:26-30). The rulers of the nations are spiritually blind to the great storm clouds now looming on the darkening horizon. Today, if anyone preaches righteousness like Noah, the world mocks them saying, "Where is Christ's return? Everything continues just as it always did for thousands of years (see 2 Peter 2:4-10; 3:3-12)." Yet when the great tribulation suddenly erupts, it will be cataclysmic and worldwide. This global calamity and worldwide economic collapse and all the events which soon follow will cause to men faint with fear for their lives and brother to betray brother to death in order to survive (Luke 21:16 & 26). This earth-shaking catastrophe will set in motion the remaining prophetic events before

Christ's triumphant return (Matthew 24:21-31; Mark 13:24-27). Since these events are the final labor pains leading to the birth of the Messianic Age, they will occur with increasing frequency and greater intensity until the Lord returns. Jesus said the generation alive during this time would see all these events come to pass (Luke 21:32).

Many Christians mistakenly believe the church will not have to go through the coming great tribulation. They naïvely believe that everyone in the church will be "raptured" and called up to heaven before the great tribulation begins. They wrongly think that God would never have His people suffer through such great judgment and suffering on the earth. Although this viewpoint of future events may be soulishly comforting to many, it directly contradicts Scripture. The Bible says that, at the close of this age, Satan will be given authority for an appointed time to overpower the church (Daniel 7:21-25; Revelation 13:7). This will be a time of great tribulation and persecution just before the second coming of Christ. Jesus Himself said the elect (His true followers) would have to endure the great tribulation. Jesus declared, "For then there will be a great tribulation, such has not occurred since the beginning of the world, and never will occur again. Unless those days were cut short, no one would survive but for the sake of the elect (whom God has chosen), those days will be shortened... for it will come upon all those who dwell on the face of all the earth (Matthew 24:21-22; Mark 13:19-20; Luke 21:35)." During this hour of great darkness, many of Christ's servants will be imprisoned and killed (Matthew 24:9). And many who profess to be Christians will fall away from the faith (Daniel 11:33; Matthew 24:10; Revelation 13:10). But even in this darkest hour, the victory is the Lord's, for Jesus declared the powers of hell would not prevail against His church (Matthew 16:18). Our God will have a faithful remnant who will spiritually endure and overcome this great crucible of fire to triumph over Satan. This much is certain! The

Bible says, "They *(the saints)* overcame him *(the devil)* by the blood of the Lamb and by the word of their testimony; and they did not love their lives even when faced with death (Revelation 12:11)."

Why would God allow His precious church to suffer persecution and death? Consider this: why would God allow Jesus, His precious Son, to suffer crucifixion and death? Because, from out of His Son's death would arise many sons and daughters of God. Then why would God allow His church, whom He loves, to be overpowered by the enemy, even for a season? The Lord will allow this dreadful calamity because, once again, He is after something of far greater eternal value. He wants a holy bride whose love and devotion to Him is pure and unadulterated. Throughout the Bible, the relationship between God and His people is compared to a marriage covenant. God's chosen and beloved people could count on His faithfulness to honor this covenant and protect and provide for them. However, God's marriage covenant was also conditional upon His people's faithfulness to Him. The Lord said, "If you will obey My voice and keep My covenant, you will be My treasured possession and you will be for Me a kingdom of priests and a holy nation (Exodus 19:5-6)."

Unbelief and unfaithfulness to God result when God's people trust in their own ability and righteousness rather than in God (Jeremiah 17:5; Deuteronomy 8:17-19). When His people abandon their love and devotion to Him for other things, God no longer calls them His bride but a harlot with other lovers (Isaiah 1:21; Jeremiah 3:1; Ezekiel 15:16). When the nation of Israel practiced spiritual adultery and broke their covenant with Him, God gave them a certificate of divorce (Jeremiah 3:8; see also 11:10). In the same way, when Christians prove themselves unfaithful and break their marriage covenant with Jesus their Bridegroom, God will give them a certificate of divorce rather than have His Son marry a harlot. The Bible says, "God keeps His covenant with those who love Him and obey Him

(Daniel 9:4)." Jesus said, "This people honors Me with their lips, but their heart is far from Me (Matthew 15:8)." During such times, God sends His prophets to warn His people to repent of their spiritual adultery and return to Him. However, if they continue in their idolatrous ways, God abandons them to lawlessness and allows them to be defeated by their enemies. Instead of God's divine protection, they are destined to experience calamity. As God said to His people of the Old Covenant: "I am going to desecrate My sanctuary, the stronghold in which you take pride, the delight of your eyes, the object of your affection... I will forsake My house, abandon My inheritance; I will give the one I love into the hand of her enemies (Ezekiel 24:21; Jeremiah 12:7)."

When the children of Israel had forsaken God, they mistakenly thought they could look to the temple to keep them safe from destruction (Jeremiah 7:1-15). In the same way, when Christians who are unfaithful and habitually practicing sin look to the false church for their security rather than to God Himself, calamity is coming. Our relationship with God may be under New Covenant grace, but we still have a holy responsibility to remain faithful in our marriage covenant to the Lord. When the church at Pergamum allowed idolatry among their members, Jesus warned if they did not repent, He would war against them with the sword of His mouth. When the church at Thyatira engaged in immorality, Jesus said He would kill those who did not repent. When the church at Sardis was spiritually dead, Jesus warned if they did not repent, He would erase their names from the Book of Life. When the church at Laodicea turned lukewarm toward the Lord, He warned if they did not repent, He would vomit them out of His mouth (Revelation Chapters 2 & 3).

Even God's faithful remnant can expect to experience the tribulation of His refining fire (Daniel 11:35). For example, Jesus told those who are faithful in the church at Smyrna: "I know your tribulation and your poverty, but you are rich! I know the slander of those who say they are Jews and are not, but are a synagogue of Satan. Do not be afraid of what you are about to suffer. I tell you, the devil will put some of you in prison to test you, and you will have tribulation for ten days. Be faithful, even to the point of death, and I will give you the crown of life (Revelation 2:8-10)." The Bible says that God scourges and disciplines His people so they might share His holiness (Hebrews 12:4-10). Peter wrote, "For it is time for judgment to begin with the family of God, and if it begins with us, what will the outcome be for those who do not obey the gospel of God? (1 Peter 4:17-18)." At the close of this age, Satan will be given power over the church until the strength of God's people is shattered (Daniel 12:7). But it is not God's power within us that will be broken; it is our natural strength. As Paul said, "We were under great pressure, far beyond our strength, so that we despaired even of life. Indeed, in our hearts we felt the sentence of death. But this happened so that we would not rely on ourselves but on God, who raises the dead (2 Corinthians 1:8-9)."

If we are willing, God will press us, even to the point of death if necessary, so we might fully embrace His Son and His completed work on the cross. God not only wants us to know Christ died for us (Romans 5:8); He wants us to know we died with Christ (Romans 6:8). Knowing we have died with Christ is the secret to overcoming Satan and enduring the great tribulation. When we know (and believe and act) on the Biblical truth that we have been crucified with Christ and that our sinful nature died and was removed from us, we will know and experience freedom from the power of sin (Romans 6:6-7). Then we will no longer depend on our own strength to overcome the fear of sin and death (Philippians 3:3; Romans 8:2). Instead, we will trust Christ, who lives in us by His Spirit, to be our overcomer, our strength, and our spiritual hiding place during the coming tribulation and persecution (Galatians 2:20).

In the final spiritual conflict of this age, during the tribulation, a great persecution will come upon the church. The Bible says the body of overcomers who triumph over Satan during this intense spiritual warfare will have one distinguishing mark: "they loved not their lives" when faced with death (Revelation 12:10). This indicates true Christians will die in this final conflict rather than forsake their bold testimony of Christ. It also indicates the final test of our faith in this end-time persecution will be our willingness to lose our lives for Christ's sake. The Holy Spirit is calling this generation of saints to prepare as soldiers of Christ for this end-time battle. However, we will only overcome Satan and his demonic minions if we train in peacetime the way we will fight in wartime. Since our fight is not against mortal men but against the spiritual forces of evil, we will not win this battle with earthly weapons. Instead, we will overcome Satan by the blood of the Lamb. This is the basis for laying down our lives. This is the key to victory.

The blood of the Lamb speaks of the triumphant work that Christ accomplished by His death on the cross. Just as Jesus Christ conquered Satan and sin by laying down His life on the cross, we also will overcome the devil and sin by laying down our lives through the power of the cross. For not only did Christ die on the cross for us, He also included us in His death, so that we might live through Him (1 John 4:9). By the divine operation of the cross of Christ, God removed our sinful nature and replaced it with His Son's divine nature (Romans 6:6; 2 Corinthians 5:21; Colossians 2:11; 3:3). Therefore, Satan no longer has any power over us to make us sin; and since sin and death no longer have any power over us, we do not have to fear what man can do to us (Romans 6:7; 1 John 3:8). The Bible says, "Since the children have flesh and blood, He Himself shared in their humanity, so that by His death He might destroy him who has the power of death; that is, the devil, and free those who all their lives were held in slavery by their fear of death (Hebrews 2:14-15)." And Paul wrote, "Who will separate us from the love of Christ? Will tribulation, or distress, or persecution, of famine, or nakedness, or peril, or the sword? Just as it is written, 'For Your sake, we are being put to death all day long; we are considered as sheep to be slaughtered.' But, in all these things, we overwhelmingly conquer through Him who loved us. For I am convinced that neither death nor life, nor angels, nor demons, nor things present nor things to come, nor any powers, nor height nor depth, nor any other created thing, will be able to separate us from the love of God, which is in Christ Jesus our Lord (Romans 8:35-39)

If we believe this to be the gospel, then we should lay down our natural soul-life every day for Christ. This is how we can prepare for the coming tribulation and end-time spiritual conflict, and for the age to come when we will reign with Christ. Although the ultimate test of losing our soul-life may be to die for Christ (since this certainly goes against our natural instinct of self-preservation), we have many other daily opportunities to practice dying to self when Christ's authority crosses our natural will and desires. For example, we may be challenged to lose our soul-life daily to serve our family. Or, we may face daily hardship at our work site that exhausts us emotionally and physically. Or, we may have to suffer an extremely difficult and painful affliction that presses us beyond our natural endurance. Or, we may have to regularly resist a strong temptation that is beyond our natural self-control. Or, we may have to love a dedicated personal enemy who is impossible for us to naturally love. The only way we can triumph in these trials and temptations is to believe our old sin nature has died and been removed by Christ's death. Then we can choose to overcome sin and die to our soul-life by faith in the power of God's resurrected Son who lives in us by His Spirit.

The great tribulation of this age is soon approaching. It is time for every Christian who hears the call of the Spirit to report for duty to our Commander-in-Chief, Jesus Christ, for spiritual warfare training. Our Lord

Jesus has already secured the victory for us by including us in His death and resurrection. If we know we have already died with Christ, let us train by laying down our lives now, so we will be ready to lay down our lives for Him in the coming spiritual war against the saints. In the coming tribulation and persecution when Satan wages war against God's people, many will fall away from the faith. At that time, let everyone who has faith fix their eyes on Jesus who will never forsake us. Men will fail us, our country will fail us, the false church will fail us; but our Lord Jesus will never fail us. Stand firm, therefore, with God's faithful remnant all over the earth, and lift your head high, for the coming of our Lord is near (Luke 21:28). We should not be surprised when this great fiery ordeal comes upon us. Jesus will use this great tribulation and persecution to purify His bride like a crucible of fire refines gold (Revelation 7:9-14). Then our Lord will return with His army of angels and overcoming saints to crush the enemy, judge the world and rule the nations. The Bible says, "Immediately after the tribulation of those days the sun will be darkened, and the moon will not give its light, and the stars will fall from the sky, and the powers of the heavens will be shaken. And then the sign of the Son of Man will appear in the sky, and then all the nations of the earth will mourn, and they will see the Son of Man coming on the clouds of the sky with power and great glory. And He will send forth His angels with a great trumpet and they will gather together His elect from the four winds and from one end of the sky to the other (Matthew 24:29-31)."

God's Divine Heart Transplant - The Miracle of Our New Birth

Jesus revealed where sin resides in man when He said, "From within, out of the heart of man, proceed evil thoughts, sexual immorality, theft, murder, adultery, greed, malice, deceit, lewdness, envy, slander, pride and foolishness. All these evil things come from within man and defile man (Mark 7:21-23)." By this statement, Jesus did not mean that sin resides in our physical heart; otherwise we would need a physical heart transplant to be freed from sin. Jesus meant that sin dwells in man's unregenerate heart since everyone is born with a heart of sin (a sinful nature). The Bible says this was our spiritual condition before we were born again of God's Spirit (Psalm 51:5; Romans 5:19).

God's solution to save us from the malignant power of sin and certain spiritual death was to perform a divine heart transplant. God used His Son's sacrificial death on the cross to spiritually remove our terminally sin-sick heart and replace it with His Son's divine heart when we were born again (Romans 6:1-6; Colossians 2:11-12). This New Covenant divine heart transplant was foretold by the prophet Ezekiel six centuries before Christ's birth when Ezekiel declared that God would remove our sin-hardened heart and replace it with a new spiritual heart when He put His Spirit within us (Ezekiel 36:26-27; see also Jeremiah 31:31-34). By this divine operation of the cross of Christ, God delivered us from enslavement to indwelling sin (by removing our sinful nature), so that His Son would dwell in us by His Spirit (Galatians 2:20). The Bible says, "God has sent the Spirit of His Son into our hearts (Galatians 4:6)." Thus God included us in His Son's death so that His resurrected Son might live in us. This is the miracle of our new birth.

But salvation is only the beginning, and not the end of God's purpose for His elect. Now that we have Christ's new heart within us, we no longer have to keep practicing sin. For through His death, Jesus once and forever dealt with the "sin factory" that was within us, by destroying and removing our sinful nature. The chief obstacle to our living by the Spirit is, therefore, no longer our sinful Adam nature (since it is dead and gone), but our old Adam way of thinking (our unrenewed mind), which needs to be transformed by the truth of God's Word. Since we have been born again of God's Spirit, how do we now live as Christ's disciples? Each day, we obey by faith Christ's command to deny ourselves, carry our own cross and lay down our natural (unconverted) soul-life for His sake and the gospel's sake (Mark 8:34-35).

In this way, we prove by our actions that we believe we are dead to sin, but alive to God in Christ Jesus (Romans 6:11; Galatians 6:14). Does this mean that we will never sin again? Of course not! Whenever we do sin, we repent and then ask and receive God's forgiveness for our sins (1 John 1:9). But now that sin is no longer our master, we are able by the Spirit to "put to death" our old habitual, sinful way of thinking and acting, and "put on" Christ's new way of thinking and acting (Romans 8:12-13; Ephesians 4:22-24). Thus, by our faith in the truth of the cross of Christ and through the sanctifying work of the Holy Spirit, we are transformed into Christ's image, and adorn ourselves with the beauty of holiness that befits the bride of Christ (Revelation 19:7; 21:2).

Seven Reasons Why Christians Do Not Have a Sinful Nature

- First and foremost, God says so. There are a dozen Scriptures in the New Testament that testify to this divine truth. The Bible is clear that when we were born again, our old sinful nature died. A number of Scriptures also make it clear that our sinful nature not only died, it was *removed* from us when we were born again of the Holy Spirit (Romans 6:6; 8:9; Colossians 2:11).

- God only creates what is good. When God created man, it was good. When God created the *new* man in Christ, it was good. God would never create a new spiritual man who still had an evil sinful nature living in him (2 Corinthians 5:17; Romans 7:21).

- God has made us into a new creation, the body of Christ. God would never allow Christ's body, the temple of the Spirit, to be inhabited by an evil sinful nature (1 Corinthians 3:16-17; Romans 7:21). Before God could make His new creation in Christ, He had to first deal with the old creation that originated in Adam.

Therefore, God not only dealt with its fruit (our sinful actions); He also removed its very root (our sinful nature). Whoever has a sinful nature is still a child of the devil (John 8:44; 1 John 3:8). That is why our sinful nature had to be destroyed and removed before the Spirit of God could inhabit us and make us children of God (Romans 6:6; Colossians 2:11; Romans 8:15).

- God would never mix what is holy with the unholy by putting His Holy Spirit into someone with a sinful nature (2 Corinthians 6:14-7:1). That is why He only puts His Holy Spirit into a new wineskin (our new holy nature), and not into an old wineskin (the sinful nature) in order to preserve both the work of the Holy Spirit and His new creation, His church (Matthew 9:17). God would never join us together in spiritual union with Christ if our body still contained a sinful nature. That would be spiritual harlotry and defile both our spirit and body (1 Corinthians 6:15-17; Romans 7:17).

- God would never create a new man who has a split personality of good and evil (Matthew 6:22-24). That would cause us to have a divided mind and a divided heart. God knew that anyone conflicted and divided against himself in this way would not be able to stand firm against Satan's attacks (Mark 3:25).

- God would never allow the devil to have a spiritual foothold in His new creation (1 John 4:4; 5:18). If God had allowed our sinful nature to still remain in us, He would have provided Satan with a spiritual connection and control within us (1 John 3:8). God knew that man's sinful nature was his Achilles heel, which Satan could use to continually snare him in sin. It is no wonder that any Christian who believes he still has a sinful nature thinks the devil has a stronghold over him in his struggle against sin?

- Finally and most importantly, Jesus did not have a sinful nature. He was born with a human body and He had a human soul (his will, intellect and emotions). However, since He was born of a virgin and God was His Father, He did not inherit Adam's sinful spiritual nature like we did. This is why He was able to obey God and live a sinless life. Now that we are also are born of God, we also no longer have a sinful nature and are capable of obeying God and not practicing sin. Thus Jesus is our divine example and the first born of God's new creation (Colossians 1:15-18; 1 John 3:9).

Note: It is essential to know (and believe and act on) the Biblical truth that your sinful nature was destroyed and removed from you when you were born again of the Spirit; otherwise you will not be able to overcome sin and the devil. The Bible says, "For we know that our old self was crucified with Him, in order that our body of sin *(our sinful nature)* might be destroyed, so that we would no longer be slaves to sin; for he who has died is freed from sin (Romans 6:6-7)."

Five Features of The New Covenant Church

- The New Covenant church normally meets in believers' homes and whenever the church grows too large to meet in one member's home, it simply multiplies from house to house throughout its geographic locality (Acts 2:46; 5:42; 20:20; Romans 16:5; 1 Corinthians 16:19; Colossians 4:15; Philemon 1:2). This eliminates the need to raise large amounts of money to buy, build and maintain church facilities. This helps ensure that God (not men and their money) will cause the growth of the church (1 Corinthians 3:6-7). This informal, home setting also encourages open participatory meetings; helps the church function in a more personal and loving way as God's family; and enables the saints to practice hospitality toward other believers and visitors (Romans 12:13; Hebrews 13:2; 1 Peter 4:9. The New Covenant church in each city or community is essentially an informal network of home-based meetings. An exception to these weekly home meetings might be to occasionally rent a building, auditorium or conference room for a city-wide meeting of house churches and/or to facilitate the outreach ministry of a visiting apostle, prophet, evangelist or teacher (Acts 19:9).

- The New Covenant church experiences intimate spiritual fellowship with the Father and His Son and experiences close-knit community life among the saints who are committed to laying down their self-will and giving up their natural *unconverted* soul-lives in *agapē* love for one another (Acts 2:42-47; 4:32-33; 1 Corinthians 12:12-27; Ephesians 4:15-16; Philippians 2:1-5; 1 John 1:3; 3:16). As members of God's household, the believers' lives are closely intertwined with one another as brothers and sisters and mothers and fathers in Christ (1 Corinthians 4:15; 1 Thessalonians 2:11; 1 Timothy 5:1-2; Titus 2:3-4; 1 John 2:12-14). This encourages mentoring and discipleship relationships to naturally develop. On the Lord's Day (Sunday), the local believers often meet together in their homes to share "the Lord's Supper" as a full fellowship meal (Acts 20:7; 1 Corinthians 11:20). The primary purpose of eating this communal meal together is to remember (with thanksgiving and rejoicing) the New Covenant provisions of the Lord's death by sharing "the bread and the cup" together, and to reaffirm the believers' bonds of love and peace with one another as God's family (1 Corinthians 11:23-26). This is why this fellowship meal is also called an "*agapē* love feast" (Jude 1:12).

- The New Covenant church has a vibrant, functioning priesthood of all believers (both men and women) who passionately love our Lord Jesus Christ, and are gifted and equipped by the Holy Spirit to do the work of the ministry together and build up the body of Christ in love. Every member of this royal priesthood personally knows and serves Jesus Christ, our High Priest, and has a vital and unique ministry role in His body (Romans 12:3-8; 1

Corinthians 12:1-12; Ephesians 4:11-13, 15-16; Colossians 2:19; 1 Peter 2:9; 4:10-11; Revelation 1:6; 5:10). Consequently, when the church meets together under Christ's headship, one member might be led by the Holy Spirit to share a prayer or a song; another member a word of knowledge or wisdom; another member an exhortation or a teaching; another member the gift of healing or miracles; and another member might share a prophecy or a message in tongues and its interpretation - all done in an orderly, peaceful and loving manner for the benefit of the whole body (1 Corinthians 14:26-33).

This dynamic priesthood of all the believers is one of the fundamental building stones ("living stones") of the New Covenant church (1 Peter 2:4-5).[14] This spiritual freedom and responsibility in the New Covenant church enables every member to grow into fully knowing God, and also helps each member learn how to exercise their individual gifts to effectively serve and care for God's family. It also enables Christ, as the head of the church, to lead His body (through a variety of members with a variety of gifts) as all the saints learn to fix their eyes on Jesus and hear and obey His voice.

- The New Covenant church has a compassionate commission to employ a variety of means to reach others with the gospel of Christ (Mark 16:15; Acts 4:20; 11:20-21; Philippians 1:5). This reflects the heart of God's love for the lost and enables Jesus Christ to employ the multi-gifted members of His church as coworkers to advance His gospel and bring His elect into the kingdom, and this outreach of *agape* love toward others also helps keep the church from becoming insular and isolated. This divine commission goes beyond just bringing new converts into the church. Jesus specifically commanded the church to make disciples who obey His commands (Matthew 28:19-20). This is why it is essential to feed newborn lambs the milk of God's Word followed by more solid food for training in righteousness as soon as they are able to digest it, so that they can exercise faith in the truth of God's Word in order to overcome Satan and sin, and be Christ's witnesses in this world (1 Corinthians 3:2; Hebrews 5:12-14; 1 Peter 2:2-3; 1 John 2:12-14).

- The New Covenant church is normally shepherded in each locality by a number of spiritually mature and humble brothers called elders. As servant-leaders, the elders are unpaid and accountable to the church and to Jesus Christ, the head of the church, to be godly examples of faithfulness; provide wise oversight (not micromanagement) to the church; help train and equip the priesthood of believers to do their God-given ministries; and provide loving pastoral care to members of God's local flock (Acts 20:17, 28; Ephesians 4:11-13; 2 Timothy 3:1-7; James 5:14; 1 Peter 5:1-4). Since Jesus is the Chief Shepherd, He personally calls, trains and, at the right time, appoints these mature brothers as His undershepherds in the local church. When a church reaches a certain size and spiritual maturity, these elder brothers will naturally emerge and be recognized by the saints, and may also be confirmed by the "laying on of hands" of visiting apostles and prophets (Acts 14:23; Titus 1:5-9).

This plurality of shared leadership helps prevent carnal authoritarian rule; stifles a "personality cult" from developing around a sole or senior pastor; and helps keep the church singularly focused on Jesus Christ as the Chief Shepherd who personally leads His body by His Spirit. This New Covenant form of local church leadership only works if the elders are truly submitted to

Christ their head and to one another in the humility of the Holy Spirit (Philippians 2:1-5). This law of the Spirit ensures these elders (shepherds) in the New Covenant church must stay vitally connected to Christ to have His resurrection life, so they can stay united in Spirit to properly care for God's flock with His wisdom, power and love; and be spiritually sensitive to discern and follow (not interfere with) the Holy Spirit's prompting and leading of the saints.

- The New Covenant church does not practice Old Covenant tithing to subsidize a special, paid priesthood or clergy (Hebrews 7:5, 12); instead its members practice voluntary giving (according to their financial means as God has blessed them) to further the outreach of the gospel and help those members of the body who are financially suffering and in need (Acts 4:34-35; 11:29; Romans 12:13; 1 Corinthians 16:1-2; 2 Corinthians 9:6-7; 1 John 3:17). This eliminates the mandatory Mosaic religious tax placed upon God's people to finance a professional clergy who are separate from the laity. It also helps ensure the basic needs of members of God's family are not lacking while other members are experiencing abundance (2 Corinthians 8:1-15; 9:6-7). This fulfills the divine command: "Bear one another's burdens, and thereby fulfill the law of Christ… when one member suffers, all members suffer together (Galatians 6:2; 1 Corinthians 12:26; see also 1 John 3:17).

The crucifixion of Jesus Christ is the most momentous event in human history. It is the foundation for the gospel and the cornerstone of the New Covenant church. Within Christianity, two doctrines are rooted in Christ's crucifixion. The first is the doctrine of justification (right standing with God). This doctrine can be expressed as: we are saved and justified by God's grace through faith in Christ's completed work on the cross. Ephesians 2:8 sums up this Biblical doctrine: "For by grace you have been saved through faith; and not of yourselves, it is a gift of God; not as a result of works, so that no one can boast." The doctrine of justification was the center of controversy during the Protestant Reformation, and now provides the basis for today's Protestant church theology. The Catholic church, which believed salvation depended on a combination of faith plus religious works, denounced the Reformation view that salvation is by faith in Christ alone, and condemned it as heresy.

The second major Christian doctrine that is directly connected to Christ's death on the cross is the doctrine of co-crucifixion. The doctrine of co-crucifixion can be expressed as: when we were born again, we were spiritually crucified with Christ, *in order to remove our sinful nature*, so that Christ might live in us by His Spirit. Romans 6:6 sums up this Biblical doctrine: "For we know that our old man was crucified with Him, in order that our body of sin *(our sinful nature)* might be destroyed, so that we would no longer be slaves to sin." The apostle Paul also expressed this doctrinal truth in his personal testimony: "I have been crucified with Christ and I no longer live, but Christ lives in me; and the life that I now live, I live by faith in the Son of God (Galatians 2:20)." The doctrine of co-crucifixion is far less known than the doctrine of justification and is rarely taught to Christians today; and when it is taught, it is usually erroneously taught. This is truly tragic and shocking since our progressive sanctification in Christ critically depends on the truth of our co-crucifixion with Christ. Just as the doctrine of justification is absolutely essential to our Christian faith, the doctrine of co-crucifixion is absolutely crucial to our Christian life. The doctrine of justification means that Christ's death on the cross has freed us from the penalty of sin *by paying the price for our sins,* whereas the doctrine of co-crucifixion means Christ's death on the cross has freed us from the power of sin *by removing our sinful nature.*

How does our on-going sanctification in Christ depend on our co-crucifixion with Christ? Our ability to stop practicing sin and live under God's sovereignty starts with our new birth and co-crucifixion with Christ. Since we were born with a sinful nature, our sinful nature had to die so we could be freed from sin. God accomplished this by spiritually including us in His Son's death, so that we could be born again into His Son's resurrection life (Romans 6:3-11). Therefore, when we received Christ as our Lord and Savior, the Bible says that our "old man" of sin died with Christ so that we would be freed from the power of sin. "For he who has died has been freed from sin (Romans 6:7)." But who died when we were born again? Did our physical body die when we were saved? Obviously not! Did our soul (our natural personality – our will, intellect and emotions) die when we were saved? Of course not! Then what died? The Bible says our sinful nature died and was removed from us (Romans 6:6; Colossians 2:11).

This divine truth is the crux of what is missing from today's church theology. As a result of this theological error, most Christians mistakenly believe they still have an indwelling sinful nature after they are born again. New Christians are incorrectly taught that the sinful nature still resides in them in some kind of inactive state, which is then powerfully reactivated whenever they sin. Unfortunately, many Christians then live with dread that their sinful nature is not irrevocably dead and removed, but instead dwells in them like a dormant volcano, which can spontaneously and explosively erupt back to life at any time and cause destruction and havoc in their lives. Because of this erroneous theology, most Christians mistakenly believe they have two spiritual natures within them, a new Christ-like nature and an old sinful nature, which continually wage war against each other. They believe their new nature loves God and wants to practice righteousness, but their old nature loves sin and wants to practice lawlessness. They are wrongly taught that this continual conflict of two opposing inner natures is the normal Christian life. This conflicted inner self-identity places the burden to overcome the old sinful nature and stop sinning on *your* shoulders and on *your* own ability, self-effort and work, instead of where it belongs: on Christ's shoulders and *His* completed work on the cross.

As a result, many Christians live under an oppressive yoke of ignorance and unbelief – worried and fearful that their daily victory over sin hinges on whichever of these two warring inner natures they yield to the most. Tragically, for many Christians, the only way out of this constant inner turmoil and sense of frustration, failure and guilt is to harden their hearts against the Holy Spirit's conviction of sin, since they are continually defeated by what they believe is the satanic power of an indwelling sinful nature. Consequently, a countless number of Christians have become hopelessly discouraged and overcome by sin because they have swallowed the lie that they have an evil nature; while many others are deceived by self-righteousness and secret pride into thinking they can overcome the old sinful nature through willpower, self-discipline and religious methods.

Thank God that this sorry "tale of two natures" is not Biblically true. Our co-crucifixion with Christ was not merely positional, conceptual or symbolic. The Bible says that our sinful nature, which was at the very core of our inner being and the seat of our self-identity and rebellion toward God, actually died and was removed from us when we received Christ into our heart; it was not merely rendered temporarily inactive, so that it can come roaring back to life whenever we sin (Colossians 2:11-12). Otherwise, how could God have completely destroyed Satan's foothold in us if we still had a hostile and deceitful sinful nature living within us? How could we spiritually fight our enemy, the devil, if we still had an enemy allied to him waging guerilla warfare within us? How could we possibly obey God's command to be free from sin and be holy in all our conduct if we still had an unholy sinful nature that always inwardly sabotaged us? And how can we believe and act with unwavering confidence in the truth that we are dead to sin if we do not know with absolute certainty that we no longer have an evil, sinful nature?

If we still had a debilitating and treacherous evil nature which gives us an indwelling propensity to sin, it would be impossible for us to live a pure life (in spirit, soul and body) for Christ's sake and the gospel's sake. God knew that man's sinful nature was his Achilles heel, which Satan could use to continually snare him in sin. That is why the Old Covenant could not accomplish God's eternal purpose to have a holy people whose hearts completely belong to Him since man's sinful nature prevented him from truly obeying God's commandments. Therefore, what the Mosaic Law was powerless to do because of our sinful nature, God did through the New Covenant by sending His Son who perfectly fulfilled the Law and became sin on our behalf when He was crucified, so that we might become the righteousness of God in Christ (Romans 8:3; 2 Corinthians 5:21). This does not mean that God expects us to achieve "sinless perfection." However, He does expect us and even commands us to stop practicing chronic sin; otherwise, we cannot know Him or abide in Him (1 John 3:6)."

Getting rid of our old sinful nature and giving us a new and holy spiritual nature was the central purpose of the New Covenant, which Jesus Christ died to give us. Because of Christ's death on the cross, the chief obstacle to our living by the Spirit is no longer our sinful Adam nature (since it is dead and gone), but our old Adam way of thinking (our unrenewed mind). There is a great difference, however, between our unrenewed mind (our unconverted soul-life) and the old sinful nature. Our unrenewed mind does not have the satanic power of the old sinful nature, which kept us permanently enslaved to sin. That is why God had to destroy and remove our sinful nature in order to decisively free us from the power of sin, so that He could indwell us by His Spirit, and our unrenewed mind could then be transformed by His Word. If we reject this precious truth of our co-crucifixion with Christ (by wrongly believing that a born again Christian still has an evil, sinful nature), we take out the very heart of the New Covenant and nullify Christ's sacrificial death on the cross. For anyone who is interested in learning more about our co-crucifixion with Christ and its practical application to our Christian lives, we recommend our introductory book, *The Meaning of the Cross.*

The purpose and meaning of Christ's death on the cross is far too important and central to our Christian faith to get it wrong. The church can be wrong about many things, but if it is wrong about Christ's completed work on the cross, it is in dire spiritual trouble. For this reason, we appeal to all Christians who are serious followers of Jesus Christ to rethink this crucial doctrine of our co-crucifixion with Christ. Some might ask how such a foundational truth of the Christian faith could have been lost from the church for nearly two thousand years. However, remember that the foundational truth of "salvation is by faith in Christ alone" had also been lost from the church for nearly one thousand years. It was not until God opened men's minds to understand the Scriptures (that we are saved by faith alone) that this truth of the gospel of Christ was restored to the church five hundred years ago. Yet even with this spiritual breakthrough, the Protestant

Reformation still only restored half of the gospel to the church: how "the righteous are *saved by faith*," but it did not restore the complete divine truth to the church of how *"the righteous will live by faith."*

In closing, let me share a personal testimony. My wife and I became Christians almost half a century ago. When we were saved, we fully dedicated our lives to Jesus Christ and consecrated ourselves to do our "utmost for His Highest." For decades, we tried to live a holy Christian life and do Christ's work in our community with all our heart and mind and strength. However, as time progressed, a prolonged series of crises adversely affected our health, family, finances, employment and church life, and pressed us far beyond our natural ability to endure. After more than three decades, this crucible of suffering finally brought us to the absolute end of ourselves and broke us of our self-confidence, false sense of moral virtue, and reliance on our natural ability to live the Christian life. It was at this lowest, most desperate point in our lives that God miraculously revealed to us the divine truth of our co-crucifixion with Christ. Twelve years have now passed since that day, and we can testify from personal experience that the truth that we have died with Christ (and no longer have a sinful nature) is not just "theological" theory. We have put God's truth of the cross into practice, and this truth has set us free us from the destructive sins that habitually entangled us in the past. Of course, we are not perfect, but this powerful truth of the gospel of Christ has set us free to live and serve God by His Spirit and be transformed by His Spirit, as we always dreamed and thought was possible when we were first saved.

Five hundred years have now passed since the Holy Spirit began to restore the power of the cross of Christ and the keys of the kingdom to Christ's church. We pray that God would now open the minds of all believers to understand (and believe and act on) the Scriptural truth of the whole gospel that God has included us in Christ's death *to remove our sinful nature,* so that Christ might sovereignly live in us - His New Covenant church - by

His Spirit. What is now needed is a Second and Final Reformation to restore the key to understanding the doctrinal truth of how "the righteous will *live by faith*," so the church can faithfully endure the great trial that will soon test the whole world. And when this crucible of fire and suffering has accomplished God's divine purpose in His church, God will crown His glorious bride with a royal diadem of pure gold for her wedding to His Son, the Lord Jesus Christ.

In that day the Lord of hosts will be a beautiful crown
and a glorious diadem to the remnant of His people...
and as the bridegroom rejoices over his bride,
so your God will rejoice over you."
Isaiah 28:5; 62:5